Richard Evans was educated at Queen Mary College, University of London where he studied law and was a City of London solicitor from 1976 until his retirement in 2014. He has had a lifelong interest in sporting history, linked to the collection of an extensive personal library. His love of cricket began at a very early age, facing bowling from his grandfather in the garden and his father on the beach. He was a very dour opening batsman, certainly not cast from the Wynyard mould. He is a member of both MCC and Middlesex, an Arsenal season ticket holder and plays golf at South Herts GC.

He lives in Kenton, Middlesex and has been married to Elisabetta for over forty years. They have three children; Marco, Francesca and Alessandra, and twin grandsons, Edoardo and Daniele.

5ᵗʰ November 2018

To my good friend John,

TEDDY

THE LIFE AND TIMES OF
MAJOR EG WYNYARD DSO, OBE

The product of my retirement!
with the author's kindest regards and
very best wishes,

Dick

RICHARD EVANS

Chequered Flag PUBLISHING

First published in the UK by Chequered Flag Publishing 2018
PO Box 4669, Sheffield, S6 9ET
www.chequeredflagpublishing.co.uk

Copyright © Richard Evans 2018
The moral right of the author has been asserted

A CIP record for this book is available from the British Library

Printed in the EU by Print Group Sp. z o.o.

ISBN 978-1-9997774-4-9

All images from author's collection unless stated

CONTENTS

PREFACE

WHO WAS CAPTAIN EG WYNYARD?

When I married in 1976 and my wife and I moved into our first marital home, I decided to develop a sports library with a particular emphasis on cricket. I will skip over my first (and last) disastrous attempt at 'do it yourself' when I brought down half the plaster on one wall in trying to put up some shelves and will simply say that I scoured the catalogues and started to make my book purchases.

In 1977 I struck gold when I saw advertised Prince Ranjitsinhji's *Jubilee Book of Cricket* published in 1897 during Queen Victoria's Diamond Jubilee celebrations. I duly made the purchase and was delighted to see it had been signed by the author with the following inscription: 'Captn EG Wynyard with the author's kind regards and good wishes.' I knew all about Ranjitsinhji, but, to my now considerable embarrassment, knew little of Wynyard. My curiosity aroused, I decided to research.

On page 426 of the *Jubilee Book* there is a photograph of him with the description 'President of Hampshire CCC'. In the section dealing with that club, Ranji commented 'at present Hants is heavily handicapped, owing to military duties depriving the county of the frequent service of Captain Wynyard, one of the finest bats in the South. In 1894 for Hants he played consecutive innings of 117 v Sussex, 116 v Leicestershire, and 108 v Essex; and in recognition of this he was publicly presented with a handsome pair of silver candlesticks.'

I decided to investigate further and discovered a fascinating story of not just a Test match cricketer who had turned down the chance to captain his country in Australia, but a soldier who had been awarded the second highest military honour and someone who had scored in one of the earliest FA Cup finals. He also had to decline an offer to play football for England.

If these were not great enough achievements, he was a pioneer of winter sports becoming a fine figure skater, an international tobogganing champion, an accomplished bandy and curling player, as well as being awarded the bronze medal from the Humane Society for bravery when trying to save a local flower seller who had fallen through the ice. He was a golfer, a rugby, hockey and rackets enthusiast who represented both the MCC – Marylebone Cricket Club – and the Prince's Club at Real Tennis along with participating, whilst an army officer, in the pursuits of bare-knuckle boxing, polo and was a whipper-in of hounds. The invention of the sweep shot has been attributed to him and when Assistant Secretary at MCC, he was a key figure in the formation of what we know today as the International Cricket Council, or ICC.

I purchased a *Vanity Fair* print entitled 'Hampshire' which now hangs in my hall and, Post Office Telecommunications used this depiction, in 1979, to advertise their Cricket Score Service. Russell March published a book entitled *The Cricketers of Vanity Fair* that contained a description of Wynyard from 1898 stating 'he can speak his mind; and he is supposed to think less of KS Ranjitsinhji than some of the public do.'

I discovered there had been a blazing row in 1897 after Ranji had eaten Wynyard's grapes, as a result of which relations between Hampshire and Sussex were so severely strained, that fixtures between them were nearly cancelled for the following season. My mind started racing. Given the *Jubilee Book* had been issued in the August of that year, was this the reason why my copy had been in general circulation around the bookshops? Life and work was a little more relaxed in the 1970s and so I was able to spend the odd extended lunch break at the Law Society's library poring over back issues of *The Times*. I read extracts from *Wisden* and thought my researches were complete when I purchased the June 1974 edition of *Blackwood's Magazine* containing an article on Wynyard by Sir John Masterman, who is best known as chairman of the Twenty Committee that ran the Double Cross System controlling double agents in Britain during the Second World War.

One sunny July day I found work was taking me to a court near Beaconsfield. The case was over by 11.30 am and so, rather than return straight to the office, I decided to go on my pilgrimage. After a relaxing pint of bitter and a sandwich sitting outside *The Crown Inn* in Penn, I walked across the road to the graveyard of Holy Trinity church and easily located the headstone bearing the inscription:

In Loving Memory of
MAJOR EG WYNYARD DSO, OBE
The King's Regiment (Liverpool)
Born 1st April 1861 Died 30th October 1936
SARAH LOUISE WYNYARD
WIFE OF THE ABOVE
DIED 24TH NOVEMBER 1972

I duly took a photograph and then drove off to nearby Knotty Green in search of the Wynyard family home called The Red House. I discovered a large new development on a road called Red House Close and concluded the world had moved on and the home was no more.

I was now ready to start writing, but work and family meant the file stayed on my desk untouched for over thirty years until I retired in 2014. Of course, in the interim, the Internet had emerged with a whole new range of information to be investigated plus an excellent statistical book on my subject by Keith Warsop with an introduction by Wynyard's daughter-in-law, Ann, who very sadly died in 2008. The time had finally come to complete my project.

Masterman had begun his article by saying 'Major EG Wynyard, DSO or Teddy Wynyard as we came to call him when age had mellowed him ... was one of the heroes of my youth.' It is very insightful about his character, describing him as 'by nature an autocrat supremely confident in his own judgment ... sometimes cantankerous and irascible ... always the leader in any group to which he belonged ... a good friend, but an awesome enemy.'

Significantly, in spite of Wynyard playing a key role in ensuring that Hampshire secured their first-class cricket status, the county's website concluded its pen portrait of him with the words 'it was said ... he was the worst tempered man in the land!' Yet he was also the person who donned a false beard to imitate WG, duped the Duke of York on parade and formed his own golf society called 'the Jokers'!

His was a complex character to try and interpret and in order to understand the man and the diverse opinions expressed about him, it is essential to examine his family roots, as well as the social values prevailing at the time of his birth and during his lifetime.

I discovered the family history was worth a chapter all to itself. As the names of so many relatives are very similar I am going to follow Sir John's lead and call the subject of this book 'Teddy', although I doubt the Major would have approved of such familiarity on my part.

Edward George Wynyard: a man who lived an exciting life and
who boasted an equally exciting family history

1

WHO DO YOU THINK HE WAS?

There are two helpful family trees, *The Family of Wynyard* prepared by the Reverend CW Bingham and 'A Family of Soldiers' which appeared in the April 1903 edition of *The Ancestor*, identifying no fewer than twenty Wynyards (including Teddy) who served in the military, ranging in rank from Lieutenant up to General. Nine of them were officers in Guards regiments and this remarkable achievement was commemorated in the Wellington Barracks Chapel in Birdcage Walk, before a V1 flying bomb wreaked devastation on Sunday 18 June 1944.

The name Wynyard is the Anglo-Saxon for vineyard, somewhat ironic given the nature of Teddy's argument with Ranji! The family trace their origins back to George Wynyard, to whom arms were granted on 2 January 1579 with the motto 'Eprouvez' (Experience).

Wynyard (or Whynniard/Whyneard, the alternative spellings of the name at that time) had a son, John, who was Groom of the Wardrobe to Elizabeth I and James I. He was keeper of the Old Palace of Westminster and had responsibility, along with his wife Susannah, for a number of properties.

This coincides with one of the most famous dates in British history, 5 November 1605, when there was the foiled attempt to blow up the House of Lords and assassinate King James I. The Whynniards leased not only a small house adjacent to, but also the ground floor vault below, the Lords Chamber to the conspirators. The gunpowder was moved to the vault but, ten days before the State Opening of Parliament, an anonymous letter was sent to a Catholic peer, Lord Monteagle, warning him of the plot.

On 4 November, rather than attract undue attention, the ruse was adopted for the search ordered by the King that Whyneard was missing 'some of the King's stuffe, or hangings' and this led to the discovery of John Johnson, aka Guy Fawkes, in possession of thirty-six barrels of gunpowder.

It has been argued that the King's Chief Minister, Robert Cecil, devised the Plot in order to drum up hatred of Catholics amongst the English population. A modern day conspiracy theorist, Father Francis Edwards, has suggested 'that if Whynniard died suddenly on 5 November, it could have been because he stumbled prematurely on something he was not supposed to know.'

So was John Wynyard murdered? There is evidence to show he was still alive on 26 November because he made his will on that date. Also, both John and Susannah took part in the official investigations into the plot and were mentioned twice in the subsequent report that is lodged at the National Archives. Bingham's family tree shows Wynyard died on 20 January 1606, by which time he must have been at least in his early to mid fifties, if not older.

Possibly, therefore, he was in bad health and that was the catalyst for him making a will and the reason for his subsequent death but the close juxtaposition of these events to the discovery of the Gunpowder Plot is certainly a remarkable coincidence.

There is though an interesting footnote to record. By 1611 Susannah had remarried and her new husband was Sir John Stafford of Marlwood who was an associate of Sir Robert Cecil. Was this just another coincidence, or evidence for the conspiracy theorists that Susannah had either been involved in Cecil's plot or her cooperation and silence was being secured?

All we can say for certain is that Susannah died in 1621. One of her and John's great-grandsons was Lieutenant General John Wynyard, born in 1682. He married Mary Maxwell and they had three children together, William, Emily and Mary.

In the foreword to Warsop's book, by Teddy's daughter-in-law, Ann, she said the family still owned three portraits by Sir Joshua Reynolds of eighteenth-century members of the family and one, of a young lady, bore a remarkable resemblance to one of her own daughters. In 1963, Teddy's son, Edward, purchased from the Boston Museum of Fine Arts the portrait of Mary Wynyard (Countess De La Warr) seated and wearing a pink dress. In 1766 (according to the National Portrait Gallery) Reynolds painted her sister, Emily, in a white dress with red sash and this was exhibited at the Royal Academy in 1883 under the simple title 'Miss Wynyard'. It is also known in later life Teddy owned another Reynolds portrait of their brother, William, when he was a Colonel in the 20th Regiment of Foot.

Their father, John, fought in the War of Spanish Succession and then in Scotland repelling the Earl of Mar's rebellion and the second Jacobite Rising. In 1742, he took command of the 17th Regiment of Foot placing him in control of Port Mahon in Minorca, and requiring him to provide assistance to Gibraltar, when needed. The regimental history recorded he 'performed the duties of commanding officer with good reputation'. He died at the age of sixty-nine on 20 February 1752 and is buried in Westminster Abbey and commemorated by a small lozenge stone inscribed 'John Wynyard Esq. Lieutenant General of his Majesty's Forces. Died Febry XXth 1752 aged LXIX.'

John's son, William, who was born in Minorca in 1732, went on to become a Lieutenant General, and was married three times, (widowed twice) and had nine children. The youngest of his children by his third wife, Sarah Lilly, was Teddy's grandfather, Edward Buckley Wynyard.

A remarkable story, however, centres around two of his half brothers. On 15 October 1785, George West Wynyard (then a Lieutenant) and Captain John Sherbrooke (later Governor in Chief of North America) were stationed with the 33rd Regiment in Sydney,

Cape Breton, off Nova Scotia. The barracks were completely blocked off by ice and so there was no communication with any part of the outside world. The two officers were in Wynyard's room that had two doors, one from the passage and the other into the bedroom. There was no other means of exit. Sherbrooke looked towards the passage door and saw, standing by the side of it, a tall youth who was pale and emaciated. Sherbrooke directed Wynyard's attention to the individual and noticed that his companion's face assumed the appearance of a corpse. The stranger passed them, looking at Wynyard along the way, and entered the bedroom. Wynyard immediately exclaimed, 'Great God! My brother!'

They both went into the bedroom but there was no one there. They told another officer, Lieutenant (later Colonel) Gore, who joined the search but to no avail. Gore suggested they keep note of the day and hour in which the event happened. Wynyard wrote home but it was not until a ship docked just under eight months later, on 6 June 1786, that a letter arrived for Sherbrooke. He was asked to break the news to his friend that George's brother, John Otway Wynyard, had died in London. Subsequent investigation revealed this had been at precisely the time and on the day the stranger had appeared in their room.

There was great interest in the story and it was widely discussed and written about in the late eighteenth and throughout the nineteenth centuries. Indeed, the story featured in a letter dated 17 March 1795, written just three months before his death by Dr Johnson's biographer, Sir James Boswell, to his son, Alexander, following what he described as 'a capital dinner at his house' with Wynyard who had the 'spirit to avow' he saw a ghost. The letter is included in the Catalogue of Papers of James Boswell at Yale University.

Teddy's grandfather was born on 23 November 1788 at Kensington Palace. He was made Captain at twenty years of age and during the Napoleonic Wars was severely wounded on 22 March 1810 at Santa Maura (now known as Lefkas). He was eventually promoted to Lieutenant Colonel and appointed Military Secretary to Sir Hudson Lowe in St Helena.

This tropical island of volcanic origin had been uninhabited until discovered by the Portuguese in 1502, but from 1651 had been in the possession of the East India Company. In 1815, it was chosen as the residence for Napoleon, following his defeat at the Battle of Waterloo. An arrangement was made between the Company and the British Government whereby Hudson Lowe was appointed Governor with responsibility for ensuring the safe custody of the deposed French Emperor.

Edward had married Louisa Warner at St Mary Abbots Church in Kensington on 1 September 1814 and the couple arrived in St Helena on 6 May 1816 on board *Adamant*. As the ship anchored at Jamestown they would have had the same view as Captains Cook and Bligh before them and, just seven months earlier on 7 October 1815, as Napoleon.

St Helena is just ten miles long and five miles wide and one of the remotest places in the world. It was a bold and intrepid journey for Louisa to make and the Wynyards set up home at Alarm House which was built into the side of Alarm Hill in Alarm Forest. Napoleon was housed two miles away, as the crow flies, at Longwood, a 1,500-acre site, 1,800 feet above sea level. Both properties still exist today and Longwood is now a museum.

There was an early falling out between Lowe and his famous guest and after just six meetings, in August 1816, Napoleon refused to see him again. One person who did form a good relationship with Bonaparte was the Irish physician, Barry O'Meara, who had been the surgeon on *Bellerophon* which was blockading the port of Rochefort when Napoleon came on board and surrendered himself to the British.

Politics were rife on the island and officers had to be careful in their dealings with their famous prisoner. Everyone was keen to say they had met and spoken with him and all visits were recorded to try and exercise some control (although there is no evidence of a formal meeting with Wynyard). In turn, Napoleon manipulated the situation to his own advantage. It was felt O'Meara had grown far too close to him and there was a serious disagreement with Lowe when the physician criticized the way in which Napoleon was being treated. Lowe dismissed him and in the subsequent dispute, Wynyard swore an affidavit supporting the Governor but the legal action never came to trial. O'Meara was forced to leave St Helena in July 1818 and published his own account which seriously damaged Lowe's reputation and Wynyard also did not escape unscathed. Just before his departure, O'Meara said he was preparing medication for Napoleon and explaining its administration to the valet de chambre, when Wynyard went to his apartments in Longwood, without his knowledge, and ordered the servants to pack up his effects as quickly as possible. O'Meara was escorted on board *The Griffon* which was being made ready to take him back to England and claimed that not only had his baggage been secretly rummaged and his papers examined but money and some of his valuables were now missing.

Teddy's grandfather had to operate in a delicate and sometimes hostile environment on the island and there was still a fear that, whilst Napoleon was alive, he might yet be a rallying point for disillusioned Frenchmen. When a known sympathiser left the island it is easy to understand why the authorities would want to check that no seditious material was leaving with him. Wynyard's actions make sense in this context, but we only have O'Meara's account as to the manner in which these tasks were performed and whether they involved any duplicity, or indeed, theft.

Meanwhile, on a much happier note, whilst on the island Louisa gave birth to three children: William (on 25 January 1817), who was Teddy's father; Edward George (on August 7 1818) and George Bingham on 14 February 1820. It is known that this third child died young and one is left to speculate whether this was the reason why the family left the island in June 1820. Napoleon died just under a year later on 5 May 1821. The couple subsequently had a further five children between 1821 and 1830.

Teddy's grandfather was appointed aide-de-camp to William IV, CB (Commander of the Most Honourable Order of the Bath) and then promoted to Major General. In September 1847 he succeeded Sir Maurice O'Connell in command of Her Majesty's Land Forces in New South Wales, Van Diemen's Land (Tasmania) and New

Zealand. Wynyard arrived in Sydney in 1848 and served on both the Legislative Council (1848-1851) and Executive Council (1848-1853). Significantly, and to his credit, it is reported that unlike O'Connell he did not insist on being addressed as 'Your Excellency'! He was regularly in dispute with British and Colonial governments over military costs and steadily opposed every proposal to reduce troops as well as refusing to allow soldiers to resign in order to become settlers. His stance was proven fully justified in 1851 when gold was discovered and each colony began to clamour for protection. In 1851 he became Lieutenant General and left Sydney in 1853, but he left his mark as Wynyard Station and Wynyard Square in Sydney, the town of Wynyard in Tasmania where he visited in 1850 and 1851 and Wynyard Street, off Clarendon Road, in Melbourne, are all named after him.

Following his departure he was made General in 1860 and back in England entered commerce as a director of the Royal Naval, Military and East India Company Life Assurance Society. He died of bronchitis on 24 November 1864, aged seventy-six, at 27 Chester Street, London when Teddy was three years old. He was buried at All Souls cemetery in Kensal Green, London and, just under six years later, on 6 July 1870, Teddy's grandmother, Louisa, died in her seventy-eighth year.

Teddy's father, William, did not follow the family's military tradition but instead joined the Indian Civil Service. In 1839, at the age of twenty-two, he was made an Assistant Under Commissioner of the Dehlee division. It is clear that whilst in India he played some cricket, although the only records relate to sixteen matches for six different clubs between 1854 and 1864 during periods when he was back in England. He played predominantly for the Indian Club and also for teams organized by the Earl of Winterton, Thomas Burgoyne (who played for MCC in the first ever match at the current Lord's ground against Hertfordshire on 22 June 1814), E Tredcroft, MCC and Margate.

On 12 August 1856, he was married at All Souls Church, Saint Marylebone, London, to 26-year-old Henrietta Ellen Willcock from Castelnau House, Mortlake. She was the daughter of Sir Henry

Willcock who was a diplomat and had been Chairman of the East India Company from 1844 to 1845. Wynyard's return to India with his new wife was to be anything but a honeymoon, although there was the joy of their first child, Eleanor Louisa, being born on 8 May 1857.

By this time William was Judge of Gorakhpur, near the Oudh frontier, and just nine days later news reached him of the mutiny at Meerut a week earlier. The Indian Mutiny is also known as the Sepoy Mutiny and the Sepoys or Sipahis were Hindu or Muslim soldiers in the East India Company's army that comprised about 300,000 Sepoys with just 50,000 British.

Kaye's and Malleson's *History of the Indian Mutiny 1857-58* is an excellent source of reference both on the Mutiny and Wynyard's part in it. He is described as 'a man of action ... recognised as the man to direct and execute plans which might be necessary for the preservation of British authority ... a lover of field sports ... fearless – a nature that knew not fear ... a mind well stored,' a description that could equally be applied to his son, Teddy, in years to come.

The Commissioner of Banaras, HC Tucker, placed Wynyard in charge of the district and gave him full authority to assume civil and military responsibility.

On 6 June the local Sipahis refused to obey orders and the following day prisoners attempted to break out from the gaols but were repelled. That night the Sipahis seized empty carts and, duly armed, marched next morning on the Treasury with the aim of stealing the money and treasure stored there. Wynyard and Capt Steel (in command of the 17th Native Infantry) confronted them and the Sipahis returned to their lines.

Wynyard proclaimed martial law and suspended ordinary forms of trial, actions that today would be viewed more critically, but at the time it was said his energy 'had an extremely deterring effect upon the disaffected'.

Between 17 and 19 June fugitives arrived from Oudh and on the following day Wynyard sent all the ladies at the station to Banaras in the hope that it would be safer. The Wynyard wives were certainly born of brave and redoubtable stock – St Helena for one generation, bloody Northern India for the next.

William must have been greatly encouraged, not only because Commissioner Tucker wrote fully approving of his actions, but by a handwritten letter sent on 28 June from the Governor General of India, Lord Canning, expressing gratitude for the excellent service rendered and expressing hope he might still hold his ground but 'if not, have no scruple as to retiring in time. You have long ago saved your honour.'

Remarkably, Wynyard did indeed continue to hold his ground for another month but, on 28 July 1857, news came through of the mutiny of the 12th Irregulars at Siguali who were now marching on Gorakhpur and so Wynyard urgently sent a message for help to the Gurkhas who arrived that evening and disarmed the Sipahis stationed there. Whilst their arrival saved the lives of the Europeans, Gorakhpur had to be evacuated because the Gurkhas were under orders not to leave a detachment behind but instead to march via Azamgarh straight on to Allahabad.

On 13 August 1857, Wynyard and his companions handed over charge of the district to the loyal landowners and rode that evening into the Gurkha camp. They marched towards Azamgarh where the rebels were strongly positioned and armed with three brass cannons. The Gurkhas, with Wynyard and Venables (a fighting tea-planter) alongside, charged with such determination that, after only ten minutes, 200 rebels had been slain and the rest were in retreat abandoning their artillery. Wynyard was nominated Chief Civil Officer of the district. On 4 September, the 'high spirited Judge of Gorakhpur', as he was described, joined up with the Gurkhas who now occupied Jaunpur.

Kaye and Malleson summarised Wynyard's role in the Mutiny in the following way:

> The state of Gorakhpur immediately upon the departure of the English officials fully justified that departure. In few parts of India did the districts become more infested with men thirsting for European blood than in the districts bordering on Oudh. To have maintained Gorakhpur for three months without assistance in the presence of disaffected

Sipahis and surrounded by turbulent landowners was a feat worthy of the highest praise – a feat which testified to the courage, the tact, the judgment of those by whom it was accomplished and which redounded greatly to their honour. But, notwithstanding Lord Canning's emphatic declaration in this respect, notwithstanding the services subsequently rendered, Mr Wynyard and his companions were not admitted within the favoured circle of official approbation. The more necessary is it then, that admiration should be accorded to them by their countrymen.

In other words an unsung hero who did not get the credit he deserved!

In the introduction to Warsop's book by Ann Wynyard she told the story of 'the Mutiny Clock' which was still in the possession of the family. This clock had been stolen by one of the rebels but when it struck, he was terrified believing it to be inhabited by foreign devils and so dumped it and fled.

The Mutiny effectively ended on 2 August 1858, but family life had clearly returned to a little more normality before then because, on 31 August 1858, William and Henrietta had a second daughter born to them who they called Lily Isabel.

On April Fools' Day 1861, Edward George (our subject Teddy) was born in Saharanpur in northern Uttar Pradesh, followed two years later, by a fourth child, William Bingham Ashton. Teddy was baptised at the hill station of Mussoorie, known as 'the Queen of the Hills' in the Gahrwal Himalayan range, and Sir George Everest, after whom the famous mountain is named, had a house built there in 1832.

In the meantime, back in England, William's younger brother, after whom Teddy must have been named as he was also Edward George Wynyard, had been asked to sit on a Court of Inquiry set up by the Grenadier Guards into what became known as the notorious Turf Scandal of 1862.

There had been an unsatisfactory Jockey Club investigation resulting in a 'not proven' verdict against a Guards officer, Lieutenant Colonel Edwyn Burnaby, who had been accused of striking a bogus bet with Captain the Hon Arthur Annesley, to try and affect the odds on Burnaby's horse, Tarragona, in a 100-sovereigns match at

Newmarket. The arguments were all played out in the press. Admiral Rous, the leading Jockey Club steward of the day, openly admitted that he abhorred Burnaby and referred to an earlier incident when he thought Burnaby had made another bogus bet, but this time it was with The Hon Randolph Stewart of the 42nd Royal Highlanders.

It was suggested they had colluded to induce the American owner, breeder and gambler, Richard Ten Broeck, to bet £100, along with others, on whether the correct spelling of the proposed new name for their horse was 'reindeer' or 'raindeer', when, in fact, they both knew the word was spelt with an 'a' in Dr. Johnson's dictionary.

Far from this situation being viewed as farcical with little sympathy for anyone who would bet £100 (£8,500 in today's money) in such circumstances, the whole affair achieved such notoriety that not only was the integrity of the officers questioned but also the very reputation of the regiments they represented. *The Times* wrote on 7 November 1862 'it is shocking to imagine that men with great names and lofty connections, occupying the most conspicuous positions, and holding high rank in our army, can be slurred with the suspicion of confederating together to cheat a companion out of a hundred pounds. Even that such a thing should be thought possible is a very unpleasant fact.'

A Court of Inquiry was duly set up comprising four senior officers of the Grenadier Guards including Teddy's uncle, who had served with distinction during the Crimean War, as had Burnaby.

It was never going to be easy to sit in judgment over fellow officers who faced likely ruin. Wynyard and his colleagues had little difficulty in exonerating Burnaby and Annesley over the Tarragona affair but they were undecided about the 'reindeer' bet. The Duke of Cambridge, who as Colonel of the Regiment had instituted the inquiry, referred the report back. Their second report also did not satisfy the Duke who referred it back yet again. At the third attempt Wynyard and his fellow Court members gave as their opinion that Colonel Burnaby had 'thoroughly vindicated his honour'.

Whilst there may have been insufficient evidence to establish guilt with regard to the Tarragona affair, Burnaby and Stewart must have been very relieved men over the 'reindeer' bet. What they could not have predicted was that a little local West Country scam would develop into a national, if not international, cause célèbre.

With Edward Wynyard's responsibilities to the Guards Inquiry completed it was back to more mundane matters for the family and by 1864 his brother William had returned to England. He played his last recorded cricket game, a three-day match on 1, 2 and 3 September at Clifton Villa Estate, Margate. This time he was playing for Margate against the United All-England Eleven. The opponents were a touring team comprising some of the best players in the land including James Lillywhite junior and Harry Jupp, both of whom were in the first ever England Test side thirteen years later.

These touring sides owed their origin to William Clarke who, in 1846, founded his All-England Eleven. By 1852, however, there was disquiet prompting John Wisden and Jemmy Dean to form a breakaway side called the United All-England Eleven. From the beginning of Clarke's day the matches attracted huge betting on their outcomes. There was such a demand to play these games that often the opposition was made up of inferior teams. In order to even up the odds (hence the description 'odds matches') these opponents were regularly increased in number with the occasional 'ringer' thrown in along the way.

Margate had twenty-two players and I can find no link between the Wynyard family and this Kent seaside resort, but if William was asked to play to bolster the home side's chance of success, it did not work.

The visitors batted first and scored 169 with Wynyard taking two catches to dismiss Carpenter and Lockyer. William went in first wicket down to be bowled by James Lillywhite junior for just 1 but the whole team only managed 72 and had to bat again. This time round, again going in at number three, he was caught Hearne bowled Mortlock ('Old Stonewall') for a duck and the side lost by an innings and 14 runs.

It is clear William was a proficient player gauged by the fact he mainly opened and did not bat lower than number four in any of the sixteen matches. Whilst his top recorded score was 46 playing for

Tom Burgoyne's Eleven at Lord's on 15 May 1855, it is important to bear in mind the condition of the pitches as they bore absolutely no resemblance at all to those of today. The grass at Lord's was kept low by sheep and the creases were cut with a knife. The wicket was described as bumpy and dangerous. The levelling out process was not properly completed at St John's Wood until 1875. Any cricket Wynyard played in India would not have been first-class and the result at Margate demonstrated the gap in standard as against the best players in England.

On 5 June 1866 William and Henrietta back in London, had twin girls, Rose Mary and Amy Eardley who were baptized at St Luke's Church in Sydney Street, Chelsea on 10 June and 14 July 1866 respectively. On the baptism certificate William's address was given as 93 Onslow Square, London and his occupation as 'Gentleman'.

Tragically, on 15 March 1868, Teddy's mother, Henrietta, died just over two weeks before his seventh birthday.

By the time of the 1871 Census, William was described as a 'retired Bengal civil servant' living at 32 Onslow Gardens with five of his children, aged between four and thirteen. To assist him he had a Bavarian Governess and five servants indicating the family had fairly significant means. The only child not listed was Teddy, because at the age of ten, he was boarding at Woodcote House Prep School in Windlesham.

Three years later on 27 January 1874, William married 34-year-old Isabella Sophia Ward who had been born in Switzerland. The marriage took place at St Peter's Church in Cranley Gardens, London. They had one child together, Henry Buckley William, born in January 1880 in Southampton, as the family had moved by then to North End House in Hursley near Winchester. In the 1881 Census all the family was living there including Teddy and they had help from seven servants with both a Governess and a schoolroom maid amongst those listed.

It is clear William threw himself into country life and helped with many charitable causes. By 1891, there were only three children (Eleanor, Lily and Amy) still living at home with William and

Isabella assisted by seven servants. William died the following year in Cannes, France on 13 February 1892. Probate was granted to Isabella and Teddy with effects of £6022 3s 5d (about £535,000 in today's money) and so there was more than enough for a comfortable lifestyle.

It is clear the Wynyard family had a strong military tradition with a deep commitment to duty, service and self-sacrifice, linked to a penchant for anything dangerous. They held positions of command and authority in connection with some of the biggest events in British history: the Gunpowder Plot, the Jacobite rising of 1715, the imprisonment of Napoleon on St Helena, the early Colonial administration of Gibraltar, Minorca and Australia, the Indian Mutiny, and there was an intriguing ghost story and turf scandal thrown in for good measure as well.

Given that cricket was also in the family, it is easy to see what an important part Teddy's heritage played in shaping and determining the course of his future life.

From Malcolm Bailey, *From Cloisters to Cup Finals*

Teddy's sporting foundation was laid at Charterhouse,
here standing far left with the 1876-77 football team.

2

A VICTORIAN EDUCATION

1861-80

The *Vanity Fair* print of Teddy entitled 'Hampshire' portrays a cricketer of military bearing, stiff both of back and upper lip. The common perception is of a brave soldier and a wonderfully versatile and able athlete albeit one who sometimes found it difficult to keep his emotions in check, if reports of his fiery temper are anything to go by.

The early years of his life, however, were emotional times for any boy to have experienced and must have played an influential role in defining the character of the man. Nothing can have prepared him for the death of his mother two weeks before his seventh birthday.

She died just as Teddy started his education at Woodcote House, Windlesham in Surrey. He was a young boy, a long way from where he was born, who had lost his mother. No matter how resilient he may have been, initially he must have been lonely, and struggling to come to terms with his new life.

By 1871, when he was ten years old, his father had retired from the Bengal Civil Service and was living in a fashionable part of London with the rest of the family. It must have made life easier for the young boy at prep school to have his family now relatively close at hand. Indeed the school clearly had a beneficial effect upon him because he started to display the early signs of a great sporting talent and in 1873, at the age of twelve, was selected to play for Woodcote House's cricket First Eleven.

There was an entry in *The Times* on 5 December 1873 to the effect that EG Wynyard was a successful candidate at an examination for navel cadetship. Clearly, he, or his father on his behalf, was considering a career in the Navy, following the route taken by his cousin, Henry Bingham Wynyard. Instead Teddy moved from Windlesham to Charterhouse School, during its Oration Quarter (early September to mid December) 1874. This was in happier circumstances, as in January of that year, his father had remarried and so there was a maternal influence to call upon again in his life.

Charterhouse was founded in 1611 on the site of the old Carthusian monastery in Charterhouse Square, Smithfield, London but had moved to its current site in Godalming, Surrey, in June 1872 and so had only been there for just over two years when Teddy joined. The headmaster was the Reverend Canon William Haig Brown and since the relocation he had almost trebled the school's size from 117 to 333 boys.

This growth was down to his fearlessness, courage and benevolence. He was popularly known as 'Old Bill' and had a reputation for possessing a good sense of humour. Whilst he could be severe, it was said he had a very humane approach to his boys, who held him in both awe and affection. He knew the name of every boy within a fortnight of any new intake and was greatly assisted by his wife, who often left flowers at the bedside of sick boys, gave friendly greetings to pupils when she met them, warmly welcomed returning Old Carthusians and even wrote and sent Christmas cards to them when they were in far off lands serving commerce or their country.

Precisely what did a Victorian public school education entail? Certainly the cost would have been relatively the same as today. AH Tod, who was at the school when Teddy joined and was also a member of the same Old Carthusian Cup Final side, wrote a history of Charterhouse up to 1900 at which time he was an Assistant Master there.

The Charterhouse register shows Teddy as 'Daviesite – Girdlestoneite'. The names of these two houses still exist to this day and 'Daviesite' was named after the Reverend GS Davies and located away from the school whereas 'Girdlestoneite' house, founded by Frederick Girdlestone, had a more central location close to the main teaching buildings. Each boy on joining the school was allocated to a house and that would be his home. Teddy would have moved on from Daviesite as he grew older.

One boy who was a Girdlestoneite from the house's inception in 1874 was Robert Baden-Powell. The difference in age with Teddy is likely to have precluded their being friends but Teddy would have known him and their paths are likely to have crossed on the football field. Baden-Powell was four years older and in the Second Boer War he commanded the garrison during the Siege of Mafeking and is still known to this day as the founder of the Boy Scout and Girl Guide movements.

Every house had a certain number of baths and a lavatory but these facilities were far from adequate for the boy's needs, not least, in terms of changing and drying wet clothes. Gas was laid on but the lights had a habit of going out leaving candles stuck into ginger beer bottles as a fallback. An attempt by the school to have its own gasworks was thwarted by neighbouring residents who secured an injunction for nuisance. When the site in Godalming first opened in 1872, the buildings swarmed with earwigs and rats and boys were allowed to keep ferrets in the houses. It all seems now and arguably, even by austere Victorian standards then, to have been a very spartan existence and a tough environment in which to grow up and spend one's formative years.

This was even more so as Tod recounts in his history that bullying had been a problem. When Teddy arrived at the school the Lemon Peel Fight was still allowed. Every Shrove Tuesday since 1850 each boy had been given half a lemon to flavour his pancake but it was used instead as a missile, loaded with pebbles and ink, in the close quarter fights which ensued between the 'Old' and 'New' School pupils, resulting in several severe injuries. The last Lemon Peel Fight was in 1877, which happened to be Teddy's last year, and its abolition was a decision of the sixth form in 1878 who described it as a 'barbarous and obsolete practice'.

Nevertheless, four years earlier, at the time when Teddy joined, it had proved necessary to curb the powers of the monitors after they had thrashed all the Under Long Room boys in one house when the perpetrator of an offence had not owned up. Until then monitors had been left largely to their own devices and could make the lives of fags very unpleasant. Teddy would have had to do his share of fagging duties, which meant complying with the monitors' bidding whatever they might have been, including the mundane tasks of cleaning studies and making tea and toast.

Tod sought to defend this state of affairs by explaining that the masters' duties ended when they left the classroom and it was for the boys to manage all other matters for themselves: 'The monitorial system taught all, first how to obey, and afterwards how to command, while the unrestricted life fostered originality and self reliance.' Teddy displayed these character traits throughout his life, but he had also been born into a family where such behaviour had already been exhibited under the most testing of conditions.

The school day began with the awakening bell in the morning at 6.45 am followed by prayers at 7.30 in the chapel (11 on Sundays). After 'banco' in the evening (the time set aside for preparing the next day's work), lights out for younger boys was at 9.20 pm. Pupils were allowed to visit Godalming at any time and did so in hordes as the school had no tuck shop.

One of the reasons Haig Brown had wanted to move to Godalming was to have enough space for sport as he felt this was an important character builder for the boys. Tod told how it had been viewed almost as a crime to study and boys (especially younger ones) who stood up and answered questions voluntarily were often persecuted. He commented that 'the boy who excels his companions in athletics is a much greater hero in their estimation than the scholar who has won every college and school distinction open to him'. It is easy to believe that within such an environment Teddy would have been held in high esteem.

At Charterhouse there was a wide variety of activities in addition to football and cricket. There are reports of Teddy playing hockey, but these were internal matches and although he was not in the school team against any outside opposition, he did go on to play hockey at county level for Hampshire in later life. He played lawn tennis and fought in single stick matches (a form of fencing using wooden rods of about thirty-five inches in length). Wednesday 18 April 1877 was Athletics Sports day and in a cold wind, he finished fourth of five to his footballing friend, Jock Prinsep, in the second-class one-mile race run on the road to Compton. He was then third of four in the half-mile handicap and so perhaps running without a ball was not quite his forte.

It is clear though that, at this time, Charterhouse really focused their attention on football, and to a very much lesser extent on cricket. Football was the main leisure activity of the whole school from September to the end of March, but the game played by Teddy, not least in its rules, was very different from the uniform version enjoyed across the world today. Malcolm Bailey has written the definitive history of Charterhouse football, *From Cloisters to Cup Finals*, which includes a comparison between the Charterhouse and FA rules; but in September 1875, a year after Teddy joined, the school did finally fall in line with the FA.

Before 1891 a referee could only stand on the touchline keeping time and arbitrating if the two umpires, one for each team, could not agree on a decision. As the game had originated from public schools it was thought honour would prevail and there was no need for a sanction, such as a penalty kick, because it was assumed, rather too idealistically, that a gentleman would never deliberately commit a foul. In 1891 penalty kicks and goal nets were introduced and a goalkeeper was allowed to handle the ball anywhere in his own half but could be challenged even when holding the ball and barged over the line.

The word 'touchline' emanates from the fact that when the ball went out of play it did not matter who last touched it, but rather who then reached the ball first. The one-handed throw-in was allowed until 1882 and it was not until 1895 that the throw-in law was changed to what is the case today.

Football at Charterhouse was organized so that there were the First and Second Eleven games and below those, all the school houses had combined into four house clubs: Cygnets (which included Girdlestoneites), Swallows, Nomads and Harpies (with whom the Daviesites played). These house clubs were formed in 1874 and 1875 at the time when Teddy joined the school. Initially their aim was to provide cricket for boys who had not reached any of the school elevens, but in the autumn of 1875 this concept was extended to football. Each house club captain had to arrange two or three games every day and provide for the participation of over 100 boys. In practice, this organisation often proved difficult and chaotic. Nevertheless Teddy would have had ample opportunity to play and his footballing skills flourished. He made the school First Eleven and acquired his colours at the age of fifteen for the 1876-7 season. Bailey comments, 'to be in the Charterhouse Football Eleven was a sort of passport to the athletic world and the school and the sport were inseparable.'

The First Eleven in which Teddy played had one of the best seasons of any team in the late 1800s. They were captained by William Page who also played with Wynyard in the FA Cup final five years later. They did not lose a single game and had a record of twelve games played, eleven wins, one draw, fifty-one goals scored with eight against.

The Carthusian assessed Wynyard as 'a heavy forward, charging and dribbling well; always middles splendidly'. It is believed Teddy was the youngest player up to that time to have gained his football colours. Given the image conjured up of a muscular centre forward it is just a little surprising that Teddy did not figure on the score sheet for any of the fifty-one goal tally that season! Admittedly Teddy did not play in all of the matches especially those early on but was in the team for 'the great match of the season' which was a 2-0 win against Westminster.

The record of this team was nearly bettered in 1880-81 but that eleven lost one game which was against the Old Carthusian team, seven of whom were to play in the FA Cup final just over three weeks later. Teddy scored twice in that 6-1 win over his old school.

Interestingly, given Teddy's success on the football field, whilst he ultimately played at Test match level, he did not also play cricket for the school First Eleven. Warsop says this was because he was only fifteen during his last season and so too young to make his mark. It was just two years later, though, that he made his county debut playing for Hampshire. An article appearing in the December 1897 edition of *Baily's Magazine of Sports and Pastimes* stated it was bad health that prevented him from gaining his cricket colours, although Teddy appeared to have played frequently between June and August in his last season of 1876.

Two other factors were the poor facilities and lack of importance given to cricket at this time by the school, even though that is now difficult to believe given Charterhouse's subsequent cricketing pedigree. A great deal of effort had been taken during 1871-2 in preparing the ground but, once complete, its maintenance was neglected for many years which coincided with Teddy's time at Godalming. Little care was taken of the pitch and as no groundsman had been appointed, the situation went from bad to worse. Tod commented the square and outfield was 'more interesting to the botanist and geologist than to the cricketer'.

Nets had to be put up by the First Eleven on the fringes of the ground but the house clubs, when formed, had to find pitches for themselves 'in arid waste'. There was only one roller and most of the school did not play any cricket at all. In these circumstances opportunities to play were limited, but fixtures were kept with other schools and also the nomadic touring side, I Zingari, for whom Teddy was to play in later life. The situation did not improve until 1881, by which time Teddy was long gone.

Nevertheless, on moving to its new location, the school had appointed the retired Surrey and England professional, Julius Caesar, as its supplier of cricketing equipment and coach to the boys. Julius was a local man, having been born in Godalming on 25 March 1830. He made his first-class debut for Surrey in June 1849 and played for eighteen seasons. He came from a large cricketing family who played as the Twelve Caesars. In 1851 he joined William Clarke's All-England Eleven and was a member of Parr's team that was the first from the British Isles to tour abroad, visiting North America in 1859-60.

His last years were not happy ones although there had been two benefit matches played for him. The first was on 12, 13 and 14 September 1864 at Broadwater Park, Godalming with Julius going in at three for T Lockyer's Eleven against W Mortlock's Eleven. Both of those captains along with Jupp and Griffith had played for the United All-England Eleven against Margate just over a week earlier when Teddy's father, William, had been in the opposition team. In the evening of the last day, at the public hall in Godalming, Caesar was presented with a gold watch and chain plus a purse of sovereigns.

A year later, Caesar was involved in a tragic and traumatic event when he was out shooting pheasant and his gun accidentally went off, killing one of the beaters. Understandably, this deeply affected him and his game deteriorated rapidly prompting him to retire when thirty-seven years old in 1867.

The second benefit was played on 17, 18 and 19 August 1868 at The Oval between a combined Surrey/Middlesex side and an England team which included WG Grace and James Lillywhite junior. Julius did not play in the game but the proceeds of the two benefits ought to have given him a little financial security.

In 1874, his wife Jane died suddenly at home and two years later, his second son, also called Julius, aged seventeen, committed suicide by throwing himself on the railway line at Peasmarsh. Caesar was a broken man, drank more than was good for him and possibly suffering from dropsy as well as gout, died impoverished and a recluse on 6 March 1878 at his lodgings in the Railway Tavern, Mill Lane, Godalming aged just forty-seven. He was buried in Nightingale Road Cemetery, Godalming in an unmarked grave but in 2004, a service was held when a new headstone carved with a bat, bail and balls was dedicated to him.

It will readily be appreciated that these tragic last four years of Julius's life coincided almost exactly with Teddy's time at the school. One must question, therefore, precisely how much coaching the famous cricketer was able to give him and the other boys at Charter-house.

Whilst Teddy may not have earned his First Eleven colours, he did get close to doing so in spite of his tender years. *The Carthusian* records that on 30 May 1875, when he was just past his fourteenth birthday, he played for HG Jefferson's Eleven against the Reverend W Romaris' Eleven. This was a practice match in which Jefferson's team consisted chiefly of those playing for the school, and so clearly Teddy was highly regarded as the opposition were Masters and Fellows at Charterhouse. He did not really have much of a chance to shine because, batting at number nine, he was bowled for just 1 out of a total of 70 in the first innings and did not bat in the second.

The following season, in addition to playing in a number of internal school matches for such wonderfully named teams as the Dissyllables, Teddy was formally made part of the Second Eleven and opened the batting against the Old Carthusian seconds and although he was run out for 7, the team scored 196 to win convincingly against opponents who managed only 42 and 66.

Teddy was moved up and down the batting order but made only one half century and so never really established his credentials. Nevertheless, the relatively low team scores were a reflection of the poor state of the pitches and it is difficult not to conclude that, had he stayed on at Charterhouse, he would have won his colours. Indeed *The Carthusian,* in 1914, when reviewing an article on Charterhouse cricket, commented, that from 1872 to 1889, there were only five pitches for the whole school but, in spite of this, both Wynyard and Smith belonged to that time.

The other pupil named was Charles (later Sir Charles) Aubrey Smith. He was not quite twelve years of age, and two years younger than Teddy, when he joined the school in the Long Quarter term (mid January to late March) 1875. He was a fag to Baden-Powell. Whilst he was not in the same houses as Teddy, their paths crossed during the next two years on the sports field as well as later on the county circuit. Also Smith was still at the school during the 1881 FA Cup competition and so will have followed Teddy's progress and that of the other old boys very closely.

Smith did make the Charterhouse cricket First Eleven for the 1880 and 1881 seasons, by which time he was seventeen years old, and took Teddy's wicket in the match against the Old Carthusians in his last year at School.

Smith led a fascinating and versatile life. He won a cricketing Blue whilst at St John's College, Cambridge in 1881 playing alongside Lord Hawke and the three Studd brothers. He was a fast-medium bowler with a high action and useful leg cutter. He had a curved approach to the wicket beginning at mid off with a delivery from round the wicket which earned him the nickname 'Round the Corner Smith'.

He played for Sussex between 1882 and 1886 and again took Teddy's wicket in the match against Hampshire in 1883. He captained England on their first tour of South Africa and played in one Test at Port Elizabeth on 12 and 13 March 1889. He took five for 19 in the first innings and two for 42 in the second, leading his country to an eight wicket victory.

He is, of course, best known as a stage actor who went on to become one of the early stars of talking pictures in Hollywood, cultivating the part of a perfect, albeit sometimes crusty, English gentleman. He formed the Hollywood Cricket Club in 1932. This came after Aubrey Smith teamed up with Boris Karloff to field a team to play a visiting Australian side captained by Vic Richardson which included Don Bradman.

Smith died of pneumonia in Beverly Hills on 20 December 1948. His body was cremated and nine months later in accordance with his wishes, his ashes were returned to England and interred in his mother's grave at St Leonard's churchyard in Hove.

Given the poor state of the Charterhouse pitches at the time and the fact that cricket was not viewed so importantly in their day, it is remarkable that these two school contemporaries, Wynyard and Smith, should both progress to play Test match cricket for England. It is also worthy of mention that both went on to lead very varied lives and achieved so much in the world beyond the bat, ball and bail.

Given their subsequent close association with the Old Carthusians it seems clear that both Teddy and Smith thoroughly enjoyed their time at school in Godalming. Whilst Charles attended Cambridge, it was a different story for Wynyard. Although Haig Brown was keen on promoting sport he also realized the importance of giving greater emphasis to academic achievement. This change would evolve over time but one regulation then was that boys had to reach a higher level than IV form in order to stay on after the age of sixteen. Perhaps the politest way to deal with Teddy's academic achievements is simply to record factually his end of year results, as Keith Warsop has done in his book.

In April 1875, when he was in Upper Shell A, he finished in an overall exam placing of thirty-third out of thirty-eight. In 1876 when he was in Under IV A, he finished thirty-first out of thirty-six. In 1877 he was in Upper IV A and was thirty-fourth out of thirty-eight. His placings that year were eighteenth in French, thirty-fifth in Natural Science and also Classics, and twenty-fourth out of twenty-five in Maths Division 1.

These results were not good enough to stay on at the school and so, in the spring of 1877, Teddy transferred from Charterhouse to St Edward's School in Oxford.

At that time the school's main aim was to educate the sons of middle-class clergy and to emphasise the teachings of the Anglican faith, and so was not an obvious choice for a boy who even then seemed to be set upon a military career.

As it happens, there were clergy in the family. Indeed, Teddy closely followed the career of his second cousin, the Reverend Frank Wynyard Wright, who had earned a reputation for himself as a more than useful cricketer playing for the Gentlemen of the North at The Oval in 1861 when only seventeen years of age. Frank also just happened to have been born in Woodstock, Oxfordshire.

The most probable explanation for the choice of school was that Teddy's father knew the headmaster, the Reverend Algernon Barrington Simeon. The Simeon family had emigrated to New Zealand in October 1851 where Algernon's father, Charles, became the Resident Magistrate and the first Speaker of the Provincial Council.

Sir Robert Wynyard (related to Teddy's grandfather) was Lieutenant Governor of New Ulster, a province of New Zealand encompassing much of the North Island. He also went on to hold the same post twice in the Cape Colony, South Africa, where Fort Wynyard in Greenpoint, Cape Town, is named after him. In 1855 the Simeon family returned to England and, although Charles died in 1867, his widow Sarah continued to live in Hursley. Given a likely connection between the Simeon and Wynyard families whilst in New Zealand, a common love of cricket and living close to one another in Hursley, it is easy to see how William could have learned about St Edward's School.

The school (coincidentally known colloquially as 'Teddies') had been founded during the previous decade in 1863 and by the time of Teddy's arrival was located in Summertown. Although St Edward's started off aiming to educate children of the clergy, it acquired a strong reputation for war heroes beginning with the Boer War and, nearly half a century later, boasted Second World War RAF pilots Guy Gibson VC (of Dambusters fame) and Sir Douglas Bader amongst its former pupils.

In more recent times, the school's entry on the Schools Cricket Online website lists notable cricketers who had been past pupils and states that foremost amongst them was EG Wynyard 'who was credited with the invention of the sweep shot' – an attribution repeated by *The Cricketer* in 'Playing Fields of England' (November 2015). Teddy's trademark shot was a hit to leg that relied more on power than finesse. He would drop onto his right knee and smite the ball over mid on, a skill that would make him an expensive acquisition in any modern-day IPL auction – today commentators would call that a 'slog sweep' with the more classical sweep going nearer square leg than long on. The ability to execute this blow successfully was perhaps facilitated by the lbw law at that time which required the ball both to pitch and strike the batsman in line with the stumps.

At St Edward's around the same time as Teddy, but slightly older than him, were Kenneth Grahame (born 1859), author of *The Wind in the Willows*, and Sir Russell Bencraft (born 1858). Bencraft was to become a life-long friend and worked very closely with Wynyard in the early development of Hampshire County Cricket.

From the very beginning, St Edward's placed great importance on sport but, in addition to cricket, it was rugby that was played and not football. Not surprisingly, Teddy took to this new game for him like a duck to water – a clear sign of his versatility, talent and willingness to try anything new.

Warsop quoted from the *St Edward's School Chronicle* which had this to say at the end of the first season, 1877/78: '(Wynyard) came out wonderfully at the end of the season as a three-quarterback, running very strongly and being a very safe tackler; also kicks well and is a brilliant forward.' In his second season (1878/79) he was top scorer with twelve goals and twenty-one tries, earning the following praise: 'one of the best all round players that the school has ever seen ... and it is partly owing to him that we have won so many matches.'

Fifty-seven years later, Plum Warner wrote an obituary in *The Cricketer* following Teddy's death and repeated the following tribute passed by a teenage contemporary: 'he was a glorious three-quarter, fast and strong, and could turn on a sixpence when in full cry. Had he not gone into the Army, he would have reached the top in the rugger world.'

Whilst the athletics records at Charterhouse did not show him as excelling in non-ball games, Warsop says 'at school he performed creditably as an oarsman and on the running track'.

If he was a 'brilliant' rugby player and one 'who would have reached the top', what superlatives could be used to describe his cricketing career at his new school?

Teddy had joined in the spring and so was just in time for St Edward's 1877 season, and he won his first-eleven colours after his very first match against St Catherine's Club. Whilst he only made a single in a total score of 16 in the first innings, he scored 38 before being run out, in a total of 138, in the second. In twelve matches that year, he played sixteen innings totalling 243, at a not very spectacular average of 16.2, but he did make a top score of 87 not out against Oriel College Second Eleven which was the highest ever made for the School at that time.

Warsop quotes again from the *School Chronicle* about their new protégé, saying he 'bats in good style, and when set scores rapidly; would do well to remedy the grave faults of being too eager to make big hits, and of getting before his wicket; the best field in the eleven; returns splendidly'. Very prescient comments when considering Teddy's future cricketing career!

Early on in the following season, Teddy had made such an impression that, at the age of just seventeen years and sixty-six days, he was asked to play for Hampshire County Cricket Club at Lord's against MCC. It would be nice to think that his father made the train journey up from Winchester to see his son perform at St John's Wood, where William had first played nearly twenty-five years beforehand.

The Times report on 7 June 1878 about the previous day's play said MCC were as strong as Hampshire were weak. By the close their correspondent felt 'the fate of Hampshire may be predicted with a tolerable amount of correctness'. MCC had batted first and began their innings at 12.15 pm; by lunch had scored 79 for four and were all out by 4.10 pm for 155 runs. Teddy caught out Mr E Bray for 13. When it was their turn Hampshire were dismissed for 24 in just one hour and twenty-five minutes. Teddy batted at number eight and scored one run. MCC enforced the follow on and Hampshire had limped to 32 for two when stumps were drawn.

The next day play resumed at 12.10 pm, and MCC needed only one more hour to finish off the match. Hampshire managed a further 33 to be all out for 65 to lose by an innings and 66 runs. Teddy's was one of the eight wickets to fall and again, GF Vernon caught him off Rylott's bowling, but this time for a duck. Arnold Rylott took fourteen wickets in the match.

The score of 24 in the first innings remains Hampshire's third-lowest total in their history. The record is 15 made at Edgbaston in 1922, and is the shortest completed first-class innings ever, lasting only 8.5 overs (or fifty-three balls). Quite remarkably, even though Warwickshire responded with 228, Hampshire went on to win!

It was not a very auspicious start for Teddy but, in truth, it was not a very auspicious performance by his county who did not call on him again that season.

The very next day, 8 June, he displayed his resilient temperament by returning to school and scoring 40. That season he played twelve matches, batted in fifteen innings, scoring 304 runs and improving his average to 23.38, better but still not great. His new top score of 88 prompted the *School Chronicle* to say 'by far the best bat in the Eleven, being a safe run-getter when once set. A brilliant field all round. Fair change bowler, with great break.'

Warsop reports that it was not until the following season, in 1879, that he bowled regularly and his figures for his entire school career were 498 balls bowled (some four- and some five-ball overs), thirty-four wickets for 184 runs (average 5.41) with best figures of five for 22.

He captained the First Eleven in 1879 and headed both the batting and bowling averages. He played in eighteen out of the nineteen matches and fifteen victories were secured with only one defeat. He set up another school record for highest score of 95 and also the largest aggregate of 773 runs, producing the excellent average of 42.94.

His complete first-eleven career was forty-two matches, fifty-one innings, five not outs, 1,320 runs, ten fifties, only four ducks, a top score of 95 and an average of 28.69. Warsop states that he played in other matches at the school including his first recorded century of 101 not out for the Football Eleven v the School Eleven.

Hampshire did not really play during 1879, but Russell Bencraft became secretary halfway through the season and arranged a match between the Gentlemen of Hampshire and MCC at Southampton. It began on 25 August but was not a first-class game. Teddy was out again to Rylott scoring 3 in the first innings before making 12 in the second.

Let the *St Edward's School Chronicle* have the final say on his cricketing career at the school:

Captain. By far the best all round cricketer that has ever been at St Edward's. Unsurpassed as a bat; very fine field with a sharp return; a good slow bowler breaking both ways. Owing to his excellent management the Eleven have experienced a far more successful season than they could possibly have hoped for, and mainly through his exertions cricket throughout the school has materially improved.

With such glowing words ringing in his ears, at the end of the 1879 summer, it was time to move on from St Edward's and he travelled seven miles to the nearby Oxford Military College in Cowley. Almost from birth, it had seemed Teddy was destined for a career in the Armed Forces and so the final stage of his education was a private fee-paying (£90-100 guineas a year) military boarding academy. Boys normally joined no later than thirteen to be prepared on a four-year course for a military commission, but Teddy was already eighteen. The college had been founded in 1876 with the Duke of Cambridge as its patron and Lord Wolseley on its Council, but went bankrupt twenty years later in 1896. The college's eighty-eight acres later housed Morris Motors (1929-32) and Nuffield Press. The main building was demolished in 1957 and the area is now the Oxford Business Park.

Teddy was afforded the opportunity, however, to play again for Hampshire during 1880. He played a total of six matches which included scores of 75 and 49, home and away against Devon, as well as 52 at Dean Park, Bournemouth, when Somerset were the opponents, but these were not first-class games. His highest first-class score to date was 24, achieved at the Antelope Ground, Southampton against MCC on 25/26 August. He also averaged 48.1 when he turned out for the Southampton club side, St Luke's, as he was now back living at home with his family in nearby Hursley.

His scores illustrate he was just starting to fulfil his potential, but it was time now to move on to the next stage of his young life, which was to continue his Army training and compete in the 1880/81 FA Cup competition.

Old Carthusians, the 1881 FA Cup winners.
Back: Richards, Norris, Colvin, Gillet, Hansell.
Middle: Wynyard, Tod, Prinsep, Page, Parry, Vintcent.
Front: Unknown.

3

THE ROAD TO KENNINGTON OVAL
1880-81

Charles Alcock was the driving force behind the creation of the FA Cup. He was secretary of the Football Association from 1870 until 1895 and secretary of Surrey County Cricket Club for thirty-five years from 1872 until his death in 1907. He had been educated at Harrow School where he remembered playing in an inter-house knock-out competition, and decided to introduce this concept to the FA. The first final was played on 16 March 1872 at Kennington Oval and was won by The Wanderers, captained by Alcock.

Over the next eight years, Wanderers won the cup another four times and the Old Etonians were beaten finalists twice before winning in 1879. Three years earlier, the Old Carthusians had formed a new football club and they played in the FA Cup for the first time in 1879/80. The Wanderers knocked them out in the second round but it was Clapham Rovers who went on to win the trophy.

For the 1880/1 season the Old Carthusians changed their colours to pink, dark blue and cerise. Would that also bring about a change in fortune? Sixty-two teams entered, eight more than the previous year, although four teams, including the mighty Wanderers, had to scratch.

The Old Carthusians began their campaign against Saffron Walden at The Oval on Saturday 23 October 1880. Teddy did not play in a convincing 7-0 win, with captain Edward Parry scoring four goals. It was not the biggest victory of the round though, as holders Clapham Rovers thumped Finchley 15-0 and Old Etonians won 10-0 away at Brentwood.

The draw for the competition in the early stages was conducted on a regional basis (London, Central and Northern districts) to try and control the prohibitive cost of travelling. In the second round the Old Carthusians were home to East London side Dreadnought on 11 December 1880. Teddy played in this match and in all the remaining ties. The Old Carthusians again ran out comfortable winners with a 5-1 score line. The Old Etonians continued on their winning way with a 2-0 home victory against Hendon.

The Carthusian reported 'in the last two matches a new forward has been discovered in EG Wynyard who played brilliantly'. The previous match had been the 1-1 draw in a friendly on 20 November away to Oxford University (beaten FA Cup finalists the previous year) which the school magazine described as the best match played so far that season.

The Old Carthusians had a bye in the third round, as did Darwen amongst others. Old Etonians enjoyed a 3-0 victory away against Herts Rangers but the best result was a 6-0 win by Royal Engineers against Rangers and the Old Carthusians drew them in the fourth round.

The match was to be played on 19 February 1881 and, because of the bye plus bad weather, Parry's men had not played since their 2-1 victory in a friendly against their arch rivals, Old Westminsters, at Vincent Square on 18 December. Only four of the team from the second round (Carter, Prinsep, Parry and Wynyard) played. The Old Carthusians were the underdogs as they journeyed to the Great Lines ground in Chatham to take on the Sappers, but they ran out the victors, 2-1, thanks to goals by Teddy Wynyard and Parry.

On the same day, Old Etonians continued on their winning way defeating Greyfriars at Dulwich, 4-0. Darwen had already gone through a fortnight earlier following a 5-2 win over Sheffield

Wednesday and a week later holders, Clapham Rovers, had beaten Upton Park 5-4. They were to be the Old Carthusians' next opponents.

The tie was played on 19 March 1881 at Kennington Oval and *The Times* reported 'the well known strength of the Clapham Rovers, and the fact they won the Cup last year, caused many to regard their chances of success as very strong'. Clapham led 1-0 at half-time, but from the restart they were pinned back and it was largely down to their goalkeeper, Birkett, they remained ahead. In the fifty-sixth minute, though, Prinsep threw in to Teddy's old school captain, William Page, whose shot brought the scores level. No further goals were scored in normal time, and so an extra half-hour was played. Perhaps because the Old Carthusians were a younger side they had greater fitness, but they were certainly quicker and further goals from Parry and Page saw them through to the semi-finals with a 3-1 win. Bailey's report concluded with the words, 'thus ended one of the best matches of the season.'

On the same day the Old Etonians won 2-1 against Stafford Road at Wolverhampton and new favourites Darwen thumped Romford 15-0. Out of the sixty-two sides that began the competition, just these three were left, which meant one team was going to be given a bye through to the final. That turned out to be Old Etonians.

Darwen FC came from the mill town of that name in Lancashire and had been founded in 1870. They were early pioneers of professional football and in 1879 had caused controversy by signing two professional players, Fergie Suter and James Love, both from Partick Thistle, thought to be the first professional players in the English game. Darwen denied they were professional, although Suter gave up his job as a stonemason as soon as he arrived in Lancashire.

There was no specific FA rule against professionals but Darwen had to overcome an official objection before they were allowed to compete. The players were working men drawn mainly from local cotton mills and they had to work full-time shifts between games. There was likely to have been no love lost between this northern, professionally linked club and their southern, old public schoolboy, strictly amateur opponents.

The semi-final was played on 26 March 1881 at The Oval. The Old Carthusians had an unchanged team but neither of their original professionals, Suter nor Love, played for Darwen. Suter had already controversially moved on again to great local rivals, Blackburn Rovers.

The original referee was to be William Pierce-Dix of Sheffield but he was unavailable and so the responsibility was given to Major (later Sir) Francis Marindin, who was one of the game's finest referees. He had officiated in the previous final and did so subsequently on another eight occasions, as well as having been FA President from 1874 to 1879.

Marindin was one of the most respected and experienced officials in the game, but the problem for Darwen was that he came from the south, as did the two umpires, CH Wollaston (Wanderers) and EC Bambridge (Swifts). They objected even though the original choice, Pierce-Dix, was known to be strongly opposed to professional football. Darwen's objections were rejected by the FA, which was hardly surprising given Marindin's pre-eminence.

When the referee went into the dressing rooms, he noticed that the Darwen players had spikes and protruding studs on the bottom of their boots, contrary to the FA's rules. Marindin reported this infringement to the Old Carthusians but, as replacement footwear could not be secured in time, they sportingly raised no objection, although a few players had reason to rue that decision by the time the game was over.

Darwen then complained about the Old Carthusians being late and took up their positions on the pitch in front of 1,000 spectators in a cold wind, shouting 'time'. The reason for the delay was that one of the Old Carthusians' best players had yet to arrive. Jock Prinsep finally appeared biting on a large sandwich!

There must be considerable sympathy with Darwen on this point. They had travelled at considerable cost to both themselves and their fans, 245 miles south, and were entitled to expect their southern opponents would at least show them the common courtesy of being ready by the appointed kick-off time.

When the game did finally get underway, Old Carthusians had a couple of early corner kicks but could not take advantage of their position, and it was Marshall who headed the opening goal for the northern side, and that was the score at half time.

There was great support for Darwen and Bailey tells how their followers sent up a cloud of carrier pigeons to spread the word. There were crowds back home in Lancashire at the newspaper office celebrating when the score became known.

Early exchanges in the second half were evenly balanced and then there was close interplay between Parry, Page and Wynyard before the final pass to Hansell, whose goal was not without controversy. Darwen claimed the ball had not gone between the posts but rather between the upright and guy rope. Let us not forget we were still ten years away from the introduction of goal nets. Marindin overruled the protest.

The Times then observed, perhaps with typical British understatement, 'the play for a time was very determined.' Matters did not improve and the Old Carthusians went into the lead with a goal by Tod that again was the subject of protest, this time for offside, but Darwen were overruled once more.

Bailey says Darwen 'lost their composure.' Doubtless this was fuelled by a sense of grievance against southern referees. Before becoming too sympathetic to the visitors, however, it is important to remember their players had spikes and protruding studs on their boots in an era when this was not permitted and also the rules did not punish foul play with a penalty kick. Two more goals by Teddy Wynyard and Vintcent wrapped the game up at 4-1.

The Times reported 'the Lancashire club brought with them a reputation for determined and skilful play and their overthrow by the Carthusians was somewhat unexpected ... The Carthusians, however, surpassed the expectations of their friends.'

One assumes no more carrier pigeons were despatched and Darwen never progressed this far in the competition ever again, which is sad, given the passion and commitment of their spectators. It is now determined the final would be Old Carthusians versus Old Etonians.

The Old Etonians had experienced a relatively straightforward passage, scoring twenty-one goals and conceding only one on the way to their fourth final. It was a very impressive record and many commentators considered this experienced side to be strong favourites, although that was by no means a unanimous view.

Whilst Old Carthusians were a relatively new team and had only played for the first time in the competition the year before, they were a young side (average age twenty years 310 days) and were fit and very much in form. They had overcome three of the sides strongly fancied as eventual winners and had also beaten the Old Etonians 3-0 in a friendly on 12 March, just under a month before the final. Page and Wynyard were reported to have done 'a lot of good work going forward' in that game.

This was a final, therefore, which was almost too close to call and the players on both sides were very evenly matched.

The Old Carthusians were unchanged from the last two ties:

Goalkeeper: Leonard Gillett
Full-backs: Elliot Colvin, Walter Norris
Half-backs: Joseph Vintcent, James 'Jock' Prinsep
Forwards, right: William Hansell, Lewis Richards
Forwards, centre: William Page, Teddy Wynyard
Forwards, left: Edward Parry (captain), Alexander Tod

Prinsep, Page and Wynyard had all played together in the same school eleven.

When Jock Prinsep played in 1879 for the losing Clapham Rovers side he became, at seventeen years 245 days, the youngest player in a FA Cup final. This record lasted until 2004 when Curtis Weston played for Millwall against Manchester United. Just seven days after setting the cup final record, Prinsep then became the youngest person ever to play for England when they beat Scotland 5-4 at The Oval. This record remained for 124 years until Wayne Rooney played against Australia in 2003 and is now held by Theo Walcott.

Teddy was Page's central attacking partner and someone he knew well. Whilst Wynyard had missed the opening tie, he had scored twice in the competition so far with a goal against Royal Engineers and another in the bruising encounter with Darwen. Bailey records the following description of him: 'a heavy forward, charging and dribbling well, always middles splendidly, with plenty of dash making himself obnoxious to opposing backs.' He was just twenty years and eight days old at the time of the final but had now reached a height of six feet one inch and weighed in at thirteen stone. A bullying handful for any defender of whatever generation!

Old Carthusians played in a formation which saw Prinsep dropping back to play centre-half and Richards, along with Parry, lying slightly deeper behind the two wingers and two centre forwards. The Old Etonians lined up as follows:

Goalkeeper: John Rawlinson
Full-backs: Charles Foley, Thomas French
Half-backs: Arthur Kinnaird (captain), Bryan Farrer
Forwards, right: William Anderson, John Chevallier
Forwards, centre: Reginald Macaulay, Harry Goodhart
Forwards, left: Herbert Whitfield, Philip Novelli

The captain of Old Etonians was The Hon Arthur Fitzgerald Kinnaird, who played one international match for Scotland, on 8 March 1873, when they were beaten 4-2 by England. He had a reputation as a tough tackler and on one occasion this prompted his wife, Lady Alma, to express concern to a friend, William Kenyon-Slaney, that her husband would one day come home with a broken leg. Kenyon-Slaney's swift reply was 'you must not worry madam. If he does it will not be his own!'

To this day he still holds a unique record. He is the only person ever to have played in nine FA Cup finals and, in the process, to have played in virtually every position, including goalkeeper, where he stepped backwards over his own line to register the first own goal in FA Cup final history.

Charles Alcock said of him in *The Football Annual of 1873*: 'without exception the best player of the day; capable of taking any place in the field; is very fast and never loses sight of the ball; an excellent captain.' That assessment had been made eight years earlier and Kinnaird was now thirty-four years of age, over fourteen years older than the average age of the whole Old Carthusians team.

What is remarkable is not just the variety and extent of the athletic prowess displayed by these twenty-two men (seven played football at international level) but their considerable accomplishments off the field in later life. At least eighteen of the players progressed on to Oxbridge whilst Wynyard and Prinsep went into the Army. It is unclear if Norris and Hansell went straight into their respective careers or not. Norris became a director of Hopcraft and Norris brewery and Hansell became a partner with Hansell and Hales solicitors in Norfolk. After further education the tally became six lawyers, five teachers (whether at school or University – albeit one reverted to making cider), three military men, two bankers, two merchants, one each of an Indian civil servant, mining engineer, brewer and police officer. Two of their number were knighted, one was a Lord and another became an MP.

All of this is not very surprising because the two teams were, after all, comprised entirely of old boys from two of the country's most eminent public schools. The players could not be said, therefore, to be representative of a cross-section of society and were quite unlike the cosmopolitan mix of the sides competing in modern day finals. This should not detract from their achievements and, on Saturday 9 April 1881, they had one common aim – to contest the tenth FA Cup final at Kennington Oval.

The forecast was easterly winds with fair weather and an average temperature of forty-five degrees Fahrenheit. It could not have been that cold because Bailey tells us the headmaster's wife, Mrs Haig Brown, was resplendent 'in a pink dress and beneath a pink parasol cheered all the players'. She, along with most of the school and up to 4,500 other spectators made the journey to the ground to watch this much-anticipated clash between the two old boys' teams.

The referee was William Pierce-Dix, whose withdrawal from the Old Carthusians' semi-final against Darwen had led to the protests about southern bias. His two umpires were Charles HR Wollaston and Ernest Henry Bambridge, who were both international footballers in their own right. At just before a quarter to four, Pierce-Dix called Parry and Kinnaird together and the coin was tossed. It came down in favour of Parry who chose the gasometer end with the wind behind his team.

Macauley kicked off for Old Etonians but Old Carthusians regained possession and went close following two throw-ins from Prinsep. The early exchanges were evenly matched with Macauley running though the middle to earn a corner kick before there was swift interplay between Parry, Wynyard and Page, resulting in Parry's shot going close on goal. The game flowed from one end to the other and Whitfield made some fine runs but Richards kept him in check.

Old Carthusians earned a corner and Teddy had a near miss with a header. When the ball ended in touch about ten yards from the corner Prinsep threw in and Wynyard raced through and his shot opened the scoring. As a result of the haphazard match reporting at the time, none of the accounts, especially in relation to the timing of Wynyard's goal, exactly correspond, but twenty-five minutes seems more likely than *The Sportsman*'s account of ten.

The Old Etonians immediately responded when a great strike from Anderson was only just saved by Gillett. Teddy responded and his shot went under the bar only to have his second goal disallowed for offside. After another corner kick for the Old Carthusians it was half time: Old Carthusians 1, Old Etonians 0.

After the ten-minute break (no one left the field in those days and there were no refreshments) it was time for Old Etonians to have the wind at their backs. Here was the opportunity for this experienced side, with five players who would ultimately perform at international level, to hit back but it was the youth and greater fitness of Old Carthusians that started to prevail. Parry had a goal disallowed for offside and then in the seventy-fifth minute the killer blow was landed. There was a combined run between Page and Parry that resulted in the Old Carthusians captain putting his side 2-0 up.

Kinnaird's men were now tiring and, five minutes later, Page made a telling run, Richards took a shot and the ball went through the posts off Tod's chest. *The Sporting Life* attributed the third to an

Old Etonian own goal, but the general consensus of opinion gives the credit to the Charterhouse historian.

The losing side kept fighting to the end and, indeed, *The Carthusian* many years later said 'perhaps the main feature of the game was the formidable charging of Lord Kinnaird, yet in all fair play, with both elbows crossed over the chest, and kicking furiously'. It was all to no avail as the result was now beyond doubt and Parry was the first overseas captain (born in Toronto) to win the FA Cup.

With the final score at 3-0, after the game both sides were entertained courtesy of Kinnaird and the Old Etonians.

Modern-day cup finals attract widespread press coverage beginning as soon as the identity of the finalists is known and extending through to the most detailed post-mortems once the match is over. The clearest possible indication that football was still in its infancy is that *The Times* made no mention at all of the final in its paper on the day of the game and the following Monday, only gave this brief report:

> This match was played at Kennington Oval on Saturday. The Carthusians were eventually hailed the winners by three goals to none. The game from first to last was of a very fast character. The winning team were in first-rate condition, and each member seemed to thoroughly understand the other's play. This is all the more creditable, as although plenty of good players yearly leave Charterhouse, the Old Carthusians is a club of comparatively recent growth.

In its succinctness, however, the essence of the Old Carthusians' success was neatly encapsulated. In all the accounts of the game the one common feature was the way in which the individual skills of Parry and his men were combined to perform as a team.

One of the best early football publications was *Association Football and The Men Who Made It* by Alfred Gibson and William Pickford, published in 1905/6, and the authors had this to say about Old Carthusians' victory:

> The winning team was described as the finest combination seen up to that time to carry off the trophy. EG Colvin, JFM Prinsep, EH Parry, AH Tod, WR Page and the brilliant Captain Wynyard were not only

players of the highest class, but they brought almost to perfection the system of combination. If one was asked to say which team deserved to rank as the first really scientific eleven that the football world knew, one would answer, the Old Carthusians.

Once again the adjective 'brilliant' was ascribed to Teddy's prowess, although this time with the round, rather than the oval ball.

One of the great Carthusian footballers, GO Smith, was a little less fulsome in his praise. Smith scored in both of the Old Carthusians' Amateur Cup successes in 1894 and 1897. He was viewed as the finest centre forward of that decade and his popularity ranked alongside WG Grace in cricket. He played for both the Corinthians and the Casuals who merged in 1939 and whose aims were 'to promote fair play and sportsmanship, to play competitive football at the highest possible level whilst remaining strictly amateur'. Between 1893 and 1901 Smith played twenty times for England, captained them on fourteen occasions and scored eleven goals. He was, therefore, a significant figure in the footballing world in his day. In Edward Grayson's book *Corinthians and Cricketers*, the author tells of the following letter written to him by Smith:

> I stayed with Teddy Wynyard at Sandhurst when I was sixteen and knew him intimately for many years. Oddly enough he never got into the Cricket Eleven at School, but, as you know, played against Australia in 1896 and was a great batsman for Hampshire for many years. He was a sturdy, forceful footballer of the old type, but not perhaps a great one. A good soldier and a magnificent all-round athlete.

The interesting feature of this judgment is that Smith was born in November 1872 and so was under nine years of age at the time of the 1881 FA Cup final. He will have played in the Old Carthusians team with Teddy after our subject returned from India in 1889. Bailey also records that Teddy played twice for the Corinthians in 1893 and scored five times, which was no mean achievement. It seems almost certain, therefore, that Smith's assessment of Wynyard is based upon his play at this time rather than when he was in his footballing prime back in 1881. He would by then have been thirty-two years old and out of serious competitive football for a decade. The game had moved on apace which may explain Smith's use of the words 'of the old type' and his reluctance to describe him as a great player. Words such as great and magnificent are much overused in any event and certainly one should be circumspect about applying them in the context of a player who was effectively only on the major footballing scene for a short period of time, however successful he may have been.

Some publications wrongly describe Teddy as an international footballer. He never played for England but the article appearing about him in the December 1897 edition of *Baily's Magazine of Sports and Pastimes* stated that an invitation for him to represent England against Ireland had to be declined. This was the match played on 18 February 1882 at the Knock Ground, Belfast when England had their biggest ever win, 13-0, in the most appalling weather conditions.

Teddy narrowly missed out, therefore, on the distinction of playing for his country at both cricket and football. Nevertheless, he is a member of a very elite club of just five men who played Test match cricket for England and also won an FA Cup winner's medal. It is even more select in the sense that Teddy was the only amateur amongst them – the other four being Jack Sharp and Harry Makepeace (both of Everton and Lancashire), Andy Ducat (Aston Villa and Surrey) and the great (in this instance few would disagree with the use of the word) Denis Compton (Arsenal and Middlesex).

What of Old Carthusians – 'the finest combination seen up to that time' – did they kick on to further glory?

The answer is that whilst undoubtedly the 1881 FA Final was the high spot in their history, they performed very creditably indeed and reached two more semi-finals and a sixth round over the next five seasons.

In the following year's competition of 1881/2, with Teddy still playing for them, they comfortably beat Esher Leopold 5-0 away and Barnes 3-1 at home in rounds one and two. Wynyard was also selected to represent London against Birmingham at The Oval on Saturday 29 October 1881. He scored off his shoulder as the opposing goalkeeper, Hobson, tried to clear but the match, refereed by Charles Alcock, ended in a draw.

Teddy also played in two other friendlies, the first of which was for the Pilgrims in a 1-0 defeat by the school on 19 November. He hit the cross bar after a splendid run and was reported to have 'played magnificently'. A week later he played for Old Carthusians in a 5-2 defeat by the school on an afternoon when wind and rain continued without any respite. Teddy crossed for Tod to score the first of his side's two goals in an Old Carthusians performance described by *The Carthusian* as 'very shabby'.

The third round, at Kennington Oval on 20 December 1881, saw Old Carthusians drawn against their rivals from the previous year, Royal Engineers. Eight of the team from the final were in the side when Parry won the toss and the Sappers kicked off at 3 o'clock. There was good combination play early on by the holders and Wynyard had a run downfield but his shot was just saved by Druitt in the opposing goal. Druitt was the younger brother of Montague Druitt, who has long had the unfortunate reputation of being one of the suspects in the Jack the Ripper murders!

Unfortunately, Teddy then contrived to score an own goal and so his side went in 1-0 down at half time. After the interval the lead was increased and although the Old Carthusians rallied with both Parry and Hansell going close, their cup heroics ended with a 2-0 defeat.

The Old Carthusians had what was effectively their swansong in the FA Cup in 1886/7, by which time Teddy was overseas. They reached round six and found themselves drawn at home to Preston North End who were to go through the whole of the following season unbeaten to earn themselves the title of the Invincibles. They lost in extra time 2-1 but only after Charles Aubrey Smith had a great chance for Old Carthusians but was tripped from behind in the act of shooting. No penalties back then!

As it was the professional teams who were now dominating the FA Cup, in 1892, the oldest football club, Sheffield, suggested a cup solely for amateur sides. The inaugural FA Amateur Cup competition was played in 1893/4 with Old Carthusians beating Casuals 2-1 in the final. With this victory, Old Carthusians became the first side to do the double of winning both the FA and the FA Amateur Cup competitions.

Just before that game an argument had broken out over the recently introduced sanction of a penalty. An Old Carthusian spokesman is alleged to have said 'penalties are an unwelcome indication that our conduct and honesty are not all it should be'. On that theme, *The Times* opined the view in 1896 that 'Cricket is a kind of synonym for generous behaviour, nor can we condemn any conduct more severely and succinctly than by saying that "it is not cricket"'.

Such sentiments may have been rather naïve, idealistic and simplistic even back then, but Wynyard played his football with Corinthian ideals and his cricket for the three leading nomadic, amateur sides whose membership was defined by the manner in which the game was played. For Teddy, respect for whatever sport he played was never an issue open for consideration but rather an expectation of all those who participated with him. He would not only have approved of that quotation in *The Times*, but lived his life by it.

After his FA Cup success though, his focus and attention was now turning to the military career that lay ahead of him.

Captain E. G. Wynyard served under me when I was comd.g the Oudh Division of the Indian army during 1858. 59. He was then adjutant of his Regiment a position requiring ability and tact as well as a good knowledge of his profession. He was highly thought of by his Comdg Officer and I considered him a very excellent and efficient officer of active and energetic habits and with much tact in conducting his Inter

C. S. Gough

General

June 9th 1897

A reference recommending Captain Wynyard
from General Sir Charles Gough VC

4

DSO: Distinguished Service Overseas 1881-89

On 1 June 1881, it was announced that Second Lieutenant Edward George Wynyard had been promoted to be a Lieutenant in the 1st Warwick Militia. At this time, he was living at home with his father, stepmother, four sisters and half brother plus seven servants at Hursley. That summer, sandwiched between his cup-winning exploits and subsequent attempts to defend the trophy, he found his opportunities to play cricket were restricted by his military training.

He only turned out once for Hampshire against Sussex at Hove between 16 and 18 June 1881. He scored just 1 in the first innings before being caught by James Lillywhite junior, bowled FJ Greenfield, who had taken his wicket twice the year before. Second time round he fared much better scoring 42 out of his side's total of only 86, with Sussex winning by 197 runs.

Teddy did play on three occasions in matches associated with his old school. On 30 June he played for Old Carthusians against Charterhouse and, according to custom, the Old Boys batted first. Going in at number five, he was caught and bowled by Charles Aubrey Smith for 11 in the first innings and was out for 16 in the second with both Parry and Prinsep also in the side. Aubrey Smith took seven wickets in the match. When Wynyard represented the Gentlemen of Hampshire against Charterhouse with Russell Bencraft also in the team, he opened the innings and made 36, with *The Carthusian* describing him as playing 'with great freedom and good style'. He also turned out for his club side, St Luke's, who said he was 'a finished bat, always makes runs; keeps wicket and splendid at cover point'.

The following year, 1882, Teddy did not play any first-class cricket at all, appearing instead in Army matches, topping the batting averages for the Aldershot Division with 258 runs at an average of 51.6 and scoring 112 in the game against I Zingari.

He was able to play four matches for Hampshire in 1883 including the innings defeat by Sussex when he found himself against Charles Aubrey Smith again and was out bowled by him for 14 in the first innings, although *The Times* said Teddy 'hit pluckily'. He made only 12 in the second innings in a match that also saw him make his bowling debut in first-class cricket with his lobs. He secured the wicket of Billy Newham ending with figures of one for 48.

Just over a week later, on 24 May, he returned to the scene of his footballing triumph at Kennington Oval to play a three-day game against Surrey. The home county ran up an impressive total of 650, but in securing a draw Wynyard scored 61 and enjoyed a fifth wicket partnership of exactly 100 with Arthur Wood. In the return fixture at the Antelope Ground, Southampton, he made 25 (out of 154) and 39 (out of 99) in a match Surrey won by 30 runs.

Teddy was meticulous in keeping photograph albums, newspaper clippings and scorecards with his annotations recording events during his career. He retained a silk scorecard of the Surrey game and their total of 650 was described as the largest made in an important match in England (up to that time).

On 16 June 1883, Wynyard turned out for the Butterflies at his old school and opened the bowling taking seven for 61 off twenty-five five-ball overs as Charterhouse were bowled out for 174. *The Carthusian* reported 'Wynyard carried all before him and with his slow curlers secured nearly all the remaining wickets'. Teddy played three more times for Hampshire before his final recorded match of 1883 for a fourteen-man military side at Phoenix Park, Dublin against an eleven-man I Zingari team that included GB and CT Studd and AG Steel. In a drawn game, Teddy scored 9 before being lbw to Steel.

By now Teddy was with the Duke of Cambridge's Own (Middlesex Regiment) and, on 12 May 1883, he received his commission and only eleven days later was selected to become a full-time commissioned officer in the Army with the King's (Liverpool) Regiment. This meant Teddy had to have achieved at least minimum standards of education and military training. He had not been a cadet at the Royal Military College in Sandhurst and, although he had been to the Oxford Military College, his 1st Class extra certificate was obtained from the Hythe School of Instruction in Kent.

Officers remained responsible for purchasing their own uniforms, furniture and equipment, which in the case of cavalry units extended to their horses. Social exclusivity remained just as prevalent because of the expensive lifestyle an officer was still expected to lead and so Teddy needed to have a private income above his army pay in order to support himself. After all, it was still necessary to be both an officer *and* a gentleman.

Teddy did have such private means and, with his commission, was now bound for his first posting overseas, back to the land of his birth in India. His Record of Service showed him to be 'acquainted with' the languages of French (one of his better subjects at Charterhouse) and Hindustani.

On 8 December 1883, *Bralabar*, having being delayed for four days to enable a number of defects in her machinery to be repaired, finally left Portsmouth harbour on her second voyage to Bombay (now Mumbai). It was arranged for her to call at Queenstown (now Cobh) in Southern Cork, Ireland in order to pick up the bulk of her passengers including Lieutenant Wynyard along with 1,038 men, fifteen women and one child.

India was the one place where it was possible to survive without a substantial additional private income because there was less to do, but boredom was seen as the great enemy of the soldier with the attendant risks of drink and women. The solution was sought in sport, and India was considered a sporting paradise for officers but, even so, it was difficult to occupy the whole day, especially as no work took place on Thursday or Sunday. The climate was problematic because in the hot season it was desirable to stay out of the sun altogether. Hockey was prevalent and Teddy was a keen player with the dry grounds making it a faster and more skilful game. Cricket was also very much to the fore and between 1883 and 1890 the King's Regiment, with Wynyard in the side, only lost one match and he averaged the astonishing statistic of 100 with his own bat.

On 9 June 1894, *The Cricket Field* published an interview with Wynyard about his time in India in which he said:

> The bowling against us was generally very easy, and it was no uncommon thing in regimental cricket for a man to have an average of over 100. Once, just as the regiment was starting on a tour, I smashed a bone in my left arm when pig sticking. However, I accompanied the team, and batted with one hand, using a very light bat. For the tour my average was 62, including three not-out innings, which will give you a very good idea of the weakness of the bowling against us. I believe that nearly the whole of the runs were made in singles, except one hit to leg for five.

In 1885, he joined the select list of those players who had scored two separate centuries in the same game, 123 not out and 106. He was playing for the Visitors against the Residents at Naini Tal in the North West Province which was 196 miles south west of his birthplace and described as one of the most picturesque sites in the Himalayas.

The surrounding forests were swarming with bears, tigers and deer which were targets for the big game hunters, and the town itself became the summer headquarters of the colonial administration of the province and was featured in Rudyard Kipling's *Story of the Gadsbys*.

On 18 September 1880 there had been a great landslide that killed 151 people and also destroyed the Assembly Rooms and the Naina Devi Temple in the town. A recreation area called The Flats was later built on the site and it was here, close to the edge of the large eye-shaped lake, that Teddy played his cricket. During the

1885 season he scored seven centuries from seventeen innings there and averaged 67 and, also when playing for the Regiment at Allahabad in Uttar Pradesh, he carried his bat for 123 not out.

Teddy was a bare-knuckle boxer and it was in the mid 1880s that organised Army boxing began in the form of officer-run contests within or between regiments. Also, in an article appearing in *Baily's Magazine and Pastimes* in 1897, the observation was made that whilst in India 'Capt Wynyard was a fairly useful member of the Mess at this time as he formed a regular member of the regimental Polo team in addition to discharging the function of whipper-in to the regimental pack of hounds.'

Teddy was, of course, serving in an infantry regiment, but equestrian sport was an essential component of officer life extending beyond just the cavalry. Officers spent an extraordinarily large proportion of their time hunting and most cavalry and some infantry regiments maintained a pack of hounds who accompanied the army to stations across the Empire. As whipper-in, it was Teddy's responsibility to assist the huntsman and help keep the hounds together, relocating any that became separated from the pack, and so a degree of resourcefulness was needed along with knowledge of the terrain.

Pig-sticking was also a popular pursuit and considered as a 'gentleman's game'. It entailed pursuing wild pigs, often over three feet in height with eight inch tusks, across country on horseback with an eight-foot spear. It was a dangerous pursuit and quite apart from having aggressive boar and the odd tiger to contend with, there were natural hazards in the lay of the land to ride over and, as previously mentioned, Teddy sustained a broken arm when participating in this activity. Spectators watched from horses or elephants as officers competed for the Kadir Cup over a course near Meerut. The winner was the first to spear the pig and Teddy's Old Carthusian contemporary, Robert Baden-Powell, was the victor in 1883. Gradually, however, the popularity of this pastime was challenged by the new sport of polo.

The British claimed to have invented the modern game near to the India and Burma border in the 1850s, and it became integral to army life. Almost all stations had a polo ground of sorts and station games were played at least two or three times a week all year round. Indeed, Tony Mason and Eliza Riedi say in *Sport and the Military: The British Armed Forces 1880-1960* that, 'it became ... an almost compulsory activity for young officers ... and potentially a major addition to their expenses.' It was also dangerous with a risk of serious injury through falls brought about by bad riding on half trained ponies on sun baked, rock hard ground.

By 1885 though, storm clouds were starting to gather over Burma. Teddy could look back at a successful cricket season especially with his performances at The Flats. Clearly he had also enjoyed the regimental field sports but by October it was time to put bat and pads away, kennel the hounds, stable the polo ponies and start preparing for war.

As a result of the First and Second Anglo-Burmese wars, Burma was split into two parts. Lower Burma was under British rule with Rangoon as capital whilst Upper Burma was under the control of King Thibaw in Mandalay.

Thibaw had secured the throne seven years earlier by having all his relatives who posed a possible threat arrested and brutally killed. The British protested but did not intervene because they were committed to a war in Afghanistan (*plus ça change, plus c'est la même chose*). In an attempt to restrain the British, Thibaw started to form close commercial ties with the French who already held a dominant position in Indo-China.

The Secretary of State for India was Lord Randolph Churchill, father of Winston. He did not have the slightest intention of dividing up Burma with France and saw annexation as the only solution. Accordingly, he issued an ultimatum to Thibaw on 22 October 1885. He only gave the King until 10 November to accept the terms, which included British control over Burmese foreign relations. In anticipation of its rejection, orders had already been issued, on 21 October, for an expeditionary force to set sail for Burma. Teddy, whose regiment was one of those called up, duly made his way to Calcutta and on 3 November boarded an ocean steamer, which arrived at Rangoon four days later.

Thibaw viewed the ultimatum as humiliating and publicly denounced the British as barbarians. He knew his response meant war and as soon as the news reached Churchill on 11 November 1885, a telegraph was sent to the Viceroy containing instructions to advance on Mandalay at once.

The Expeditionary Force was under the overall command of Lieutenant General Sir Harry Prendergast, KCB VC, who was a veteran of the Indian Mutiny. Brigadier General HH Foord was in command of the 1st Infantry Brigade that was made up of Teddy's 2nd Battalion King's (Liverpool) Regiment plus the 21st and 25th Madras Infantry. Many accounts refer to Teddy as serving with the 8th Regiment of the King's Liverpool but following the army reforms by Edward Cardwell and Hugh Childers, the two battalions of the 8th became the 1st and 2nd Battalions of the King's (Liverpool) Regiment.

The Expeditionary Force sailed on board twenty-four steamers and twenty-three flatboats equipped with awnings and adequate living quarters, chartered from the Irrawaddy Flotilla Company. When Wynyard's sea steamer arrived at Rangoon on 7 November he was immediately transferred to the steamer *Yankeentaung* which was towing two flats transporting the telegraph equipment and stores. Space was at a premium with each British serviceman allotted twenty square feet!

Yankeentaung left Rangoon on the ninth and arrived at Thayetmo, near to the border with Upper Burma five days later. At noon on 14 November 1885, Prendergast ordered IMS *Irrawaddy* and two launches to reconnoitre upriver where they came under fire from two stockades at Nyaungbinmaw and Sinbaungwe that lay on opposite sides of the river.

On 15 November, the remaining boats then crossed the border in a single column about two cables apart. *Yankeentaung* was twelfth in line and navigation was difficult with the steamers often going aground causing obvious problems in staying together. The following day all the steamers weighed anchor at daybreak and, at 9.15 am, landed detachments, including the Liverpool Regiment, at Zaunygyandaung, a village on the right bank two miles below the stockades and concealed from view. The official despatch stated 'nothing could be more picturesque than the advance of the Liverpool Regiment from hillock to hillock while the batteries were kept amused by the shells from the *Irrawaddy*.' Whilst both stockades were seized, the Burmese fled panic-stricken and were not captured.

Minhla lay ahead and through intelligence gathered, it was known there were two forts there, which Prendergast decided to attack at the same time. Brigadier General Foord's 1st Infantry brigade including Teddy's regiment, commanded by Col AA Le Mesurier, were landed at Patango, nearly two and a half miles below the Gwegyaung-Kamyo fort. They marched through steamy heat for nearly three hours via a narrow path over hills and through dense jungle to the white pagoda of Gwegyaung where the fort held a commanding position 250 feet above the river.

The British encountered two pickets of the enemy who gave no resistance and fled northwards, but not to the fort. As the flotilla rounded the bend, both forts opened up with gunfire but the Royal Artillery on board the *Irrawaddy* responded with devastatingly accurate hits. The Liverpool Regiment then occupied the high ground east of the fort and the Burmese were completely surprised by the attack because all their guns were pointed in the opposite direction. As the British soldiers advanced with a rush, the Burmese fled by the north-west gate and of the 1,700 men present under the leadership of Maung Sanhla Sin Bo, only his second in command and a lieutenant and two soldiers, all of whom were wounded, remained in the fort.

The attack on the other fort at Minhla was not as straightforward but eventually it was successfully stormed. Prendergast left garrisons, including two companies of the Liverpool Regiment, in the ruins of each of the two forts. Mr Robert Phayre, who had previously been Assistant Resident at Mandalay, was left behind as Civil Officer.

Prendergast continued sailing upriver and, on 23 November, two companies of the Liverpool Regiment, along with other detachments, were landed at Pagan. He then pressed on and easily captured Myingyan.

At 4 pm on 26 November, near Nagaung, a Burmese state barge paddled downstream flying the King's flag and also one of truce. Prendergast responded by saying that if the King and his army surrendered and European residents at Mandalay were uninjured, the King's life would be spared. A deadline was set of 4 pm the following day. King Thibaw knew he was beaten and agreed to surrender himself and his army.

Prendergast then anchored at Mandalay on 28 November and the British troops marched in separate columns with bands playing up to the capital, entering through each of its different gates. The next day, at 3.30 pm, Thibaw and the ladies in his family were led from the palace through the throne room, between avenues of British soldiers, to the bullock carriages prepared to carry them to SS *Thooreah*. Thibaw's formidable wife, Supayalat, who was heavily pregnant, was determined to retain her dignity and nonchalantly asked a British soldier to light her cheroot.

On board the steamship, the King's retinue was guarded by two companies of Teddy's Liverpool Regiment and conveyed to Rangoon. Thibaw and his queen were exiled to Ranagiri fort near Bombay. Thibaw died in 1916 and his death saw the end of the Burmese monarchy forever. The Indian Government then allowed Supayalat to return to Burma where for some years she lived in a modest bungalow in Rangoon.

As at 28 December 1885 there were two companies of the King's Liverpool garrisoned at Minhla, where it is likely Teddy was based, and another two at Myingan.

The whole operation had lasted under a fortnight and the official despatch recorded:

> By rapidity of movement, by skilful energy, and by the exercise of humane forbearance, Sir Harry Prendergast has succeeded, with comparative little loss to the force under his command and without unnecessary bloodshed or undue severity towards the enemy, in occupying Mandalay, in capturing its King and taking possession of the whole of Upper Burma.

If only life were really that simple! The speed of the British advance meant that a significant part of the Burmese army had not been obliged to fight but instead had escaped into the jungle with their arms intact. Following the capture of Mandalay, the British showed little respect for their surroundings and there was a collapse of the traditional administrative system because the monarchy had been Buddhism's patron and focal point. This upheaval in custom and beliefs sparked off Burmese brigandry. Disbanded soldiers formed wandering bands called dacoits. As guerrilla warfare expanded, Prendergast ordered harsh punitive measures, shooting anyone with arms, burning villages where there was resistance, and flogging suspected members of dacoits.

The formal British proclamation on 1 January 1886 that Burma would now become a province of British India only aggravated the situation. The Secretary for Upper Burma wrote to the Chief Commissioner that 'the people of this country have not, as by some expected, welcomed us as deliverers from tyranny' – words that reverberate through history to this day.

The expeditionary force was wholly inadequate to occupy the entirety of the country. Upper Burma extended over 140,000 square miles with a population of three and a half million. A considerable part of this vast expanse was impenetrable jungle and even in the populated districts there were no roads or bridges. During the rainy season large areas would be under water for weeks.

The guerrilla leaders (who were called 'Bos') were swift and unmerciful in dealing with their fellow Burmese whom they thought were assisting the British. Two of the most prominent Bos were Maung Swe and the yellow-robed monk, Oktama (also known as U Ottama or Oo Temah) and their strength increased substantially after they joined forces.

Robert Phayre had been left in charge at Minhla and its surrounding district including Minbu, supported by a small force. Bo Swe had control of the southern regions of Minbu and Bo Ottama the northern areas of the town. Early in June 1886, Phayre along with about 100 men started from Minbu to attack Bo Swe at Taunggauk Camp, Padein. The guerrilla leader reinforced his strength overnight with a further 200 to 300 men and when Phayre led the attack, on 9 June, he was shot dead by Bo Swe. When he was about to fall from his horse, another dacoit, Bo Nay Mee, dashed towards him and cut off his head. Phayre's death prompted his men to fall back leaving his body to be carried off by the Burmese and a search party later found his remains. Not only had he been decapitated but also quartered. His head and quarters were found suspended from the branches of different trees. A truly horrific spectacle, but his body was taken back and buried at Minbu where his wife Edith, along with their baby son Robert, who was barely six months old, had been awaiting his return.

Since the turn of the year the King's (Liverpool) Regiment had operated in small groups seeking out the guerrillas in the jungle. The terrain was ideal for the enemy with dense terai jungle making pursuit virtually impossible. Often the men would have to march for five to six hours, withstanding intense heat and cutting a path through the undergrowth. It was imperative they pushed on as fast as they could, making straight for the believed position of the enemy because, if they rested for a moment, they would very easily lose touch with the dacoits. The incessant forced marches and exposure took its toll on the troops, not helped by the serious lack of fresh food and scanty nature of the supplies with little to forage off the land.

In June 1886 Teddy was at Salin, a town in the Minbu district. There had been great outrage at the manner of Phayre's death and three days later, on 12 June 1886, Captain Dunsford of the 2nd (Queen's Own) Bengal Light Infantry, who was in command at Salin, received information that rebels led by Oktama were collecting to the north and west of the town with the aim of attacking it.

Dunsford, with 200 men from the Bengal Infantry along with another 200 men from the King's Liverpool led by Teddy Wynyard, armed with about forty rifles in total, headed five miles to the north where they saw about 160 insurgents on their left flank moving on Salin. Dunsford ordered a change in direction to the left and attacked them. Oktama's men were successfully driven out of their position but retired to a high hill and pagoda two miles south of

Salin where he joined up with his other forces to make around 500 dacoits in all.

The British held higher ground and were able to shoot down on the rebels, taking the hill without casualty but inflicting heavy losses on their enemy in the process. Oktama then regrouped and took up a strong defensive position in the walled pagoda.

Brisk fire was exchanged and Dunsford, assisted by Teddy, led the charge until Oktama shot Dunsford through the head in the final rush. One of the rebels was able to cut off the Captain's head as he lay dying. When the same barbarous act had been committed on Phayre, his men had been forced back. The attack was now at a pivotal point. If it faltered there could be ruthless retribution at the hands, guns and swords of Oktama and his men.

This was Wynyard's moment. At just over twenty-five years of age, he took overall command of his near-exhausted troops and pressed home the charge, amidst a scene of carnage, taking the pagoda with only the losses of Dunsford and one private of the King's Liverpool. The precise extent of the enemy's losses are unknown but inevitably were much higher, although Oktama escaped to fight another day.

It was a highly emotional moment when Teddy Wynyard and his men recovered Dunsford's headless body and took it back to Minbu for burial there, alongside Phayre, in the British cemetery.

Ten days later details of the incident appeared in *The Times* although the paper heeded the sensitivities of its readers by sparing them details of the horrific decapitation as they read the news at their breakfast table. The report for 22 June 1886 stated in a very matter of fact way:

> Rangoon 20 June: On the 12th inst. Captain Dunsford of the 2nd Bengal Infantry and Lieutenant Wynyard with 40 rifles of the King's (Liverpool) Regiment attacked 500 Dacoits at Salon [sic], on the western bank of the river, 50 miles north of Minhla. The Dacoits were driven out but Captain Dunsford was killed and 3 men of the Liverpool Regiment were wounded. These Dacoits formed part of the force of Bosweb, who recently killed Mr Phayre.

There was, though, an even greater enemy than the dacoits, namely disease. There had been an outbreak of cholera as the troops advanced upstream, and this developed into a raging epidemic in Mandalay and then spread further afield, eventually killing 154 men out of 271 sufferers. There was the constant fear of jungle malaria that proved fatal to the British troops as well as a high risk of diarrhoea, dengue fever, and typhoid fever, to name just a few of the infectious illnesses that lay in wait, while the climate was the worst possible for anyone with respiratory problems.

On 28 June 1886, just sixteen days after his heroic efforts, Teddy, who had fallen ill, left Burma never to return there on active service. He stayed for three weeks back in India before boarding ship for home on 20 July 1886 in order to recuperate.

Meanwhile Oktama had besieged Salin, but after three days he was driven away by the 2nd Hampshire Regiment, led by Captain Atkinson who was killed in the process. Oktama was finally captured near Legaing in October 1889 and hanged for his crimes but, just before his execution, he asked for some paper and composed a verse which is still read to this day, stirring emotions of Burmese patriotism.

Teddy's efforts in the campaign at Salin warranted a mention in despatches. On 10 March 1887, Major General White wrote to the Adjutant General in India telling how Brigadier General Low had commanded in two of the most turbulent districts in Upper Burma. In turn, Low named a number of officers and amongst those specially selected was: 'Lieutenant Wynyard, Liverpool Regiment, on the death of Capt. WG Dunsford, 2nd Bengal Infantry, proved himself to possess a quick appreciation of what was needed on an occasion of considerable danger and by bold leading converted a critical situation into an assured success.'

On 25 November 1887 the *London Gazette* contained a notice stating: 'The Queen has been pleased to direct these distinctions shall take effect from 1st July 1887 ... DSO – Lt EG Wynyard King's Liverpool Regiment.'

The Distinguished Service Order was at that time a very recent military decoration having only been instituted during the previous year. The Order was established to reward individual instances of meritorious or distinguished service in war, normally under fire. Prior to 1943 the honour could be given only to someone mentioned in despatches and was not normally bestowed upon officers below the rank of captain. Where a junior officer was honoured with the DSO, this was often regarded as an acknowledgement that the individual had only just missed out on the Victoria Cross.

Wynyard was, of course, only a Lieutenant at the time of Salin and so it shows just how courageous his conduct was considered to have been and how close he came to being awarded the very highest military decoration for gallantry.

In addition to the DSO, Wynyard was also awarded a Burma medal with clasp, but there was another treasured relic that makes a fascinating footnote to this part of the story. In the introduction to Keith Warsop's book, Teddy's daughter-in-law, Ann, wrote:

> A more present-day link we have with EG Wynyard himself is an ornamental sword which was a souvenir of his involvement in the Burma campaign of 1885-7 in which he won his DSO. It is a huge weapon with a richly ornamented carved handle and would take a lot of strength to wield. When I had it examined by an expert he said its greatest value lay not in the handle but in the fact that it had a genuine Saracen blade. This is razor sharp so we always keep it in its scabbard and when our three daughters were young they were warned strongly not to attempt to play with it!

Very wise counsel indeed knowing what we do about the grisly outcome to both Mr Phayre and Captain Dunsford.

While guerrilla warfare continued to rage in Burma, on his return home Teddy had recovered sufficiently to play for Hampshire against Surrey at The Oval, beginning on 16 May 1887. By this time Hampshire matches were no longer counted as first-class. Although Surrey won the match comfortably by seven wickets with scores of 253 and 92 for three, Teddy made a great impression scoring 75 in the first innings out of a total of only 132 before being caught by Bobby Abel, off the bowling of George Lohmann.

On 16 June 1887, Wynyard's portrait and biography had appeared in the magazine *Cricket* and the article stated:

Those who remember Mr Wynyard's exceptional promise as a bat when he made his first appearance for Hampshire as a boy some nine years ago, will, we are inclined to think agree with us that with the opportunities offered to some other cricketers, by this time he would, in all probability, have been in the front rank of batsmen ... Mr Wynyard has every physical advantage as a cricketer. Quite six feet high and strong withal, he has not only reach to help him but powers of hitting, which he utilizes fully when opportunity occurs. He plays in good style with a very straight bat, and, as he showed against Surrey at the Oval last month, has excellent defence. On that occasion, indeed, he batted with great judgment and with more practice in good cricket we should expect to see him make his mark effectually. He is a splendid field anywhere, and has also been of use as a bowler in minor matches.

After the Surrey game Teddy took himself off for a few weeks to the fresh air of the Italian lakes in order to further his convalescence, but was back by 24 June to play for his county as well as MCC, Old Carthusians and United Services. On 11 August he scored a fine 63 representing the Gentlemen of Hampshire in a close draw against the Gentlemen of Canada at Southampton. His best innings by far though that month was a knock of 233 for Incogniti against Phoenix Park in Dublin.

As far as Hampshire was concerned it was a very disappointing season and he played five more times for them and all were defeats. They lost against Sussex, Essex, Somerset (home and away) and Surrey. He scored 43 against Essex and 46 against Somerset (away) but his final match back against Surrey proved to be a particularly low point. At Southampton, on 25 and 26 August, he bagged a pair bowled by Lohmann again in the second innings and his side lost by the very wide margin of an innings and 290 runs. He kept wicket in this game though and secured two dismissals, one stumping and a catch.

Doubtless he would have liked to score some runs before boarding ship, rehabilitation over, on 8 September 1887, to return to his army service in India. Upon his arrival there he soon made up for his two ducks by scoring 237 for his Regiment against the 23rd Royal Fusiliers.

Teddy was made adjutant of his regiment and was now based at Lucknow, the capital city of Uttar Pradesh which was the state of his birth.

His stay in India did not last long because he left again, on 4 April 1888, in order to keep his appointment with the Prince of Wales at St James's Palace. On Friday 11 May 1888, Teddy wore his full dress uniform as he waited in the Throne Room for his name and rank to be called. He then stepped forward, and bowed to the Prince of Wales who was seated on a dais with male members of the Royal family and officials of the Royal Household behind him. The Adjutant General to the Forces, Viscount Wolseley, who, by coincidence had been closely involved with the Oxford Military College where Teddy had started his military training, presented Teddy with his DSO.

While back in England his opportunities to play any cricket were limited. Three days after receiving his medal he turned out for MCC against Kent at Lord's and played five times for Hampshire but did not score well. In his final county game at Hove, Sussex won again by an innings and 63 runs, with Teddy making only 3 and a duck. He did, however, bowl his lobs and took two for 11. Both wickets were bowled and one of his victims was his Old Carthusian contemporary, Charles Aubrey Smith.

His last recorded match for the year was the Hampshire County Challenge Cup final, on 14 September 1888, at the County Ground, Southampton, when he opened for Winchester against Portsmouth Borough making 26 and 38 in a comfortable victory. He also took three wickets, including Arthur Conan Doyle batting at number seven, stumped for 13. The author then took two wickets and top scored with 32 in Portsmouth's second innings.

On 2 October 1888, Wynyard made his way back to India and so only overlapped by five days with the arrival in England of the first ever New Zealand Maori national rugby union team – also the first to wear all black and perform a haka. The squad included three members of the New Zealand branch of the Wynyard family: George ('Sherry'), Henry ('Pie') and William Thomas ('Tabby'). This side made such a significant impact on the development of New

Zealand rugby that they were inducted into the International Rugby Hall of Fame in 2008.

Not only did Teddy miss seeing his visiting cousins play but he was still overseas when his uncle, General Edward George Wynyard, died aged seventy-one, at 5 Portman Street on Sunday 29 September 1889. Teddy inherited his uncle's gold hunter repeating watch.

Meanwhile, in India, Teddy continued with his various sporting pursuits and made something of a name for himself in his new role. I recently purchased from a dealer in manuscripts a reference letter that, whilst dated 9 June 1897, related to Teddy's time as an adjutant. Its author was General Sir Charles Gough VC who came from a remarkable family as both his brother and son were also awarded the Victoria Cross. He wrote the following glowing recommendation on United Service Club, Pall Mall notepaper:

> Captain EG Wynyard served under me when I was commanding the Oudh Division of the Indian Army during 1888,89. He was then adjutant of his Regiment a position requiring ability and tact as well as a good knowledge of his profession. He was highly thought of by his Commanding officer and I considered him a very excellent and efficient officer of active and energetic habits and with much tact in conducting his duties.

Unfortunately Teddy suffered a recurrence of his ill health and on 8 November 1889 had to leave India, thus bringing to an end his distinguished service overseas.

COUNTY CRICKET GROUND, DERBY.

AUGUST 6th, 7th, and 8th, 1894.

DERBYSHIRE v. HAMPSHIRE.

Batsman's No.	HAMPSHIRE.	First innings		Second Innings.	
1	Mr A J L Hill	c and b Davidson		0 b Davidson	6
2	Mr C Robson	b Hulme		1 b Hulme	7
3	Barton	c Wright, b Davidson		1 l b w, b Sugg	29
4	Capt Quinton	c Storer, b Hulme		20 c and b Davidson	17
5	Bacon	c Storer, b Davidson		4 b Sugg	14
6	Mr H F Ward	not out		61 not out	12
7	Capt E G Wynyard	c Davidson, b Hulme		90 not out	9
8	Mr A H Wood	c and b Hulme		5	
9	Mr D A Steele	c sub, b Hulme		10	
10	Baldwin	c Evans, b Davidson		5	
11	Cave	b Hulme		3	
		wds 1 bys 3 lb nb		4 wds bys 4 lb 3 nb 1	8
		Total		204 Total	102

Fall of Wickets.—1st Inns.

1	2	3	4	5	6	7	8	9	10	1	2	3	4	5	6	7	8	9	10
1	2	2	9	32	159	176	194	199	204	13	13	60	66	91	...	...	...	...	...

2nd Inns. (for right columns)

Bowler's No.	DERBYSHIRE.	First Innings.		Second Innings.	
3	Mr L G Wright	b Baldwin		86 b Baldwin	2
4	Hulme	run out		24 c Quinton, b Baldwin	7
7	Bagshaw	c and b Hill		5 c Quinton, b Baldwin	10
5	Chatterton	l b w, b Baldwin		11 b Hill	16
1	Davidson	b Baldwin		0 c Robson, b Baldwin	9
2	Storer	b Baldwin		0 b Baldwin	10
6	Sugg W	run out		27 c Hill, b Barton	77
8	Mr F Evershed	b Baldwin		0 c Hill, b Baldwin	19
10	Evans	b Steele		2 run out	23
9	Malthouse	not out		6 c Robson, b Baldwin	4
11	Mr G G Walker	b Hill		6 not out	2
		wds bys lb nb		... wds 1 bys 7 lb 2 nb	10
		Total		117 Total	188

Umpires—
G Atkinson & F Coward

Fall of Wickets—1st Inns.

1	2	3	4	5	6	7	8	9	10	1	2	3	4	5	6	7	8	9	10
45	55	73	75	75	82	84	95	109	117	17	19	29	82	83	106	139	147	178	188

2nd Inns. (for right columns)

LUNCHEON *provided at the Grand Stand from* 12 *till* 3, *at* 2/6 *each.*

Printed on the Ground by S. B. Smith, of 24, Back Sitwell-street, Derby.
Price 1d

Teddy played a key role in Hampshire's victory over Derbyshire in 1894 – a win that helped propel Hampshire into the County Championship

5

INTO THE GOLDEN AGE

1890-94

Back in England, as recognition for his efforts in Burma and India, Teddy was promoted to Captain and on 19 March 1890 transferred to the Welsh Regiment. On 22 August he was seconded to the Royal Military College at Sandhurst and appointed an Instructor in Tactics, Military Administration and Law in the place of Major F Luttman-Johnson. There was a strong connection between Sandhurst and the Wynyard family. Teddy's cousin, Lieutenant Colonel Montagu Wynyard, was the Assistant Commandant and Secretary and Montagu's younger brother, Rowley Wynyard, had been on the instructional staff between 1883 and 1890 when Douglas Haig had been one of his cadets.

On 20 April 1891, in recognition of their respective appointments, Teddy and his cousin, Montagu, along with Captain Richard Daymer Wynyard (another of Montagu's brothers), attended a Levee at St James's Palace where Major General Clive (Governor and Commandant at Sandhurst) presented Teddy to the Prince of Wales with the Duke of Cambridge in attendance.

As an instructor Teddy had responsibility for training the cadets in their respective classes, maintaining good order and discipline, and there was a specific direction stating 'great care must be taken that no waste of materials takes place'. Each month he had to send a report to the Professor of Tactics, for onward transmission to Montagu, detailing the work carried out and highlighting any cadet who was not progressing satisfactorily.

On 1 January 1891, Wynyard was transferred to the Fortifications branch where one of the cadets to receive tutelage was a former Harrow public schoolboy who had not distinguished himself academically and had twice failed the Sandhurst entrance examination, finally passing at the third attempt. Winston Spencer Churchill entered the RMC in September 1893 and revelled in his new environment, writing in *A Roving Commission My Early Life* that 'I was no longer handicapped by past neglect of Latin, French or Mathematics. We had now to learn fresh things and we all started equal. Tactics, Fortifications, Topography (map making), Military Law and Military Fortification, formed the whole curriculum.'

Churchill graduated in December 1894 with honours finishing eighth out of his batch of 150. Two months later the 21-year-old Winston was commissioned as a second lieutenant into the 4th Hussars, and so began the career of this country's greatest ever wartime Prime Minister.

In *The Story of Sandhurst*, Hugh Thomas wrote that none of the staff officers of this period stood out as individuals 'except perhaps for Major Wynyard (known as "Blood Orange") a celebrated cricketer in his day'. Thomas did not elaborate on how Teddy earned this nickname, but one imagines it was a combination of his natural appearance and his reaction when something displeased him!

There was plenty of sport also on offer for the cadet. Cricket, football, rugby, athletics, fives, golf, polo (abolished in 1894), boxing and fencing were all activities that were available, along with a gymkhana, point-to-point races and a gun club. Hockey had not been played for nearly forty years, having been superseded by football, but, in 1897, Wynyard reintroduced it and became secretary, organising nine matches that year.

Teddy was also honorary secretary of the association football side for the seasons 1894 through to 1896, with matches arranged, amongst others, against his own eleven and Charterhouse School. There was also a special athletics race for officers and he won at the meeting on 19/20 May 1892, which was an improvement on his performance at school! Hence, there was no shortage of sporting activity for Teddy, but his return to England also provided an increased opportunity to play cricket, not only putting together his own team against the college, but as Sandhurst was only fifty miles away from Southampton, it meant he could play more regularly for his county.

The period beginning 1890 through to the outbreak of the First World War in 1914 is widely regarded and known as the 'Golden Age of Cricket', and Wynyard played with virtually everyone of note, both amateur and professional, and of all nationalities during that time.

It may seem strange to say about a man who had already won an FA Cup medal and the DSO before he was even twenty-six years old, that Teddy was only now about to start upon the decade of his greatest achievements, both from a sporting and an humanitarian point of view. Certainly this is the time for which his cricketing exploits make him best known.

1890 was not only the start of the Golden Age and the year when the Long Room was erected as part of the Lord's pavilion, but also when the County Championship took on a formal structure for the first time. The counties playing in the new competition were Gloucestershire, Kent, Lancashire, Middlesex, Nottinghamshire, Surrey, Sussex and Yorkshire. The 'County Champions' (a slight variation from the term 'Champion County' used for those who had won the pre-1890 competitions), would be the side that had the most points after subtracting defeats from victories with draws being ignored. It was Surrey who won in the first year with nine wins and three losses producing a total of six points.

Teddy's county, Hampshire, was not one of the eight original participating counties, and so their matches would no longer be first-class – although not all of them had been treated as such up to this time in any event.

The literary and statistical might of HS Altham, John Arlott, EDR Eager and Roy Webber combined in 1958 to write a superb

Official History of Hampshire County Cricket. Harry Altham wrote the first section dealing with the period from formation through to the outbreak of the First World War.

The County's revival really began in 1882 with Francis Lacey and Dr Russell Bencraft playing key roles. Lacey was a Cambridge blue at both football and cricket, played for Hampshire between 1880 and 1897 and captained the county from 1888 to 1889. He went on to become Secretary of the MCC from 1898 until 1926, for which he was knighted. Teddy was an old and close friend and described Lacey as 'one of the finest hitters in the world, his off-driving being in particular superb'.

Henry William Russell Bencraft was appointed both Secretary and Treasurer in 1887 and Altham said he was 'the man to whom, as we shall see, the county was in course of time to owe the greatest debt in its history'. He had attended St Edward's School, Oxford (as had Teddy) and qualified as a doctor. He first played for Hampshire in 1876 and in the years that followed held every important position by way of service to the county including Captain, Chairman and President. He became a member of MCC's Committee and was knighted in 1924.

In 1884, when Captain James Fellowes was still Secretary, a lease was negotiated for a new County Ground on Northlands Road, not far from Southampton Common and to the south-west of where the university is now situated. The County moved there the following season, vacating the Antelope Ground which was just over a mile away and had been named after the inn on St Mary's Road.

Wynyard was back for the 1890 season and HW Forster took over from Lacey as captain. Forster went on to become President of MCC in 1919, at which time Lacey was the Secretary. He became Baron Forster of Lepe and was only one of two men (Lord Griffiths, an Old Carthusian, being the other) also to be made Captain of the Royal and Ancient Golf Club. He was appointed Governor General of Australia in 1925.

On 19 May, Teddy played for AJ Webbe's team in a three-day game against Cambridge University at Fenner's. It was twelve-a-side and although the scorecard on the Cricket Archive website shows

Wynyard's name batting at number five, scoring 91 and also wicketkeeping, Warsop says Teddy actually played under the pseudonym of SM Whittle 'for very good reasons'. *The South Australian Register* reported that SE Whittle made '91 not out free from blemish'. There seems to be confusion even over the correct initials for the assumed name and no explanation for the deception, although the opponents would have known only too well who was really playing. He took four catches in a comprehensive victory by eleven wickets against a strong Cambridge side that included Gregor MacGregor, the Hon FS Jackson, Digby ('The Lobster') Jephson and AJL Hill (who went on to play with Teddy at Hampshire).

Immediately afterwards on 22 May, Wynyard played for Gentlemen of England in another twelve-a-side game at The Parks against Oxford University. He took another five dismissals behind the stumps; Teddy regarded this as his best ever week as a wicketkeeper and he fulfilled that role for his county throughout the 1890 season.

After being dismissed for a duck playing for the Lyric Club captained by AE Stoddart against MCC, he appeared for Hampshire for the first time that season, against Somerset on 26 June at Southampton. It turned out to be one of the most thrilling matches of the season. The visitors won the toss, batted and made 127 with Wynyard securing one stumping. When Teddy batted, he went in at number three and top scored with 22 out of 94. Going in again, Somerset scored only 99 with Wynyard taking two catches. The home team needed 133 to win and got off to a great start. This time Teddy opened with Bencraft and they made 20 and 52 respectively, but only one other player reached double figures and the side were all out for 130, losing by just 2 runs.

Forster (57) and Wynyard (29) steered Hampshire to a winning second innings score of 143 for two against Sussex and Teddy then made 33 of his side's miserable second innings total of 54 to lose by 169 runs to Somerset. After playing Devon in Exeter, Wynyard's last two matches of the 1890 season for Hampshire were real tests against the Championship counties of Sussex (again) and Surrey.

The return fixture at Hove began on 21 August. Wynyard opened and made 40 towards a total of 238. The home side were quickly in trouble on 69 for seven but Charles Aubrey Smith then mounted a recovery scoring 61 and steering his team to 182. Hampshire had a lead of 56 but second time round they were 48 for four when Wynyard and Easby came together. They put on 74 runs by what *The Times* described as 'good cricket' and the score had progressed to 122 for four when stumps were drawn at the end of the second day with Teddy on 42 not out.

On the Saturday, rain delayed play until 1 o'clock and when Easby was out, Soar joined Wynyard and the home bowlers were severely punished. In just seventy minutes, 105 more runs were added and Hampshire declared on 234 for five with Teddy, who *The Times* reported as playing 'brilliantly', on 114 not out including twelve fours. This was his first century for his county. Sussex began their second innings at 3.35 pm needing 291 to win but a draw looked the most likely result. Nine wickets then fell in an hour and three quarters for just 85 runs and although the last pair showed some resilience, Sussex were dismissed for 126 with stalwart, Harry Baldwin, taking five for 49.

Two days later, Surrey were the visitors at the County Ground and, in a drawn game, Wynyard scored 1 and 27 not out as well as making two stumpings. In the nine matches in which he turned out for Hampshire, they won four times (including two victories over Sussex), drew on three occasions (one being against that year's County Champions, Surrey) and had two losses both at the hands of Somerset, who because of their performances, were about to be elected into the elite of the County Championship.

At the time of the Census on 5 April 1891, Teddy was staying with his cricketing friend, Albert Leatham at 7 Miserden Park, near Stroud in Gloucestershire. Leatham had been educated at Eton and Magdalen College, Cambridge and gave his occupation as a farmer. He was a left-arm slow-medium bowler for Gloucestershire playing alongside the Grace brothers (WG and EM) and had been selected with Teddy for AJ Webbe's side the year before against his old university. He emigrated to New Zealand and died there in Christchurch on 13 July 1948, just before his eighty-ninth birthday.

It is little wonder that Leatham and Wynyard were friends as they were cut from the same cloth. In 1912, Leatham published *Sport in Five Continents*, a fascinating account of his travels, hunting, fishing and living off the land in remote parts of the world. Wynyard would himself go caribou hunting with another friend, Hesketh Vernon Hesketh-Prichard, in Newfoundland after his retirement from the Army, and perfectly fitted Leatham's description of 'the man who will most enjoy and perhaps most benefit by a trip to the wilds is he who has learnt to do practically everything for himself. Nor is this self-dependence a difficult lesson to learn. Necessity and experience are able teachers and-so runs an Arabian proverb-when a man makes up his mind to a thing, it becomes easy for him to do it.'

Unfortunately Sandhurst claimed Teddy for virtually the whole of the 1891 season and he was only able to play for his county in the last of their eleven matches which was against Staffordshire. Hampshire suffered badly as a consequence losing seven of those games, two by more than an innings and two by ten wickets.

On a quite different sporting note Teddy, accompanied by Major James Spens, travelled from Sandhurst to Godalming to play rackets on Saturday 20 November. They gave a close game to the school pairing of Price and Hotham but narrowly lost out. Spens, apart from being at Sandhurst, was also a county cricketer with Hampshire having made his debut and played for them in the 1884 season. He did not turn out for them again for another thirteen years until 1897. He was, however, a formidable rackets partner for Wynyard to have because, along with Julian Marshall, Spens had been responsible for drawing up the rules of the sport for the first time in 1890, and was an acknowledged expert.

In later life, Spens became a member of the British Fascists but died in Folkestone in 1934, over five years before the outbreak of the Second World War, and so never had to witness the consequences of his political beliefs. As a generalisation, it was not uncommon for members of the aristocracy and military at that time to hold views that were, shall we say, some way to the right!

1892 started off badly for Teddy as his father, William, died in February in Cannes. Unfortunately the year also followed the same cricketing pattern as the previous season. Bencraft took over the captaincy from Forster but Teddy was only able to play in two out of the eleven county matches (six lost, three won and two drawn) and to make matters worse Surrey refused to renew their fixtures.

Teddy played in a drawn game against MCC, scoring 32 and taking five catches in the match, but only scored 2 and 7 in a six-wicket defeat by Leicestershire. He did play some further cricket though that summer. On 7 June he represented the Old Carthusians against the Staff College at Camberley alongside EH Parry. He went in at number eight and scored 44 not out. A month later he was playing for the Free Foresters against his old school and, batting at number five, made 64 out of 219 for six. He then turned out for the RMC Staff against the 69th Welsh Regiment at Sandhurst on 20 July. *The Carthusian* described this as a day of 'unalloyed triumph'. He batted brilliantly for 123 and took eleven wickets in the game.

A week later both Charles Aubrey Smith and Wynyard were selected to play on the Old Carthusians' tour in a two-day game against the Old Wykehamists but 'Round the Corner' had to drop out. Teddy took five wickets plus a splendid catch in the deep. He did not go to the Domum Ball in the evening with their opponents and *The Carthusian* said the rest of the team should have followed his good example. This was because only Wynyard could cope with the bowling next day and scored 24 as the side was all out for 98. Old Wykehamists had made 420 and second time round the Old Carthusians still only made 144 but 'Wynyard showed that to a batsman of his calibre run getting was as easy as shelling peas. He hit the bowling to all parts of the field and by the most brilliant cricket shown in the match scored 100 not out.'

Sadly for the Old Boys, Teddy could not play on the rest of the tour. In the autumn he did find time though to play some football. He was selected along with GO Smith for AH Tod's Eleven against Charterhouse on Saturday 24 September, scoring two goals in a 5-1 victory, and a fortnight later scored again, this time for the Old Carthusians in a 3-2 win against the school.

In March 1893 he was elected to Corinthians FC and played twice for them, scoring an impressive five goals. The biggest football match for Teddy that year was when he played in the final round of the London Charity Cup against the holders Crusaders in front of a 5,000 to 6,000 crowd at the Essex County Ground, Leyton. It was a warm day and, with both GO Smith and Wynyard in the team, the Old Carthusians were favourites to win. Even though their opponents were reduced to ten men through injury, they led 2-0 before Smith pulled one back. Teddy then had the goal at his mercy but shot wide and 2-1 was the final score. The man of the match was the Crusaders goalkeeper, Leslie Gay, who also happened to play wicketkeeper for Hampshire.

Teddy was elected President of Hampshire Hogs Cricket Club which had been founded in 1887. In the early years the club only played eight to ten matches a season because most of its members played for the county. Wynyard followed Francis Lacey and was in turn succeeded by JC Moberly and then Russell Bencraft. The club is still going to this day.

1893 did see Teddy able to play a little more often, although he did not turn out for Hampshire until the third week of July. On 8 July he hit vigorously for 54 not out playing for the F Dames Longworth Eleven at Charterhouse. In the same side was Prince Albert, Duke of Schleswig-Holstein, who was a grandson of Queen Victoria. He became a Lieutenant Colonel in the Prussian Army but because of his British connections, the Kaiser excused him from fighting in the First World War and he served instead on the staff of the Governor of Berlin.

Hampshire lost their first three games of the season but Wynyard was then available for five of their next six matches, of which they won two and drew another. On his return against Sussex at Hove on 20 July, he made 79 (which was the top score) and 41 in a drawn game. 412 runs and fourteen wickets were served up for the spectators on the last day – indeed a Golden Age! On Teddy's travels Warwickshire won by an innings and then, in spite of his scoring 95, Hampshire lost to Derbyshire by eight wickets.

Warwickshire were the visitors for the return game at the County Ground starting on 10 August. The scores were fairly equal after the first innings. Hampshire made 204 (Teddy scoring 8 before being bowled by Shilton) with Warwickshire replying with 182. Wynyard, fielding at slip, caught Shilton for the last wicket with Robson fulfilling the role of wicketkeeper. Teddy walked to the wicket at 22 for two and was out caught by Docker bowled Shilton at 258 for five having made 154 including sixteen fours and two fives. This was his best score for the county to date and Hampshire went on to win by 267 runs.

Warsop recounts an anecdote which Wynyard himself told about the game. When he took the catch to dismiss Jack Shilton, the retreating batsman retorted 'Ah, Captain if you had let that one go, there would always have been a bottle for you whenever you liked to call.' Shilton had bowled Teddy in the first innings and when Wynyard reached the wicket second time round joked 'I've got another special one up my sleeve for you, Captain.' Teddy duly hit him twice to the boundary in the first over and then out of the ground.

Unfortunately Wynyard was unable to play in the last three matches of the season, but after their poor start Hampshire had definitely picked up in the second half of the year once Teddy had been available to play for them. He had scored 450 at an average of 50 and topped the second-class county averages for the season in the process.

He did play one first-class match when he was selected to represent the Second-Class Counties against the visiting Australians at Edgbaston on 21, 22 and 23 August. The match was played five days after the tourists had suffered an innings defeat in the second Test at The Oval. The first Test at Lord's had been drawn and the third, which was to start as soon as this game finished, was scheduled for Manchester which was also drawn, leaving the home country victors, 1-0.

Australia played exactly the same side for the last two Tests and there was only one change for the game against the Second-Class Counties, namely Jarvis coming in for Blackham at wicketkeeper. The home side made only 147 with Teddy batting at number six and being bowled by George Giffen for 10. Indeed Giffen took seven for 53 in the innings. It was enough on a rain-affected pitch to give his team a four run lead as Jack Shilton responded with three for 26.

McLeod then caught Wynyard, off Hugh Trumble's bowling, for 2 in the second innings and Australia progressed to victory by four wickets.

In May 1894 the MCC agreed that matches played by Derbyshire, Essex, Leicestershire and Warwickshire should be regarded as first-class even though it was too late for those counties to be included in the County Championship for that season. Hampshire had not been invited and so the fight to join the elite had to be renewed with fresh vigour.

Again Army duties intervened for Wynyard that summer but he was able to play some sport even if his performances for Hampshire were limited. On 2 June he was selected for a strong I Zingari side who inflicted a severe defeat upon Charterhouse. Teddy batted at number three and made 111 before being caught in the deep.

By August and with two thirds of the season gone, Hampshire had secured only one victory. The tide turned with a very narrow 9-run win away to Essex at Leyton, and then Wynyard returned for the remaining matches.

On 6 August the side travelled up to Derby. Hampshire started badly on a slow wicket affected by rain and had only reached 32 for five when Wynyard, batting at number seven, put on 127 runs with Ward, in two hours and a quarter. At one stage 60 was scored in thirty minutes before Teddy was caught in the slips for 90, which included two sixes and eight fours. Derbyshire were skittled out for 117 and so failed by just 7 to avoid the follow on. Second time round they made 188 and Hampshire lost five wickets chasing down the 102 they needed with the two heroes of the first innings, Wynyard (9 not out) and Ward (12 not out), together at the crease when the final runs were polished off.

Next stop was back down in Southampton for the return game against Warwickshire beginning on 9 August. Although Teddy scored only 3 and 20, the home side won by two wickets.

It was then the turn of Sussex at the County Ground, on 16 August. They batted first for a total of 142 with Wynyard catching CB Fry off the bowling of Soar for 8. When it was Hampshire's turn, they secured a first innings lead of 109 but Teddy, batting at number three, made only 2 of them. Sussex then turned a losing position into a potentially winning one when the former Australian captain and now skipper of his county, Mr WL 'Billy' Murdoch, scored 172 having already made 42 in the first innings. During the interval when he was still not out and with his side on 349 for eight, he decided to declare.

Murdoch was chasing victory and set Hampshire 241 runs to win in three hours. Remarkably, they made their target for the loss of six wickets in 74.3 overs. *The Times* reported 'the chief credit for this performance belonged to Captain Wynyard who made his 117 in two hours and hit a six and thirteen fours'. Eventually, he was out when Fry caught him off the bowling of Brann. This match goes down in history as the first recorded win for a side after a declaration had been made against them.

The following Thursday, Leicestershire were the opponents in Southampton. They won the toss and scored 166 with Teddy taking three catches. 81 of those runs were made in a brilliant knock by opening batsman Mr CE de Trafford. Hampshire responded with 306 for four and for the second match in succession Wynyard made a century. He had scored 116 when he was out at 160 for three. At the close his county was in a strong position as they were 140 runs ahead with six wickets in hand. Unfortunately there was no play on the final day and so Hampshire were denied another possible victory.

The final match of the season was another home game against Essex. Hampshire won the toss and opted to bat. Let *The Times* on 28 August tell us what then happened:

> Captain Wynyard who has played so prominent a part in the recent fine cricket of Hampshire scored his third consecutive 100 for the county at Southampton yesterday in the beginning of the return match with Essex ... Capt Wynyard who went in first wicket down at 25 made a splendid stand of over 100 with Mr. Robson and was ultimately caught at square leg for 108 the result of two and a half hours cricket-twice he hit the ball out of the ground and six fours.

What *The Times* did not mention was that Essex had a strong attack with Kortright and Mead opening their bowling.

Hampshire were all out for 282 but Essex only managed 146 in reply. Teddy weighed in with six overs, one for 13, securing the wicket of CP McGahey who top scored with 45. Forced to follow on, Essex only scored 75 and Hampshire won by an innings and 61 runs in just two days.

At lunchtime, on what turned out to be the final day, the Chairman of the Hampshire Committee, Mr John Moberly, made a presentation to Teddy of a pair of silver candlesticks in recognition of his achievement of three consecutive centuries. They still remain in the family's possession to this day.

Lord Harris, who was elected President of MCC for the following year of 1895, then took up Hampshire's cause. He was a hugely influential figure in cricket administration until his death in 1932 aged eighty-one. Although born in Trinidad, he was a 'Man of Kent' and was closely associated with the 'Man of Yorkshire', Lord Hawke, who many considered to be Harris's disciple. The two of them played key roles in the management of cricket from the 1890s through to the 1930s.

With the weight of Lord Harris's opinion behind them, Hampshire were duly given first-class status and elected the fourteenth county in the Championship with effect from 1895.

There can be no doubt that this recognition was as a result of the enormous contribution of Dr Russell Bencraft dating back to 1876 when he first played for the County, but Wynyard's efforts also should not be underestimated. Clearly Hampshire's performance in August when they had beaten Derbyshire, Warwickshire, Sussex and Essex (twice), all of whom already held first-class status, had been decisive. In turn these victories had coincided (all bar the first win over Essex) with Teddy's return to the side and his prolific batting performances.

At the Annual General Meeting of Hampshire County Cricket Club held on 6 December 1894, the decision was taken to elect a new President for the first year in the Championship. His name was Captain EG Wynyard DSO.

Teddy with his trusted tobaggan and the Symonds Shield,
the 1895 International Road Tobogganing Champion

6

A Man for All Seasons

Teddy's stepmother, Isabella, had been born in Switzerland and so she may well have been the source of encouragement and inspiration that persuaded him to seek out the benefits of fresh alpine air during the winter months. It will undoubtedly have assisted his recuperation after he was invalided home from India. The lure of meeting new challenges, with not just a little danger attached, will have proved simply too hard to resist, especially if old school friends and army colleagues were already participating.

When military duties permitted, therefore, Wynyard travelled south to the resort of Davos in the Swiss Alps. The city is best known today for hosting the annual meeting of the World Economic Forum. Even now Davos is not an easy place to reach, but 120 years ago it would have taken a good two to three days to travel from England to Switzerland alone before then embarking upon a slow train journey and/or an arduous sleigh drive to reach the resort.

The first winter guests were two German visitors, Hugo Richter and Dr Friedrich Unger, who arrived on 8 February 1865 and, as a result, Davos began to obtain a reputation as a health spa. The microclimate in the high valley, located at a height of 5,120 feet, was deemed excellent for lung disease patients. A British colony grew there and a small alpine village developed that, by the middle of the 1890s, had 5,000 inhabitants.

There were a number of different activities to attract Teddy, but he decided to begin gently and, in 1891, passed one of the figure skating tests introduced by the National Skating Association.

Two years later, on 9 December 1893, Wynyard was skating on Lake Davos with an old cricket and footballing friend, GR Wood. It was 2.30 pm when a thirty-year-old local edelweiss gatherer, named Munkert, was returning across the lake. Suddenly he found himself in an area that was only partially frozen and fell through into the icy waters beneath. Wynyard was a quarter of a mile away but, seeing what had happened and without any further thought, skated to the spot followed by Wood. He found a rope and tied it round his body and passed the other end to his companion. Disregarding the freezing temperature of the water and the treacherous currents below the surface, Teddy dived into the place where Munkert had gone down. His initial search was in vain but he would not be defeated and continued his rescue attempt. He was then seized with cramps and lost consciousness. It was only because of the bravery of Wood, who stuck to his place on the thin ice even though he was very nearly dragged in himself, that Teddy was finally hauled to the surface exhausted, insensible and near death. Tragically, all his efforts were to no avail and Munkert could not be saved.

The residents of Davos were so impressed by Wynyard risking his own life for their compatriot that they gathered together and sent a Memorial to the Royal Humane Society. The case was considered at a meeting held at the society's offices in Trafalgar Square on 15 January 1894. Captain AB Hawes was in the Chair and, in spite of a strong recommendation, the extract from the case book records that case number 26,907 was unsuccessful, although a bronze medal was awarded. No reason was given for the refusal to give a higher award, but at least there was some recognition of Teddy's courage, and the local people did not forget his unselfish conduct.

Regrettably, very little is known about Wood, whose own courageous actions need to be properly recorded because, without his intervention, Teddy would undoubtedly have died below the ice on the lake.

As the news of Wynyard's bravery spread around Davos Platz it would have reached the ears of the author Arthur Conan Doyle and his first wife Louise (nicknamed 'Touie'), who were staying at the Kurhaus Hotel that winter. Five years earlier Teddy had taken Conan Doyle's wicket in the Hampshire County Challenge Cup final and they were to play together several times for MCC in the early 1900s.

It was in December 1893 that *The Strand* magazine had published 'The Final Problem', Doyle's account of the apparent demise of Sherlock Holmes in a fight to the death with Professor Moriarty at the Reichenbach Falls, 220 kilometres away from Davos. Doyle thought that once and for all he was rid of his detective and could concentrate on more serious literature. Sadly he had other more important matters on his mind as Touie had just been diagnosed with rapid consumption and there was little hope of a permanent cure. In his biography *Memories and Adventures* Doyle said he 'then set all my energy to work to save the situation'. They left their home at 12 Tennison Road, Norwood, sold the furniture they had just bought and made for Davos 'where there seemed the best chance of killing this accursed microbe'. The clean fresh air appeared to work, at least for a period of time, because Louise had been given only a few months to live but survived for another thirteen years and did not die until 1906.

Davos became a regular winter haunt for Mr and Mrs Doyle (he was not knighted until 1902) as it had already become for Teddy. In 1889 Tobias Branger arranged for a pair of skis to be sent from Norway and, along with his brother Johann, they were the first locals to teach themselves the technique of skiing. In 1893 the brothers undertook their first major ski tour lasting seven hours over the 2,445 metre Maienfelder Furka Pass to Arosa. The history of Davos records they took Doyle with them in 1894. Doyle was particularly flattered when they arrived at a hotel and he had to state his profession in the register. Tobias Branger insisted on entering 'Sportesmann' alongside his name. Probably this pleasure was not surpassed until he took his only first-class wicket playing for MCC against London County in August 1900. The scorecard read: WG Grace, caught Storer bowled Conan Doyle, 110.

Whilst Doyle took up skiing, Teddy, in the winter of his valiant rescue attempt, decided to learn how to toboggan. On 7 February 1883, the Davos Toboggan Club had been founded, followed five days later by the first international and timed toboggan race on the main post road from Davos to Klosters. Twenty-one athletes competed and, remarkably as this was a race against the clock, the result was a dead heat between the Swiss P Minsch and the Australian GP Robertson. They both finished in a time of nine minutes fifteen seconds. Minsch was the local Klosters postman who rode his toboggan every day along the road delivering his letters. John Addington Symonds, a founder member of the club, acted as referee.

Minsch won the race again the following year and the success of these events led to the introduction of the silver Symonds Cup in 1885. There was no comparable road in the rival resort of St Moritz and so a specific run had to be created. Hence the Cresta Run was constructed for the first time and the Davos tobogganers were invited across to compete in the Grand National; Minsch finished second.

The sport was developing rapidly in many ways, particularly the equipment being used and the riding positions that were adopted. The Davos sledge was effectively the original amongst toboggans and is still in use to this day. It was slow though and the initial competitions were run using Swiss wooden toboggans called handschlitten. During the winter of 1887/8, LP Child visited from New York and introduced his 'America' machine and rode headfirst, steering with the toe of his moccasined foot. This toboggan was longer and lower thereby producing greater stability, and the next development was to replace the wooden framework with a steel skeleton frame. It had greater spring, making it a more comfortable ride, especially as there was a cushion on the platform.

In 1890 this resulted in John Symonds introducing a fresh trophy, the Symonds Shield, the rules for which allowed flexibility in the use of machine and riding position. The Symonds Cup remained for competitors on the Swiss wooden handschlitten toboggans and a year later riding in an upright position was made compulsory for that event.

In spite of his enthusiasm and commitment to tobogganing, Symonds was not himself a sportsman. He was born in 1840 and attended Harrow School at the age of fourteen but was excused games because of his delicate constitution. The headmaster was the Reverend Charles Vaughan who suddenly, without any warning, resigned on 16 September 1859. It was not until a very long time after Symonds had died and the injustice of homosexuality being a criminal offence had been removed by the Sexual Offences Act 1967 that his memoirs were published. These revealed that on Symonds' father learning of affectionate letters sent by Vaughan to a boy at Harrow, he threatened to inform *The Times* unless the headmaster resigned. Some have questioned the motives of Symonds junior on grounds of jealousy because of his own homosexuality.

Symonds became an English poet and literary critic specialising in the Italian renaissance. He married Janet North and they had four children together. Accounts relate how the stress of repressing his true sexuality affected his already frail health and he moved to Davos where he built his own home, named Villa Am Hof. Robert Louis Stevenson also went to Davos because he was suffering from haemorrhaging of the lungs and, whilst there, became a good friend of Symonds. He observed the latter's double life and it has been suggested this possibly provided, at least in part, a model for the concept of a split personality in the *Strange Case of Dr Jekyll and Mr Hyde*.

Symonds died of tuberculosis aged fifty-three in 1893 and is buried in Rome. Nevertheless his name lived on in Davos with the two trophies for the annual international toboggan races.

In 1894, the Hon Harry Gibson had won the Symonds Shield in five minutes and seven seconds and immediately afterwards wrote his book *Tobogganing on Crooked Runs*, which was both historical and instructional. Teddy would almost certainly have benefited from his experience and tuition.

Gibson wrote about an English friend who described the sport as 'a form of lunacy which consisted in sitting on a thing like a tea tray and letting yourself slide to the bottom of a hill'. Modesty and self-deprecation is much to be admired but this was a gross oversimplification. On a haughtier note he wrote:

> It is a sport that appeals to an Englishman as it calls into play all those qualities for which England as a nation is famous. The decision quickly called for and instantaneously carried out, the opportunity of exercising pluck, nerve, resource, and activity, the quick eye for a curve, the necessity for hand and eye to work exactly together.

These were qualities that Teddy had already displayed in Burma, on the cricket field, and at Davos earlier that winter. He might well be ideally suited to his new sport but there was a lot to learn in terms of technique and strategy.

Gibson expressed the opinion that whilst many beginners would feel it safer to start on a Davos sledge riding upright, this was a waste of time if the person wanted to compete in the Symonds Shield. It was better to start in both a headfirst, racing position and upon a racing machine from the outset. Teddy heeded this advice and started out on the steel-skeleton-framed toboggan.

The first essentials he had to learn were perfect balance and the power to shift his weight quickly, accurately and smoothly. If he put his left foot down the toboggan would steer to the left and vice versa. The amount of turn would be determined by the amount of pressure applied and so it was easy to exaggerate the movement and then overcompensate. Often the beginner would be seen zigzagging, at which point it was vital to keep one's nerve or a fall would almost inevitably ensue.

At the greater speeds on ice the rider had to control the machine as it had its own momentum whereas at the slower pace on the road, the tobogganer had to use his skill and energy to propel it. The basic way of achieving this end was 'to peg' which entailed moving onto his side and holding on with one hand whilst using the other, either by a side or an overhand stroke, through the snow to gain momentum.

If the toboggan was still not going fast enough, and a great deal of speed would be lost on difficult corners, then Wynyard was taught how 'to punt'. This was the most rapid method of gaining momentum and required the rider to kneel on one knee and effectively kick the machine along using the sole of his other foot.

Both punting and pegging required not only great technique but also tremendous physical effort. Furthermore Wynyard had to be able to coordinate these exhausting activities with cornering. In order to take a bad corner it was necessary to drop weight back until the bows were left clear and then swing them around in the new direction using the foot on the inside of the curve. When shifting weight it was vitally important to find exactly the right position and Teddy will have made marks on the side-bars so that he knew precisely where his hands should be placed. If he was to be competitive, he must also learn the art of the running start. Not only did all of these individual techniques have to be mastered and then combined together but he had to familiarize himself with the course and plan a strategy. There was no other option than to do a great deal of practising.

Teddy would rise early enough in the morning to breakfast and then catch the nine o'clock train to Wolfgang, a little hamlet three and a half miles away, then either toboggan or walk to the top of the road before riding down to Klosters. He would then walk two-thirds of the way up again to try another run down the last part of the course and, if he wanted, then catch the train back for lunch. Alternatively, he could travel by sleigh back up the road so that he could practise all day, not returning until late in the evening.

It was necessary to be careful if attempting to ride the entirety of the course because this was a normal post road. It was perfectly possible as he came hurtling out of a corner or curve to find a stationary horse and sleigh blocking his path, requiring an emergency stop using the rakes on his boots as the rules prevented any mechanical means of steering or braking. It was essential, therefore, to walk the road in order to appreciate the full extent of its twists, turns and changes in height.

After only starting the sport in the winter of 1893/4, Teddy entered for the Symonds Shield the following year. He would be competing against the greatest international specialists, as well as locals who had ridden toboggans and the road almost since birth. The size of the task facing him cannot be overstated.

A friendly rivalry existed between Davos and St Moritz and there were now three great annual events in the tobogganing world – the two international races at Davos for the Symonds Cup and the Symonds Shield which were normally run in mid January, with the Grand National race taking place at St Moritz on the Cresta Run a month later. It was the winner of the Symonds Shield, however, who would be the International Road Tobogganing Champion of the year.

The importance of the Davos races can be appreciated by the fact they also became the focal point of the social season. Over a week-long programme of balls and dinners was organised to keep the spectators and competitors occupied when the sport for the day was over. Teddy could not allow these distractions to affect the serious business at hand, at least not until his event had been completed.

The morning of the Symonds Shield race in January 1895 finally arrived and Teddy set about making sure he was properly equipped for his ride. In true British fashion a collar and tie was worn under a white woollen sweater. Gauntlet gloves were an absolute necessity and gaiters running from above the knee down to the foot were recommended over trousers in order to keep dry. Elbow and knee-pads helped protect other vulnerable parts of the body. There was no such thing as crash helmets, and no Health and Safety Executive to intervene, simply men pitting their bravery, daring and skill against the elements.

In competition, rakes would not be attached to the boots as this would slow down a running start and, on the road course, there were only three corners where the best riders found it necessary to use their feet. India rubber boots were therefore the suggested footwear to assist with the sprint at the beginning and to aid deceleration when the foot did need to be used on a corner.

Teddy travelled with his steel toboggan to Grüne Bödelli for the start. The length of the course was 160 yards short of two miles with a fall of 860 feet. There were three very difficult corners but all were natural features with no man made banking although the authorities did all they could the night before the race to make the course as fast as possible. Their efforts were thwarted just before the start by a heavy fall of snow which meant the times would be slower, placing a greater emphasis on athleticism with the need to peg and punt all the harder.

As it was not possible for the riders to race side by side against one another on the road, they had to compete instead against the clock. One stopwatch could not be used because there was no point along the course at which both the start and finish were in view. Hence two ordinary watches (not stopwatches) were carefully set some days before they were required so that both the minute and second hand corresponded exactly. On the morning of the race the watches were tested to ensure they were still synchronised, whereupon the two timekeepers separated, one going to the top and the other to the bottom of the run. At the agreed time, the watch holder at the top started the first competitor with the remainder following at exactly one-minute intervals. The watch holder at the bottom then took the exact time at which each competitor passed the winning post. When everyone had finished the two men met to calculate the precise time for each rider.

There was just one heat and lots were drawn to determine the running order. When Teddy received the signal from the starter he sprinted and stooped down to lie in the headfirst position. The initial thirty to forty yards were very flat and so there was no natural momentum. This meant that, almost immediately, he had to peg, punt or both before reaching the first difficult 'bridge' corner after two thirds of a mile. Wynyard had a quick look back to the mark on his side bar and then moved his hands there as he transferred his weight onto the rear, causing the bows to lift up as he then swung around the corner. The toboggan was running on the blade of the ungrooved runners at speed and he was trying to maintain control, with his feet barely touching the ice, if at all. The smaller the amount of foot pressure, the less would be the braking effect and the greater the momentum around the bridge. This was important because the road then became a level strip of ground which required further vigorous pegging and punting, especially given the recent snowfall. Once momentum had been regained, Teddy had to ensure his weight was as far forward as possible, head down to reduce wind resistance, with body and legs kept rigid, feet close together and well up from the ice.

There then followed four very sharp curves interspersed with innumerable lesser ones, which were a constant source of trouble requiring great concentration and care. Each curve was different from the last, demanding individual treatment and with a quick look to find the right mark on the side bar, Teddy then transferred his weight backwards again, but not as far as for the difficult corners. A gentle movement of the head and shoulders to the right would ease the machine to the right of the curve and vice versa with the wrists sensitively pulling the bows in the intended direction. The way these curves were taken would often determine whether seconds were lost or saved, which could be decisive by the end of the race.

The worst corner on the course was known, rather unoriginally, as 'the last corner but one'. At this point the road formed an elbow turning right and back on to itself. Here it was necessary for Teddy to use his feet as a brake and this produced an inevitable loss of pace as the road levelled out once again. Nearing the end of the course it was vital for him to start punting, but many a rider had then entered the 'last corner' (another true but unoriginal name) too fast and been caught out by the drop of six feet on the outside of the curve. Teddy was sufficiently aware to avoid this pitfall and briefly punted on the flat to pick up pace again before ensuring he was perfectly balanced to maximize his speed through until the finishing post in the village of Klosters.

When all the riders had completed the run, the two timekeepers compared notes. Teddy had recorded six minutes and twenty-two seconds, travelling at an average speed of twenty miles per hour, and no one had beaten it. The winner of the Symonds Shield of 1895 and the International Road Tobogganing Champion at his very first attempt was Captain EG Wynyard DSO.

The March 1895 edition of *The Carthusian* proudly reported Teddy's victory as 'the highest honour that Davos can offer to the tobogganer'.

A year later, Teddy was back to defend his title. The Symonds Shield race, organized by the Buol Toboggan Club, was run on 14 January 1896 and started at 11 o'clock. There were twenty-seven competitors and Wynyard finished fourth.

Teddy kept returning to Davos and on Thursday 27 January 1898 he was one of the timekeepers when fellow Old Carthusian and President of the Oxford University Speed Skating Club, C Edgington, skated fifty-five yards short of nineteen miles, breaking the world record for the distance covered in one hour.

It had been a remarkable fourteen month period for Wynyard, beginning in the winter of 1893 with his bravery and heroics on Lake Davos, followed by the 1894 summer which saw three consecutive centuries, leading to Hampshire gaining County Championship status, and ending in the winter of 1895 with his international tobogganing success. He was the veritable man for all seasons.

The side that competed in Hampshire's first County Championship match, against Somerset in 1895.
Back: H Baldwin, CG Barton, GW Lewis (scorer),
C Heseltine, T Soar.
Middle: C Robson, EG Wynyard, R Bencraft (captain),
AJL Hill, HF Ward.
Front: FH Bacon, VA Barton.

7

A Test Debut Beckons

1895-96

Hampshire's elevation to the Championship encouraged 400 new members to join the club. As there were now fourteen sides, it was no longer logistically possible for everyone to play each other, although a minimum of sixteen games per side was set. The scoring system was also modified, and the points total was now to be divided by the number of finished games (won or lost). The side with the highest percentage would be the new County Champions. Hampshire played sixteen matches that summer and Teddy was able to turn out for them on eleven occasions.

The first game was away at Taunton, against Somerset, beginning on 30 May 1895. The home side won the toss and batted first making 221 with Lionel Palairet scoring 96 but Hampshire were swiftly dismissed for just 94. Teddy went in at number three, which, for this season, was his normal batting position for the county. He was caught by Palairet off Sammy Woods for 1 and following on, did not make many more, registering 11, but his county reached 314 leaving Somerset 188 to win. At 166 for five the game looked over. At this time Wynyard was keeping wicket because Robson had injured his thumb and when he caught both incumbent batsmen, the tide turned and Hampshire sprang a surprise victory by 11 runs to get their Championship campaign off to a good start.

Teddy did not play in Hampshire's next five matches but was selected for a formidable I Zingari side against the Gentlemen of England in a game arranged at Lord's to mark the wandering side's jubilee. I Zingari had rigidly preserved the amateur traditions of their organisation since their formation in 1845 and Wynyard was a proud and enthusiastic Zingaro, playing a vast number of games as well as running sides for them until he was nearly seventy. He was still a committee member at the time of his death in 1936. Regardless of what team he was playing for he would often wear his I Zingari cap balanced at the military angle with a strap under the chin – a famous 1905 print by Albert Chevallier Tayler depicts Teddy wearing his I Zingari colours. The historian David Kynaston also records another feature of Teddy's cricketing paraphernalia, namely a belt of flannel worn around his abdomen, which he told all who would listen was effective against both extremes of heat and cold – perhaps a notion he picked up whilst out in India!

There is an excellent history of I Zingari written by Bob Arrowsmith and Bud Hill that has been updated by Tony Winlaw. They had this to say about Teddy:

> His contemporaries were unanimous that, had he been able to play first-class cricket uninterruptedly in his prime, he would have been remembered among the great but he was thirty-three when Hampshire became first class and forty-two when he retired from the Army, so his opportunities were severely restricted ... A splendid attacking bat, he had a complete armoury of strokes and in an age when amateurs especially tended to look for runs mainly on the off, he was equally strong on the leg and particularly expert at the pull, played as WG and George Hirst used to play it, by dropping on his right knee and taking the ball at the pitch from just outside the off stump over or wide of mid-on. He was a fine driver and, if the bowler shortened his length, would cut or hook him. Left-handers he constantly drove for four over extra cover or cover. He was a brilliant field anywhere, an adequate wicketkeeper in a crisis and a good enough lob bowler to pick up quite a few wickets even in first-class cricket.

High praise indeed, and there were a number of equally fine players alongside him for this Jubilee match – the Hon FS Jackson opened, AE Stoddart went in at number three with Teddy at number five, followed by Sir Timothy O' Brien, with all-rounder AG Steel (who played in the first ever Test versus Australia in England) going in at number eight. *The Times* described the team as 'one of the most brilliant that could be put together'. Dr WG Grace captained their opponents with his son, WG junior, also in the team along with CB Fry and Gregor MacGregor as wicketkeeper.

On Thursday 20 June 1895, I Zingari won the toss and elected to bat. The wicket was in the very best condition and the Lord's pavilion plus Members' enclosure was crowded with a total of around 5,000 in the ground. Amongst those present were two of I Zingari's original founders, JL Baldwin and Sir Spencer Ponsonby-Fane. The latter was a familiar figure at Lord's as he was Honorary Treasurer of MCC. Indeed he remains a permanent feature to this day as he is depicted on one of the moulded terracotta heads supporting the consoles of the upper terrace of the pavilion.

HT Hewett and FS Jackson started well and had added 75 when WG senior, bowling lobs, had Hewett stumped by MacGregor for 51. Fry then took the ball, dismissing Jackson and Stoddart for 34 and 38 respectively. It was reported that I Zingari were hitting at almost everything. Teddy was the next man in and had partnerships of 42 with O'Brien and 52 with Steel. He progressed to 56 before being caught by Hill off the bowling of WG Grace junior. His driving had been clean and of great force as he hit nine fours. When he reached 34, he passed 500 first-class runs.

By 4.30 pm, the side were all out for 289 with Fry taking five for 75. It should be noted though that Fry had a decidedly suspect action. His bowling career ended in 1898 when he was no-balled by three of the leading umpires of the day.

WG Grace senior opened with Arthur Sellers (father of Brian, the successful Yorkshire captain of the 1930s) at 5 o'clock and by close of play, two hours later, the Gentlemen had progressed to 148 for five. The wicket was as hard as iron and playing truly. As a result the bowlers were not allowed to escape and brilliant batting accompanied by fast scoring was the order of the second day with the Gentleman of England reaching 411. Wynyard bowled and had figures of no wickets for 22.

At lunchtime, JL Baldwin presented each member of the I Zingari Eleven with an edition of the jubilee record of the club detailing its origin and progress.

Hewett and Jackson started the second innings 122 runs behind but it was Stoddart, going in at number three, who set the crowd alight. He made 92 in just 100 minutes, including a cut for which he ran five, and was particularly severe on the Doctor's lobs. Nevertheless I Zingari were decidedly second-best on Friday evening and Wynyard, along with Steel, had to bat carefully for the last few overs of the day. By the close they had made 24 and 5 towards a total of 224 for five.

The third and final day was a Saturday and it was hoped there would be a full house and equally enthralling denouement. In the morning Wynyard treated the spectators to some fine hitting and he was seventh out, caught and bowled by Fry, for 51. In all he had batted for an hour and his total included four fours. When Steel reached 14 he had amassed exactly 7,000 runs in first-class cricket. He was then out for that score in what was to be his last ever first-class game. I Zingari were all out for 293 and Fry had taken five for 102 (ten wickets in the match).

The Gentlemen of England needed 172 runs to win and achieved this with Grace senior and Sellers still at the crease scoring 101 and 70 respectively, although the Doctor was dropped by O'Brien and then Stoddart. It was Grace's fourth century at Lord's that year and his sixth in all first-class matches for the season so far. Teddy had performed very creditably, exceeding 50 in both innings.

During the luncheon interval, as a permanent reminder of the occasion, Baldwin had his photograph taken with the whole of the Jubilee I Zingari side. He died the following year at his home in Tintern, aged eighty-seven.

Three days later Teddy was back at Southampton for the three-day game against reigning champions, Surrey, who won by seven wickets with Wynyard scoring 24 and then 69 before being run out in the second innings.

On 25 July Essex were the visitors in a remarkable game. Drizzling rain prevented a start until 4.30 pm and Hampshire, winning the toss, elected to bat making 246 with Wynyard bowled by Mead for 10. In reply, Essex were skittled out for 128 saving the compulsory follow on by just two runs, with Baldwin taking six for 36. In the second innings, it was Hampshire's turn to be dismissed cheaply, making only 136, with Teddy falling lbw, again to the bowling of Mead, for 20. Walter Mead trundled in for 77.3 overs and took seventeen wickets (including Wynyard twice) for 119 runs in the game.

Essex had been set 254 to win but the target was never threatened as Baldwin followed up his first innings performance taking seven for 42, to dismiss the opposition for just 83. Essex's defeat meant that Mead's bowling performance remains the second best for a losing side in the history of first-class cricket. The record is held by William Mycroft who took seventeen for 103 in 1876 when playing for Derbyshire also against Hampshire.

Hampshire won their next two matches away against Leicestershire and Yorkshire. It was a comfortable win by 342 runs at Grace Road, with Wynyard contributing 53 and 44 and taking one catch. The game at Bramall Lane was a low scoring and close run affair. Yorkshire made only 110 and 111 with Teddy taking one catch in their second knock. Hampshire scored 127 with Wynyard lbw to Bobby Peel for 15 and then they struggled to their target of 96 for the loss of eight wickets with Russell Bencraft and Baldwin finally seeing them home. Teddy was again out to Peel being bowled for just 5 and the Yorkshireman took eleven wickets in the game for 95 runs.

This was the high point of the season because the next four matches were all lost against Derbyshire, Warwickshire (home and away) and Sussex. Hampshire then moved across the county to play their first ever Championship game at the United Services Ground in Portsmouth against Leicestershire. Wynyard was captain for this game and secured a narrow victory by three wickets. Their last game was away at The Oval to Surrey, and the result of the Championship hung in the balance. If Surrey lost, Lancashire would be champions by the merest fraction under the new proportionality rule. The match began on 2 September and Wynyard was again Hampshire's captain. He won the toss and batted, but was caught by JM Read off the bowling of Richardson for 21. His side was all out for 182 with Richardson taking six for 85. Surrey responded and by the end of the first day were 163 for two. 10,000 people were present for day two and Surrey advanced to a handsome total of 374 (JM Read 131) with Teddy bowling two overs for six runs. He opened the batting second time, marching to the crease at 3.25 pm in the afternoon, needing 192 to avoid an innings defeat. He was swiftly dismissed, caught by Street off Richardson again, for just 1. The team progressed to 100 for two when Richardson was brought on at the top end. Haze descended on the ground and he took eight out of the last nine wickets coming down the slight incline at great pace. The weather was fine and play was allowed to go a little beyond the time for drawing stumps and at 6.10 Wootton was bowled by Richardson for 37. Surrey had won in two days by an innings and 20 runs, securing the County Championship in the process for the second year in succession.

The Champions had played the maximum possible twenty-six matches, won seventeen, lost four, producing a winning +61.91%. By contrast Hampshire had played the minimum sixteen matches, had six wins, nine losses and total of -20%. They finished tenth out of the competing counties, below average but just about respectable. The difficulty with every county having different fixtures was that it could be very misleading to make comparisons especially if some counties avoided the tougher sides (Surrey, Lancashire, Yorkshire and Gloucestershire) and instead played against predominantly weaker opposition.

The Times in their summary of the season referred to Hampshire as 'the county that can boast of being the birthplace of cricket' and reported that Wynyard had batted 'exceedingly well'. His Championship aggregate of 465 runs off twenty-two innings with a top score of 69 produced an average of 21.13 which was only sixth for the County. In fairness to him, however, apart from the opening match he did not play until mid July just as the good batting weather was about to end. For all first-class games that season he scored 581 runs, at an average of 22.34.

On Tuesday 10 December 1895, Wynyard and Bencraft represented Hampshire at the meeting of County Secretaries held at Lord's. There was a discussion about the programme for the Australian tour during the following summer and it was agreed there should be three Test matches. Charles Alcock of Surrey said the usual precedent would be followed whereby the home county kept the profit for the Test. There was great anticipation for the visit by Australia as the last Ashes series was one of the greatest ever played. AE Stoddart had led the team down under in 1894/5 and after leading 2-0 it was all square by the time of the last rubber at Melbourne beginning on 1 March 1895. England were set 297 to win and thanks to JT Brown of Yorkshire, who hit the fastest fifty in Test cricket at that time in under half an hour and went on to make 140, England coasted home with six wickets in hand.

Before the 1896 season began, Wynyard attended MCC's 109th AGM in the Long Room at Lord's, on 6 May 1896, followed in the evening by the annual dinner held in the Members Dining Hall, located in the Tavern. The very next day he travelled up to Fenner's to play for CI 'Buns' Thornton's Eleven against Cambridge University.

Thornton's team for the match was an impressive one including, in addition to Wynyard, Arthur Shrewsbury, AJ Webbe and Albert Trott. The University had Gilbert 'the Croucher' Jessop playing for them and on the first day he took two quick wickets to leave Buns' team at 45 for six but Teddy, going in at number nine, made 26 not out and steered the side to 219. On day two, Cambridge were all out for 289 with Teddy catching Jessop off Davidson's bowling for 25. The chief honours of the day went to Wynyard, who played splendidly for his 121 in the second innings including sixteen fours. At the close, Thornton's team were 315 for five and on the following morning progressed to 440 thanks to some magnificent hitting by Albert Trott who made 58. The University were 231 for nine at the end of the day to scrape a draw.

Teddy was clearly in great form because at the end of the month, on 30 May, he scored 261 not out when playing for Royal Military College Staff against the Staff College at Sandhurst. A fortnight later he was back at Charterhouse playing against his old school for the Free Foresters and made 87.

For this Championship season, Hampshire again played sixteen matches although the minimum number of games had been reduced to twelve as Australia were touring and playing a number of the counties. Teddy was now not only President but also captain as he had taken over from Bencraft. He missed the opening four games in which his county lost twice and won once but was back in charge on 29 June for the match against reigning champions, Surrey, at Southampton. Hampshire lost heavily by 380 runs, with Wynyard dismissed twice by George Lohmann.

On 6 July 1896, Teddy captained his county against the touring Australian side. He won the toss and decided to bat. He went in at number three and was caught by Trumble, bowled Trott, for 37 and his side collapsed from 119 for three to 134 all out (McKibbin, five for 41). The tourists amassed the large total of 462 with Iredale making 106 and Griffin 130. Wynyard bowled six overs which cost him 18 runs but he took the wicket of Eady, caught by Barton, for 11. In the second innings he top scored with 68 before being caught and bowled by McKibbin but his side were all out for 203, to lose by an innings and 125 runs, in just two days with Harry Trott taking five for 66.

This comprehensive defeat meant Wynyard had a day's break before Somerset were the visitors at the County Ground. Somerset secured an easy eight wickets victory thanks to an outstanding innings of 292 by Lionel Palairet. In contrast Teddy made just 14 and 2. He then made the short journey along the south coast to Hove and on 13 July won the toss and elected to bat. He scored his first century for his county in first-class cricket making 112 before being stumped by Butt off Hartley in a total of 356. Sussex replied with 225 and Wynyard bowled three overs for 12 runs. The second day was not without its controversy as the Sussex captain, Billy Murdoch, thought there might be an advantage to his side if they followed on leaving Hampshire to bat last on a wicket that could well break up. Accordingly, last man Butt, shortly after arriving at the crease, hit his wicket off the bowling of Ward. The ploy did not work because, although Sussex did follow on, Hampshire comfortably made the 129 they were set to win, with Teddy contributing 35.

Hampshire's next opponents at Southampton on 16 July were the very strong Yorkshire Eleven led by Lord Hawke. Teddy's luck with the coin continued and going in at 27 for one his team had progressed to 350 for three by close of play with his own personal contribution standing at 211 not out. This was against a bowling attack that included Hirst, Haigh and Peel. He started steadily but then, as *The Times* described it, he 'forced the game in vigorous style' batting for four and three-quarter hours: 'He timed the ball beautifully and apart from a difficult chance in the long field when 155, he made scarcely a bad stroke. Driving was his strong point.'

Day two saw Wynyard continue to flay the Yorkshire bowling and he had made 268 when caught by Moorhouse, off Wainwright's bowling. He had given just one further hard chance when on 257, and this was the second highest score of the season at that time (behind Palairet). It was to be Teddy's career-best in first-class cricket and also the highest first-class score by any Hampshire player at that time. In his innings Wynyard hit two sixes (which meant out of the ground), thirty-eight fours, five threes and twenty-three twos with fine driving and cutting being the major source of his runs. *Wisden* described it as a 'grand innings ... which far surpassed anything previously done by the Old Carthusian'.

Yorkshire responded to the Hampshire total of 515 and had reached 206 for six by close of play with Teddy taking two catches to cap a magnificent two days for him. On the last morning they progressed to 307 and had to follow on, with Teddy having bowled three overs towards the end for 16 runs. His side ran out of time in a drawn match with the visitors on 235 for eight, just 27 runs ahead. Let *Wisden* have the final word: 'During his long stay Wynyard only gave two chances and after playing so finely it was extremely hard for him to see his county just robbed of victory.' They could have added against the team that went on to be the 1896 County Champions!

Hampshire then beat Essex at the Lyttleton Ground in Leyton although Wynyard was bowled for 17 by a ball he did not attempt to play from fast bowling amateur, Charles Kortright. This easy eight wicket victory, with the match over in two days, allowed Teddy an extra twenty-four hours to prepare for the game at Lord's beginning on 23 July against the visiting Australians in which he had been asked to represent MCC. He was part of a strong side led by Stoddart that included MacLaren, Ranjitsinhji, William Gunn and JT Hearne.

The Australians won the toss and elected to bat but began badly with Wynyard catching Iredale off Hearne before there was any score on the board. They eventually made 202 with a century (103) from their skipper, Harry Trott. MCC responded well and had reached 119 for two with MacLaren 42 not out and Gunn on 10 by the close. The second day saw fine weather and attracted a crowd of 10,000 even though it was a Friday. MacLaren did not add to his overnight score and Wynyard strode to the wicket but for a time he was a little uncertain, whilst Gunn cut and drove beautifully. The Nottingham professional was then caught at short slip and was followed by Ernest Smith and then Pougher. By now Wynyard was well into his stride and played vigorously, although *The Times* said 'he mingled a lot of fine strokes with sundry chance hits'. In one and three-quarter hours he made 58 including eight fours. Jones then caught him off the bowling of Trumble, when the score was 249 for six. Pougher stoically kept up his end for 51 not out and MCC were eventually dismissed at 367. There was still more than three hours to play and Australia progressed to 113 for two by the close.

Play began on the Saturday at 11.35 before a 7,000 crowd, but there was a little rain around. When Iredale was out, Gregory played too soon at a ball from Attewell and the ball popped up towards mid-on but Wynyard was very alert, ran in and just reached it low down with his right hand. *The Times* described it as 'a wonderful catch'. Teddy also splendidly caught Donnan when he ran in from short mid on and managed to extend one hand under the ball but still held on to it even though he fell over in the process. 184 for five and it was 1 o'clock, but the tourists batted through until 4.50

pm reaching 331. There was only eighty minutes playing time left before the scheduled finish and MCC needed 167 to win. MacLaren and Ranji were both out, bowled by Trumble, trying to hit good length balls to leg. Stoddart hit 59 out of 80 in an hour before being caught and bowled by Trumble. Nine runs later Wynyard came in and added 8 with Gunn in the last ten minutes before stumps were drawn. MCC had run out of time on 99 for three with Gunn 26 not out and Wynyard 4 not out. They needed just another 68 to win with seven wickets still in hand. The Times said the day had been dull until the last hour but 'two wonderful catches at mid-on by Captain Wynyard were among the best things done in the way of fielding at Lord's this year'.

His performances, both batting and fielding, not least for MCC and his county against Australia, along with his 268 against the champions, Yorkshire, had brought his name to the attention of the Surrey Committee who would be choosing the team for the third and deciding Ashes Test at The Oval starting on Monday 10 August.

The 1896 series had not been without a modicum of controversy. Australia were captained by Harry Trott but his younger brother, Albert, was not selected in spite of his performance at Adelaide in the 1895 Test when he made 110 runs in the match without being out and took eight for 43 in the second innings.

The first Test was at Lord's and so selection was a matter for MCC. The in-form Ranjitsinhji was not picked leaving a suspicion of racial prejudice, albeit Lord Harris when Governor of Bombay (1890-95) had been the promoter of matches between the Parsees and Europeans. It is said he did not want 'birds of passage' playing for England though, and Ranji's biographer, Simon Wilde, says Harris came under pressure from Lord Salisbury's government who did not want Indian involvement in British domestic affairs. WG Grace captained the side and secured a six-wicket win.

The second Test was at Old Trafford and the Manchester selectors looked upon matters differently, as Ranjitsinhji was selected, coming in for William Gunn. There were two further changes with Archie MacLaren and Johnny Briggs replacing Tom Hayward and George Lohmann. Australia made two alterations with Frank Iredale opening the innings and bowler Tom McKibbin being chosen instead of Graham and Eady.

The *Wisden* editor, Sydney Pardon, when commenting on the 1896 series, condemned the bowling of both Jones and McKibbin as unfair. The warning was heeded because in October 1897 Australian umpire Jim Phillips did no-ball Jones at Adelaide and then did the same in the January Melbourne Test making him the first bowler to be called for throwing in Test cricket. Phillips subsequently called both McKibbin and England's CB Fry – a fearless official!

The Test began on 16 July and Australia won the toss making 412 in their first innings and went onto win by three wickets. Ranjitsinhji scored 62 and 154 not out and *Wisden* described his innings on the third morning as 'marvellous' with 'wonderful strokes on the leg side'. He had 'the Australians quite at his mercy'. Tom Richardson had also bowled for three hours on a pitch affording him little help and in the whole match he delivered 110.3 overs taking thirteen wickets for 244 runs. In spite of these two gargantuan performances, Australia had by far the better of the game and the series was now level, nicely setting up The Oval to be the deciding match for the destiny of the 1896 Ashes.

The Morning Post on Saturday 1 August 1896 reported the decision made twenty-four hours earlier that nine men had definitely been selected to represent England in the game: Dr WG Grace, AE Stoddart, FS Jackson, KS Ranjitsinhji, Abel, Lilley, Richardson, Gunn and Hayward. The last two places would be chosen from Peel, Lohmann, JT Hearne and Captain EG Wynyard DSO.

In spite of the fact that Teddy was not definitely in the team, on the same day, Russell Bencraft attended at the Bull Street, Birmingham Post Office and sent a telegraph to him at Heybridge in Essex. Wynyard's younger brother, William, lived at nearby Langford Parsonage. The telegram read: 'Congratulations on your selection for England from the Hampshire eleven. Bencraft.'

BOBBY ABEL, TO W. G.:—"LOOK HERE, WE PLAYERS INTEND TO BE SUFFICIENTLY
PAID, AS WELL AS THE SO-CALLED GENTLEMEN !"

Punch's take on the 1896 strike, a tense stand off during which
Teddy made his Test debut

8

THE STRIKE AND THE ASHES

1896

The naming of thirteen men for the squad meant that JT Brown, Archie MacLaren and Johnny Briggs had been left out from those who had played at Manchester. During the next ten days events occurred that potentially threatened the game even taking place, although it has also been argued that what happened actually secured Wynyard's spot in the team.

On Saturday 8 August, *The Times* ran a story with the heading 'Withdrawal of England Professionals'. The paper disclosed that earlier in the week George Lohmann, Tom Richardson, Tom Hayward, Bobby Abel and William Gunn had signed a written demand that they be paid £20 instead of the usual professional fee for these matches of £10.

Wynyard told his friend John Masterman, as recorded in the June 1974 issue of *Blackwood* magazine, that 'this was the match when all the professionals struck for higher pay and when England would have been hard put to it to field eleven men if rain had not delayed the start'. A common, but as we shall see not entirely accurate interpretation of a dispute whose origins were deeply rooted, extending back well over thirty years or more.

The advent of William Clarke's All-England Eleven saw the professional in the ascendency in terms of influence within the game during the middle of the nineteenth century up to the 1860s. Whilst MCC had been responsible for the laws since 1787, cricket was regionalized and there was no effective central or national control. A power battle started to evolve between the amateur and the professional over who would be the driving and dominant force going forward.

On 18 July 1848, William Gilbert Grace was born. In Simon Rae's biography of WG he observed that Grace's father had risen to his position in the medical profession from humble origins and, having fought hard to achieve some status in society, was absolutely determined his sons would be brought up as gentlemen. It meant they must play as amateurs and this, perhaps more than any other single factor, determined the course of cricket's development up to the end of the century.

As the eminent cricket writer, commentator and historian EW Swanton observed, 'cricket was largely a country pastime when Grace started his career but had become a national institution by the time he retired.' WG's pre-eminence and public popularity ensured that it was the amateurs under the auspices of MCC that held sway over the future running of the game. It is also true to say the professionals were simply not equipped to maximize the opportunities afforded whereas the largely public school and Oxbridge educated amateurs did have the qualities so required.

The major difficulty was that Grace and his family did not have sufficient private means to support him as a full-time cricketing amateur. Simon Rae estimated that during the 1870s WG earned a minimum of £1,000 (£80,000 in today's money) from domestic cricket per season comprising sums paid for organising United South matches, a share of profits for each match paid plus expenses for Gloucestershire and Gentlemen v Players games. In addition he went on highly profitable overseas tours.

The issue of remuneration, including what was reasonable to pay an amateur by way of expenses, prompted MCC in November 1878 to define amateur status by saying 'that no gentleman ought to make a profit by his services in the cricket field and that for the future no cricketer who takes more than his expenses in any match shall be qualified to play for the Gentlemen against the Players at Lord's'.

In reality this was no more than a restatement of the existing position and prompted the following stinging criticism from *John Lillywhite's Companion* that the scandal of payments to amateurs should have been 'long since ... nipped in the bud' and, with WG firmly in their sights, 'one well known cricketer in particular has not been an absentee from the GENTLEMEN's eleven at LORD'S for many years past and that he has made larger profits by playing cricket than any Professional ever made is an acknowledged fact.'

Teddy Wynyard, whilst a man of private means, was nevertheless a serving and paid Army officer and his cricket had to fit around his military responsibilities. The only solution to playing regularly without an adequate private income was to find a way to work around the strict definition. Perhaps then we should not be too censorious and judgmental about those, for Grace was far from being alone in this regard, who took a pragmatic approach towards its interpretation.

It is hardly surprising though that this caused friction with and resentment among the professional players. Their life was not an easy one. In addition to playing, often there were other duties to perform such as maintaining the ground and being available to bowl to club members as long as there was daylight by which to see the ball. Their earning power lasted only so long as their health and form held up, with drink often taking its toll on both counts.

It was not just remuneration that was an issue, but also social status and respect. This was why many amateurs baulked at being openly paid for playing the game. Scorecards and match reports referred to amateurs as 'Mr' whereas players were described by their surname only. The professionals had separate dressing rooms (often without a view of the pitch), different entrances onto the playing arena, separate travel (third as opposed to first class), accommodation (lodging houses rather than hotels) and separate tables and menus (if permitted). In later life, the great Yorkshire professional,

Wilfred Rhodes, was to compare this discrimination with apartheid in South Africa.

There was no such gentleman and players division in Australian cricket. Before the First World War, profit sharing of tour proceeds was common, and for the 1896 series the distribution was made between the tourists and the home county hosting the match. Nevertheless, Australian cricketers touring England were considered amateurs and it was a source of considerable resentment amongst the English professionals that the tourists benefited from the gate receipts whereas they did not.

For the first England v Australia Test in 1880, the Surrey Committee had voluntarily paid £20 to Shaw, Morley and Barnes but by 1896 the rate for those professionals selected for representative and England matches had been reduced to a consistent fee around the country of £10. It was this sum that Abel and company were seeking to increase for the final Test of that year. This era was known as the Golden Age but, in truth, it does not take much scratching of the surface to see how easily the metal beneath was tarnished. In these circumstances, the authorities cannot have been entirely surprised when these simmering undercurrents bubbled to the surface.

On Monday 3 August 1896, Abel, Gunn, Hayward, Lohmann and Richardson sent the following letter to the Surrey Committee:

> Sir, We the following players having been asked to represent England v Australia on August 10 and two following days do hereby take the liberty to ask for increased terms viz. twenty pounds. The importance of such fixture entitles us to make this demand. Trusting this will meet with your approval.

It was not until the following Saturday, 8 August, however, that *The Times* reported the Surrey Committee had 'without discussing the merits of the case, naturally refused to be dictated to by professional cricketers who had played at Lord's and Manchester under regular terms' and had re-invited the men to play on the original terms. When they refused the Committee reconstructed the England team which was now Grace, Stoddart, Jackson, Ranjitsinhji, MacLaren, Teddy Wynyard, JT Hearne, Pougher, Lilley, Peel and either Mold or Hirst. In other words Wynyard, Peel and JT Hearne were selected for the team from the original squad with MacLaren, Pougher, Mold and Hirst having been drafted in as replacements for the rebels.

Whilst there was some support for the players' cause, the press was largely critical of the timing and manner of the protest which was depicted as opportunistic brinkmanship, waiting until the eve of this decisive Test before threatening not to play and thereby exerting maximum pressure to drive home their pay demand. *The Times* felt very strongly that, as four of the rebels were from The Oval, they should have shown 'loyalty to the Surrey Club' and their 'patriotism for English cricket should have been a sufficient incentive to the players to have practiced self denial a little longer'.

The men upon whom responsibility fell to handle the dispute could not have been more experienced. They were the Surrey Secretary, Charles Alcock, and Sir Richard Webster, Chairman of the Surrey Committee. It was Alcock who had created the FA Cup competition and also presided over the introduction of professional football in 1885. He was widely viewed as being diplomatic, pragmatic and fair. Webster, an Old Carthusian, was the Attorney General and one of the foremost lawyers of his day. He briefly became Master of the Rolls in May 1900 (as Baron, later Viscount, Alverstone), before moving on to be Lord Chief Justice of England from October 1900 until 1913, presiding, in the process, over the murder trial of Dr Crippen (of whom it is said Bobby Abel bore a close physical resemblance). He also played a prominent part in cricket administration being both President of Surrey (1895-1915) and MCC (1903).

Alcock received the letter a full week before the Test was due to begin and by coincidence Nottinghamshire were Surrey's opponents at The Oval until Wednesday 5 August. Although neither Lohmann nor Gunn played in the game, there was an opportunity to speak with the other three professionals, if not all five of them, but this appears not to have happened. Instead the Committee waited for their next meeting, which was the day after the game had finished, and then sent a telegram to the four Surrey players stating 'fee for playing England v Australia £10 or you are out of the match'. William

Gunn was simply told his 'terms were not accepted'. Alcock sent the telegrams on the Thursday but the professionals did not receive them until the following day. The timing of the message and the requirement now for the Surrey players to confirm their availability was an astute playing of their hand by the Surrey executive.

There was just the weekend remaining before the Test started and so the players had been left with no time in which to manoeuvre. Matters might have been very different had the substitute professionals joined arms with those making a stand. This, linked to the fact that not all of the England professionals had made the demand in the first place, meant the rebels were effectively left with no negotiating power whatsoever.

Monday's *Times* reported that, by late on Saturday, Abel, Richardson and Hayward had reconsidered their position and 'unreservedly placed themselves at the service of the Surrey officials'. Although Alcock received this news on the Saturday night, he said the whole Committee needed to discuss the position on the morning of the match.

The Surrey Committee convened at 10 o'clock on the Monday morning and, if that conveyed the impression they had not left themselves very much time, it also demonstrated they were confident of being now back in control of events. This was a miscalculation, however, because over the weekend the issue had escalated when stories appeared about the payments being made to amateurs, especially Grace and Stoddart.

They both arrived at The Oval in high dudgeon and there was a serious risk they would not play. What one would have given to be a fly on that Committee room wall! The four Surrey professionals (Gunn was back in Nottingham) came in to face the Attorney General of England and Wales and the principal sports administrator of his day. A case of David v Goliath, but destined not to have the same biblical outcome!

In spite of the assurances given on Saturday, the three Surrey players were now asked to sign a letter – 'the Committee letter' – in the following terms:

10 August 1896
Gentlemen,
We extremely regret that you could not see your way clear to grant the request we made but as you know the Australians have made and are making large sums by these fixtures. It seemed to us only reasonable that we should participate in a small way out of the large amount of money received at representative matches. But after further consideration we desire to withdraw our refusal to play and beg to leave the matter in your hands, and we trust in future when these matches are played the matter will not be lost sight of, and at the same time we hope this will not destroy the good feeling which has existed between us in the past.
We are, Gentlemen.
Yours obediently,
T Richardson, R Abel, T Hayward.

As the Committee had insisted upon the meeting, it is likely Webster and Alcock had already decided in advance what terms they would insist upon and it is easy to see how in such an alien environment the three players felt they had no choice other than to sign, especially if playing was made conditional upon their compliance. Lohmann refused to sign but was not one of the original definite selections to play, in any event. Gunn was quite a different proposition and not one who could be intimidated in the same way. He did not play for Surrey and had attained financial independence with the success of his sports business, Gunn and Moore. He had prospered to the extent that he lived in Nottinghamshire's fashionable residential area, The Parks. By this stage of his career (he was now thirty-seven years of age) he did not need the money but expected proper recognition of his worth. When Gunn died in 1921 he left an estate valued at the considerable sum of £57,392, equivalent to nearly £2 million today.

Meanwhile, the Committee also had to consider the grievances of Grace and Stoddart. Given the Doctor's status within the game and his public popularity he was able to prevail upon Alcock, who also happened to be a good friend, to issue the following official statement that day:

The Committee of the Surrey County Cricket Club have observed paragraphs in the Press respecting amounts alleged to be paid, or promised to, Dr WG Grace for playing in the match England v Australia. The Committee desire to give the statements contained in the paragraphs the most unqualified contradiction. During many years, on the occasions of Dr WG Grace playing at The Oval, at the request of the Surrey County Committee, in the matches Gentlemen v Players and England v Australia, Dr Grace has received the sum of £10 a match to cover his expenses in coming to and remaining in London during the three days. Beyond this amount Dr Grace has not received, directly or indirectly, one farthing for playing in a match at the Oval.

Signed on behalf of the Committee
CW Alcock
August 10, 1896.

Interestingly though, Keith Booth asserts in his biography of Alcock, basing his information on an article by Frank Keating in *The Guardian*, that the amateurs Jackson, Ranji, Stoddart and Wynyard had been promised £25 and Grace £40 as expenses for the match. This places the payments to the professionals into proper perspective and raises the serious question of how Alcock could sign his name to such a letter.

His honour preserved, Grace agreed to captain the side but no such exoneration was given for Stoddart and he withdrew from the match. Newspaper reports attributed this to ill health as he had a very heavy cold that lasted over a week. MacLaren said much later, in a 1921 edition of *The Cricketer*, that 'Drewy' graciously stood aside to let him play. The authoritative voice on Stoddart is the renowned cricket historian David Frith, who has written two superb biographies on his subject. Frith states, 'by far the most likely reason for his withdrawal was the recently published suggestion that he was being paid far more than simply expenses by the Oval authorities.' He was never to play for his country in England again.

Abel being reinstated into the team meant England now had one surplus batsman until Stoddart withdrew and Frith said it seemed Wynyard had been the beneficiary of the dispute. Teddy, though, had been in the original pool of players selected ten days earlier whereas MacLaren had been omitted and so it seems that on this occasion, Archie was the more likely candidate to have missed out. Indeed, his own testimony was that Stoddart stood aside to let him play and *The Times* of the next day said the place was between Stoddart and MacLaren.

Gunn was no longer in London, having returned to play for Nottinghamshire against Kent. When he learned about the happenings at The Oval, he immediately put pen to paper. His response, which was published in *The London Standard* on Wednesday 12 August is very enlightening:

> So far as I am concerned in the matter, I only acted, along with others, in asking for an extra payment in consideration of the importance of the match, and the increased strain involved in playing such a fixture. What was asked was a sum of twenty pounds per man, the same as paid in such matches a few years back. In the request forwarded to the Surrey Committee it was not stated that I would not play for the ten pounds offered, neither did I refuse to play on those terms, but merely solicited the Committee to consider the payment of the higher sum. In reply to this I received the following telegram: 'Committee regret they cannot accept your terms – Signed, Alcock, Oval.'
>
> Up to this moment I have received no further communication whatever. I also wish to state that the remarks in the papers, said to be made by myself and others, respecting the payment of amateurs' expenses and the Australians' share of the gate money, are entirely erroneous, no such remarks ever having been made. I feel these are matters with which neither I nor any other player has anything to do.

The four Surrey professionals also wanted to set the record straight about what had really happened and they wrote another letter which was published in *The Times* on the same day. They stressed their original communication was sent as soon as three of them had received official notification of their selection. They were told the matter would be considered on the following Thursday. They were clearly upset that the public appeared to think they had waited until the Friday before making their request whereas, not only was that untrue, but they had actually already made a similar application after Lord's, which had been refused, and were still awaiting reimbursement of their expenses for the Old Trafford Test.

Wednesday 12 August 1896 was a very busy day because there was another specially convened Surrey Committee meeting at which an apology was accepted from Lohmann. He said he had declined to sign the Committee letter along with his three fellow Surrey professionals until he had spoken with Gunn. He had been told he would not be selected for Surrey until the matter was resolved. Not surprisingly in the light of this threat, the Surrey fast bowler backed down and agreed a letter could be sent to the Press in which he said, 'I would add that when the original letter was drawn up my idea was that a request was being preferred instead of a demand being made, and that the expression "demand", which I now see to have been so unfortunate, was inserted against my wish and better judgement.'

Alcock subsequently stated he was concerned because a 'peremptory demand had been made rather than a request for consideration' – this may well have had a significant influence on Alcock's interpretation of events. Lohmann came from a different background to most of his fellow professionals. His father was with the Stock Exchange and he may, therefore, have appreciated more than others the subtle significance of the language used. By making a demand it would automatically be seen as the professionals behaving in a manner above their station in a class-driven Victorian society. Abel's biographer, David Kynaston, thought Lohmann was the leader of the group, but, if so, it appears he did not have the final say on the wording of the letter.

Close scrutiny of the letters places the dispute in a different light from that portrayed in the press and down through history. The original letter, and Gunn emphasises this point, had not mentioned any refusal to play, but merely been a request or demand for improved remuneration. The telegram received by the Surrey players stated if they did not accept the £10 they 'would be out of the match'. In other words, rather than the professionals threatening not to play unless they were paid £20, the evidence points to the authorities issuing an ultimatum that the players would not be selected unless they confirmed their acceptance of the money on offer. When Abel, Hayward and Richardson told Alcock on the Saturday night that they unreservedly placed themselves in the hands of the Committee, such a response was entirely consistent with being in reply to the Surrey telegram, but the Committee letter clearly refers to a 'refusal to play', in which case, when was that refusal made?

The report in *the Times* on Monday 10 August stated:

> The English professionals never dreamed of the trouble that their demand for extra payment would cause but confidently hoped that the Surrey Committee would fall in with their views. But it was the clumsy and almost arrogant manner in which their demand was made which left the Surrey Club only one policy to adopt and that was to re-invite the men to play on the £10 and expense terms and then on their refusal to look to other quarters for the completion of the England side ... Whatever the outcome of the dispute that has occurred and however beneficial to the professionals in the end, the 'strike', as it has been termed, has been a great grief to the best lovers of the game.

The clear inference is that in the short period of time between receipt of the telegram on Friday and the communication to Alcock on the Saturday evening, the Surrey professionals had initially rejected the ultimatum. In *The Haywards: The Biography of a Cricketing Dynasty*, Keith and Jennifer Booth said 'negotiations continued by telegram from Leyton' where on Friday Surrey were losing by an innings against Essex inside two days. No mention of any such refusal of the terms emerges though from the letters detailed above, nor from Alcock's own subsequent account of events.

A rejection would explain, however, the wording contained in the Committee letter and, in the process, create the impression that the original pay demand had been accompanied by a threatened strike. Alcock was not about to persuade people otherwise because six years later he wrote, along with Webster (by then Viscount Alverstone), *Surrey Cricket: Its History and Associations*. They had this to say:

> The subject even at this distance revives rather unpleasant memories, and one would like to ignore it, but the faithful chronicler has a duty to perform ... A very few days before the match a communication was received by the Surrey executive to the effect that Lohmann, Gunn, Hayward, Richardson and Abel would not play unless each received a fee of £20. The Surrey Club Committee very naturally felt that such an

ultimatum ought not to have been hurled at them on the very eve of the match, and by their own men ... The manner in which the application was made to the Surrey Committee left them no alternative but to refuse. As a consequence arrangements were made to fill up the places of the five irreconcilables. At the same time opportunity was given to the four Surrey men to withdraw the letter they had written ... Gunn, one of the signatories to the letter, being a Notts man, was outside the jurisdiction of the Surrey executive.

As we have seen 'a very few days' was in fact a week and it was Alcock, and not the players who had issued the ultimatum. No reference was made to any rejection by the players of the terms contained in the Surrey telegram and, if that had been the case as suggested by *The Times*, surely some mention would have been made of this in the book? Instead Alcock, and he of all people knew what really happened, clearly states the refusal to play was in the original communication but as we have seen the letter of 3 August only asked for more money. It appears (and Lohmann's comments are consistent with this view) that Alcock regarded the use of the word 'demand' as a threat to withdraw labour and if that is the basis for suggesting a strike then, he, along with Webster, had demonstrated themselves to be early masters of spin without ever having to bowl a ball. It should be borne in mind that in addition to Webster's skills as a lawyer, Alcock was also a professional journalist, and together they succeeded, from their point of view, in putting the best possible gloss on events for public consumption.

Closer in time, but still permitting an opportunity for reflection, what did *Wisden* think of this affair? The editor, Sydney Pardon, wrote in the 1897 edition:

The players quickly withdrew from the position which, without thoroughly weighing the consequences, they had taken up. I thought at the time, and I think still, that the players were right in principle, but their action was ill-judged and inopportune ... Out of their revolt, however, I hope and believe that good will come ... I hope when the Australians pay us their next visit, it will be agreed to pay every professional chosen for England in the test matches, a fee of £20.

As it happens Pardon was granted his wish because at a meeting held at Lord's, in October 1898, ahead of the Australian tour the following summer, agreement was reached officially to increase the remuneration of the professionals to £20. The efforts of Abel, Lohmann and company had not, therefore, been in vain. Pardon neatly side-stepped the issue of amateur expenses because he lacked 'the necessary information' but he had it on good authority that:

> There were no more than half a dozen men playing as amateurs who make anything out of the game, the evil would not seem to be very widespread. *Mr WG Grace's position has for years, as everyone knows, been an anomalous one but 'nice customs curtsey to great kings' and the work he has done in popularizing cricket outweighs a hundredfold every other consideration.* [Emphasis added.]

It is remarkable how very little is new in life. *The Daily News* had said on 8 August 1896 that 'some of the players have struck for £10 … but how much we wonder of the so called increased interest now taken in cricket is due to the game and how much to the money in it and on it'. Compare that question with one by Australian cricket writer, Gideon Haigh, concerning the Indian Premier League nearly 120 years later: 'does cricket make money in order to exist or does it exist in order to make money?' Today, more than ever before, the answer to that question is likely to determine the future of Test cricket as we know and love it.

What did Teddy think of the dispute that nearly thwarted his Test debut? He had an autocratic reputation and was clearly one of those born to lead. Public school educated with a distinguished military career; Duty, Queen and Country were at the heart of everything in which he believed. He was very much a man of his time in that respect, and so the natural inference is he would have been a supporter of the Surrey Committee. Furthermore, Webster was an Old Carthusian and Alcock an old footballing acquaintance. It is pure guesswork whether it triggered one of his famed temper outbursts, but as he awoke on the morning of the Test, there was a different threat facing him as there had been a series of rainstorms on the Sunday and further downpours were forecast for the first day.

Play was scheduled to begin at 11.30 am and the gates opened at 10 o'clock, also the time the Surrey executive had scheduled to start their meeting and their prolonged discussions were hardly ideal preparation for the most important match of the season.

Australia, on the other hand, had no such problems and selected an unchanged side from the Old Trafford Test. They did have one choice to make, however, because a certain Frederick Spofforth had approached Harry Trott and pleaded with him to play. 'The Demon' was not part of the touring party but was now living in London. When he saw the weather, memories flooded back to the same venue in 1882 and he wanted one last chance to get at WG and the English! The opportunity was denied him though and the Australians lined up as follows: Darling, Iredale, Giffen, Trott (captain), Gregory, Hill, Donnan, Kelly, Trumble, Jones and McKibbin.

Alcock and Webster, having finished their deliberations, finally announced the England side: Grace (captain), Jackson, Ranjitsinhji, Abel, MacLaren, Hayward, Wynyard, Peel, Lilley, Hearne and Richardson.

The modern day player has a unique identification number on his shirt below the three-lions crest representing their place in the chronological list of players appearing for England. Had such an arrangement been in place back in 1896 (albeit Teddy would not have approved of all the sponsors' logos), Wynyard would have been 106. The man before him at 105 was Ranjitsinhji who had made his debut in the previous Test at Manchester. WG was twenty-four.

Now that the team was known, they had a little time to compose themselves because, before lunch, there was a downpour of rain that swamped the pitch. In spite of the weather, by midday, 10,000 people had been admitted into the ground. Even after the storm the crowd kept growing and by the end of the day the attendance was 16,000 with 13,411 having paid their shilling admission.

The umpires for this, the fifty-second Test match, were Australian-born Jim Phillips and Englishman William Hearn. They had a difficult day ahead of them. The pitch was incredibly soft, especially at one end, and they were very reluctant to allow play. Nevertheless the sun came out and started to shine and the large crowd wanted to see some cricket (shades of the Centenary Test in 1980) and their wish was finally granted. After numerous inspections, the ringing of the bell at 4.30 in the afternoon to indicate play could commence was greeted by loud applause. It then took another twenty minutes to mark up the creases (the frustration of being a cricket spectator is not a modern day phenomenon) and so a start was not made until just before 5 o'clock limiting the first day to only one and a half hours' play.

Grace won the toss and elected to bat. As the pitch was soft, the ball cut through the surface but it was vital to register as high a score as possible before batting conditions deteriorated with the drying out of the wicket. Grace walked out down the steps accompanied by FS Jackson and they progressed the score to 54 when Grace played forward to Giffen and Trott took a low catch, tumbling over in the process, at point.

Ranjitsinhji was next man in and was given a hearty reception by the crowd. Trott recognized his strengths and so adjusted the leg side field and Ranji survived two lbw appeals from both Giffen and Trumble. By close of play England had advanced to 69 for one with Jackson 39 and Ranjitsinhji 5 not out.

On Tuesday the weather was more settled and there was a larger crowd of 29,000 with 25,367 paying at the gate. Play began at 11.30 am and Jackson was soon out for 45. The next man in was Bobby Abel and he was applauded all the way out to the wicket, demonstrating there was no public animosity towards him for the stance he had taken. Before any runs had been added, though, Ranji played back to Giffen and was completely beaten.

The ball was not coming evenly off the pitch, either in terms of bounce or direction, but England progressed on to 113 for three when Trott made a crucial bowling change bringing on McKibbin with his slow off breaks and replacing Giffen with Trumble at the Pavilion End. Trumble took the wickets of MacLaren and Hayward in quick succession and the score was now 114 for five.

Exactly fifteen years and 122 days after Wynyard had walked out onto the Kennington turf in Old Carthusian colours to win his FA Cup medal, he now stepped onto the Oval grass again, but this time in his cricket whites, completing the second leg of a unique double by making his Test match debut in an Ashes finale. The pitch was getting worse by the minute as it continued to dry out. Teddy was determined he was not going to be bogged down and stroked the ball well, especially with a fine off drive to the boundary. He had just reached double figures and was facing McKibbin's off breaks. The genial, moustachioed bowler from New South Wales had a very suspect action and was deadly when aided by a damp wicket. Wynyard decided to lay down the challenge and chanced his arm but skied the ball to a great height only for Joe Darling to run in from long off to take a fine steepling catch behind the bowler. The 'Hampshire crack' (as he was described by the *London Standard*) was out for 10.

The score was now 131 for six but the tail folded and England were all out by 1.15 pm for 145. *The Times* was critical of England's batting, perhaps with Wynyard in mind, for being too attack minded. Their correspondent observed England's usual 'hitting game was not profitable' as it was a day to scrap for runs.

Darling and Iredale opened the batting at 1.25 pm and had a nasty twenty-five minutes to face before lunch. Grace started with Peel from the Gasometer (Vauxhall) End to a five-four field and Teddy was placed at short leg. Jack Hearne came on at the Pavilion End and was given a quite different seven-two offside-dominant field with Wynyard still in an attacking position at forward short leg. While England had their chances, Australia progressed quickly to 45 without loss by lunch.

Grace restarted with the right arm medium pace combination of Hayward and Hearne. After bowling only two overs, Hayward was swiftly replaced by Richardson as the Australian opening partnership added another 30 runs. *The Times* commented that '75 on such a false piece of turf in forty-five minutes against Peel, Hearne and Richardson was simply wonderful'. Quite extraordinarily, Iredale then attempted a fifth run off a snick by his partner Darling, only to be dismissed in a moment that completely changed the course of the Australian innings. It was Ranji who chased the ball to the boundary's edge and obviously surprised the Australian openers by throwing the ball over 100 yards, straight into Lilley's gloves above the bails. Ranjitsinhji reportedly presented the wicketkeeper with a gold cigarette case by way of thanks although MacLaren says another fielder had to intercept Ranji's throw and relay it to the stumps at the bowler's end but, in fact, it probably must have been to Lilley. In any event the rot quickly set in and 75 for one became 83 for 4.

Giffen was joined at the crease by Clem Hill, who was to become one of the most distinguished of all Australian left-handed batsmen. There was a heavy expectation on his shoulders as this young protégé took guard. He got off the mark and then played his favourite nudge around the corner and set off for a single but Wynyard, fielding at backward short leg, pounced and effected the second crucial run out of the day. It was now 84 for five. Wickets continued to tumble and Australia were all out for 119.

Hearne had bowled for nearly two hours taking six for 41 and missed two hard caught-and-bowled chances in the process. Undoubtedly though he had been bowling when the pitch had been at its worst, at least, so far!

Just after 5 o'clock, almost exactly twenty fours after Grace and Jackson had marched down the pavilion steps to start England's first innings, they were now making the same journey to begin the second. They were just 26 runs ahead and there was one and a half hours play left in the day. Trott opened the bowling with Trumble and McKibbin, again preferring the slower option to that of Jones.

Trumble dismissed both openers and the score was only 12 for two. Kelly then stumped Ranjitsinhji and MacLaren joined Abel with forty-five minutes still left in the day. After a cautious period of batting, Trott turned for the first time to the pace of Ernie Jones. He came on at the Gasometer End and promptly removed MacLaren's leg stump. Tom Hayward arrived and cut Jones for four but then Abel was well caught by Giffen high up and right handed at short mid on.

It was 56 for five and England were only 82 ahead with just five wickets remaining on a treacherous pitch. What a test of nerve and character for debutant, Captain EG Wynyard, as he made his way to the wicket! Teddy said, 'I batted for about twenty minutes and was not out and I can assure you that I never batted better in my life.'

Hayward stayed with him and so there was no further loss by the time stumps were drawn. England had progressed to 60 for five in their second innings with Hayward on 9 and Wynyard yet to score.

It had been a truly remarkable day's play for the large crowd – twenty-four wickets had fallen and 255 runs scored!

A great deal would depend on Wynyard and Hayward batting long into the next day but it was a tough ask for them to swing the runs and time equation back in favour of the home side. It appears WG saw matters differently though.

Let Sir John Masterman now take up the story. Teddy was one of the spymaster's boyhood heroes and, when they played cricket together in later life, Masterman asked him who Wynyard thought the best cricket captain was. Without pausing for a moment's reflection Wynyard replied, 'WG, of course!' and went on to tell the tale of the 1896 Oval Test. He referred to the wicket as a pig and having survived the ordeal of Tuesday evening was 'hoping to make a good score on the next day'. The following morning, however, WG pressed his thumb several times into the pitch and pronounced, 'I'm sorry for you boys, for I know you'd like to make runs in a Test match, but you've all got to be out in half an hour. I must be bowling at them by 12.30 at the latest.' Teddy added that Stoddart, who was not playing, argued with Grace that England would need every run they could muster, but the Doctor could not be swayed from his view.

The pitch was damper than anticipated when play began at 11.35 am with McKibbin bowling the first over. Hayward ran a single leaving Wynyard to face and a snick onto the leg side produced three runs. Hayward then picked up another three from a cut.

Trumble was now bowling and off his first ball the Surrey all-rounder gave short leg a gentle catch. Bobby Peel came in and was missed by Giffen at mid-off. The score did not change for the next twenty balls, when Wynyard was well caught behind by the wicketkeeper chasing a wide offside delivery. The manner of his removal was consistent with what one might expect of a military man, namely following his captain's orders as he recalled them, to score runs and be out in half an hour. Nevertheless, if that was the case,

WG could not have been happy with the four maiden overs that had preceded Teddy's dismissal. Kelly had caught Wynyard, off the bowling of McKibbin, for 3 and England were 67 for seven. This very quickly became 84 all out in just two hours spread over the Tuesday afternoon and Wednesday morning. Trumble had taken six for 30 and McKibbin three for 35.

Wynyard was adamant it was all part of the Grace master plan, but only 24 more runs had been added and the tourists needed just 111 runs with the pitch likely to grow better as the day wore on.

At 12.35 pm Darling and Iredale walked down the pavilion steps hoping they could emulate their 75-run first-innings opening partnership which would all but guarantee their side victory in this deciding Ashes Test. Grace sprang an immediate surprise by opening the bowling from the Pavilion End with Tom Richardson. Normally the local paceman would have been the logical first choice to spearhead the attack, but this pitch had not favoured speed with Jones and Richardson having bowled only eight overs in the match to date. Nevertheless, Tom sent down a maiden to Iredale and Jack Hearne took the ball to start bowling from the Gasometer End. He immediately found his length and his third fast-medium delivery broke across the body of left-handed Joe Darling to strike the top of off stump.

Grace immediately replaced Richardson with Peel. Wynyard was in later life to say, 'yes, of course, Grace was the greatest of all captains, though I never really understood why he gave Richardson that one over.'

Iredale and Giffen had swiftly followed Darling back to the pavilion and Australia were 7 for three. Hearne had bowled 24 balls, four maidens and taken three wickets for no runs. Surrey's Bill Brockwell was fielding as substitute for Ranjitsinhji who, CB Fry said, had indulged in a 'leisurely uprising' that morning having had a bad night with asthma and then stood on an upturned nail at the hotel. He also did not have a good reputation for punctuality at the best of times, but Brockwell, on the other hand, had an excellent reputation as a smart fielder and when Trott hit a hard drive towards mid off he took a tremendous catch low down and leaning sideways.

There had been only thirty minutes of play and yet Clem Hill, number six, was already walking out to join Syd Gregory. He was completely beaten by a Peel leg break. Donnan, Gregory, Kelly and Jones all then succumbed to Peel and in no time at all the score was 25 for nine. Quite remarkably McKibbin was now at the crease as the last man in. He decided to hit any and everything before Abel took a fine right-handed catch at slip to dismiss him off Hearne's bowling.

The whole innings had lasted one hour and fifteen minutes and only number eleven had reached double figures. Twenty-six overs had been bowled and 44 remains, at the time of writing, the third-lowest score of all time in Ashes matches (36 by Australia at Edgbaston in 1902 is the lowest). England had won by 66 runs and retained the Ashes with Peel taking six for 23 and Hearne four for 19.

This was the last match in which WG Grace led England to success over Australia. There were great scenes as thousands of the excited crowd rushed onto the pitch and congregated outside the pavilion. They would not leave until the players from both sides had appeared, and the cheering was at its loudest for Hearne and Peel. How tragic, therefore, that barely twelve months later the hero, Peel, should be dismissed by his county for drunkenness. This was to be his last Test for England but it was a great performance to finish on, even though he had been out for a pair! The Surrey Committee rewarded both players with an additional £5.

What price before the match started that Richardson would not take a wicket in either innings? Instead, Peel who had the ability with his left-hand slow bowling to break the ball both ways, had taken eight for 53 and Hearne ten for 60. It should not be forgotten though that the other two wickets had been run outs at crucial times courtesy of Ranjitsinhji and Wynyard.

There is one final and significant postscript to this memorable and historic Test. Over the three days more than 48,000 people had paid for admission, resulting in what *The Times* described as 'a very lucrative match for Surrey and the Australians'. Guess what? Whilst the official Surrey minutes are silent on the matter, Alcock and Webster disclosed in their history of Surrey, written six years later, that '*as a mere matter of detail,* it should be mentioned that the professionals playing in the match, including the reserves, received £20 each from the Committee of the Surrey County Cricket Club' [emphasis added]. So, at the end of the day, Abel and his fellow players were paid, by way of a win bonus, the amount they had 'demanded' and for which they had been publically vilified.

It is a sad reflection on the Golden Age that the English professionals were not rewarded openly in recognition of their worth but, of course, that would only have served to highlight the legitimacy of their original claim.

Ranjitsinhji demonstrated his particular way to play the leg glance in his *Jubilee Book of Cricket*; Teddy's portrait in the book was a more formal one

9

THE GRAPES OF WRATH

1897

After the Test, Teddy returned to the County Ground for the visit of Warwickshire. He kept wicket, stumping Forrester off Baldwin for a duck, and made 3 and 111 with the bat. In the process he completed 1,000 runs aggregate for the season. He held the team together in the second innings, hitting sixteen fours, but in spite of his efforts Warwickshire ran out easy winners by ten wickets.

Wynyard was selected to play at the Scarborough Festival for a very powerful CI Thornton Eleven against the Australians in the penultimate match of their tour, beginning on 31 August. He only scored 6 but was again prominent in the field, running out Iredale with a smart return and taking three catches to dismiss Giffen, Donnan and Gregory, which, added to another five-wicket haul for Peel, saw the tourists all out for 140 in their second innings giving Thornton victory by an innings and 38 runs.

So came to an end by far and away Wynyard's best season. He had scored four first class centuries, 268 (v Yorkshire), 121 (for Thornton's Eleven against Cambridge University), 112 (v Sussex) and 111 (v Warwickshire). He played twenty-three innings, made 1,038 runs at an average of 49.42 (which placed him overall second with only Ranjitsinhji ahead of him) and had made his Test debut. This was a great achievement in the Golden Age of Cricket.

On 27 November 1896, Hampshire's AGM was held in Southampton and Wynyard was reappointed Captain. There were two developments, with Lancashire being added to the fixture list for the first time since 1870, and also a cricket week to be played at Bournemouth.

Yet 1897 was an unsettling year for Teddy, marked initially by uncertainty over his military career and later by frustration of his cricketing aspirations. There was a common cause centring upon his seven-year tenure as an instructor at Sandhurst expiring on 22 August, and so there were important decisions to make or to be made for him.

By accepting the captaincy of his county for another year, though, Teddy clearly hoped for a good summer's cricket before having to move on. Hampshire continued to suffer from their inability to call upon their best players on a regular basis and they were especially vulnerable in the bowling department.

Wynyard did not play in the first five Championship matches but turned out on 10 June against Cambridge University at Fenner's in a match for the benefit of Robert Carpenter who had been in George Parr's team on both the first English tour overseas to America in 1859 and the second tour of Australia four years later. WG said, 'Carpenter may be safely placed as one of the finest of our great batsmen.' Carpenter had been dismissed, caught by Teddy's father, William, when on 54 in the United All-England v Margate game in September 1864. Unfortunately the weather was unkind to the beneficiary who umpired the match. Cambridge inflicted an innings defeat on Hampshire inside two days with Wynyard scoring 31 and 22.

On Friday 18 June, Teddy was a steward at the Old Carthusian dinner held in the Whitehall rooms of the Hotel Metropole to mark twenty-five years of Charterhouse at Godalming. Other stewards included old school friends and footballing teammates Robert Baden-Powell, AH Tod, GO Smith, EH Parry, FG Leatham and AW Walters. The price of the dinner tickets including wine and cigars was twenty-two shillings and sixpence (£120 today). It must have been a good evening!

Wynyard played his first Championship match for Hampshire at Southampton against Yorkshire on 5 July. He contributed 63 before being stumped off Bobby Peel's bowling towards a total of 251. Yorkshire responded with 293 with Teddy using no less than eight different bowlers including himself (nought for 9 off three overs with one wide). In the second innings Teddy batted again at number three, but fell victim to Hirst's bowling for 33 on a rain-affected pitch. Reigning champions Yorkshire ran out easy winners by ten wickets.

Wynyard's next match was his debut in the Gentlemen v Players fixture starting at The Oval on 8 July. It was also the first time Warner and George Hirst had been selected to play in the game. The Gentlemen were short of bowling whereas the Players were at full strength including five from the third Test in 1896.

Wynyard came in at number three and joined WG with the score on 56 for one, Plum Warner being the man out. He made a steady 33 before again falling victim to Peel. The Gentlemen made 284 but the Players responded with 431 before 5,000 spectators on the second day. Wynyard took two catches to dismiss Tom Hayward and George Hirst and bowled, taking Wainwright's wicket, ending with figures of one for 12. At 5 o'clock the Gentlemen started their second innings, 147 behind. WG and Plum were quickly dismissed and Teddy again made 33 before being caught by Hayward off Wainwright's bowling. The Players easily managed the 29 they were set to win.

The next county game was at the United Services Ground in Portsmouth against Somerset. Twenty wickets fell on the second day as the ball was flying about in a dangerous fashion. *The Times* reported that 'a notable exception to the general batting failures was a fine display by Capt Wynyard and Victor Barton, the two men putting on 130 runs in just over 1.5 hours for the fourth wicket. They had to contend against many difficulties but surmounted them in wonderful fashion, scarcely a mistake being made.' Wynyard made 80, hitting twelve fours, his highest first-class score of the season. In the second innings he was out for 32 leading his side to a win by three wickets.

On 10 July the formal announcement was made that Captain Sir Charles Cuyler of the 1st Battalion Oxfordshire Light infantry had been selected as an Instructor in Fortifications at the Royal Military College to replace Wynyard. Mention has already been made of the reference letter Teddy secured from General Sir Charles Gough VC on 9 June 1897 relating to his period as an adjutant in Oudh. Teddy obtained this because there was an opportunity to return to India as he was being considered for the post of Chief Constable in Oudh, a role with which his father had been familiar.

These were uncertain times for him as he pondered what the future, cricket aside, might have in store for him. After scoring 1 and 23 in a rain-affected draw against Surrey, Wynyard did not play in the next Championship match away at Hove against Sussex but, nevertheless, he appears to have left his imprint on the game.

Masterman makes mention in his *Blackwood* article and both Frith (in his two books on Stoddart) and Simon Wilde (in his biography of Ranjitsinhji) refer to the incident, although none of them give a precise date for when it happened. Masterman says a fine bunch of hothouse grapes had been placed on the pavilion table for Teddy's benefit. Ranjitsinhji, who had been out after a good innings some time before the close of play, had seen them and, not knowing to whom they belonged, ate a few before going up to change. Teddy was told this when he came in and 'his language was sulphurous and his wrath unquenchable, and soon, in spite of the courtesy of Ranji, a minor incident developed into a major altercation. Things went so far that fixtures between the two counties were cancelled for the following season.'

They were subsequently reinstated and both Masterman and Frith agree that it was Stoddart who was the peacemaker. He made it clear that, as he had asked both players to go on the England tour under his captaincy to Australia during the following winter, he would have to cancel the invitation if Teddy did not apologise.

It was not part of Wynyard's character to take a step backwards or ever to say sorry. Masterman said he had never done so to anyone in his life and did not know how to do so. Some of his friends then drafted a letter which 'on a very liberal interpretation could be construed as an apology and this he was induced to sign'. Apparently, Ranjitsinhji readily accepted it.

1897 was the year of Queen Victoria's jubilee and Ranjitsinhji published his *Jubilee Book of Cricket*. It was 'Dedicated, By Her Gracious Permission, To Her Royal Highness The Queen-Empress' and he sent a personally signed copy to Teddy. Doubtless this was also an effort at peacemaking but, as that book has been in my possession for nearly forty years, it is pure speculation whether Wynyard, still incensed, simply gave it away or kept and read it. There are immaculate pencil notes in the margins on some pages and I would like to think they might just have been made by Teddy's own fair hand!

On 15 August 1896, Stoddart, from his then address at 30 Lithos Road, South Hampstead, wrote to Wynyard saying:

> Dear Wynyard,
>   I was very pleased to hear that the War Office had given you leave and that you accept the invitation to join the team. I feel certain you will enjoy the tour immensely and I shall be glad to do all in my power to make things happy for you.
>   Yours ever
>   AE Stoddart

There were further handwritten details of 'colors [sic] for the day we leave England'. Stoddart also enclosed a tie and hat ribbon and an order for tour caps and coats (blazers) with instructions to have them made in plenty of time. He said he would look after 'all the other things in the shape of colors' and had arranged a berth 'Cabin 43 and 44' which was inside 'but very comfortable'. Only a week later though, on 22 August 1897, Stoddart had to write the following letter of commiseration:

> My dear Wynyard,
>   I cannot tell you how sincerely sorry I am to get the news of the War office cancelling your leave. I was looking forward with the greatest pleasure to having you with us and can only tell you that I am almost as disappointed as you are. Possibly you may be able another year to

visit Australia with a team but this is no consulation [sic] to me. About the inconvenience caused please don't let this add to your trouble. I can easily get another man, I had intended to take 14 but now I think that if Briggs takes your place that will be enough. I only wanted another good bowler to add to the 13 which appeared in the papers to have a rare side. As my object in accepting your invitation to dine with you was only with the view of helping you re the tour, and I am very much busy I will ask you to excuse me. I shall hope to see you somehow before we leave and in the meantime can only repeat how sincerely sorry I am you cannot join us.

Yours ever,

AE Stoddart

The date of Stoddart's second letter coincided exactly with the day Wynyard's seven-year tenure as an instructor at Sandhurst came to an end. Next day there was an announcement in *The Times* that he had been ordered to rejoin his regiment in India and consequently he would be unable to accompany Stoddart's team to Australia. He was to return to the Welsh Regiment following the vacancy caused by the retirement of Captain JRP Clarke.

Hampshire played Sussex both home and away in 1897 but Teddy did not play in either game. The second match did not start until 19 August and Ranjitsinhji scored only 3 and 21 not out. As this was so close to Wynyard's withdrawal there was hardly time or need for Stoddart's peacemaking initiative, which points to the game at Hove on 22 July as being the scene of the 'Grapes of Wrath' incident. There is further evidence in support as Ranji scored 149 in that match and Masterman said he was out after a good innings. Simon Wilde also referred to an article in the August 1897 issue of *Vanity Fair* that mentioned the 'well publicized argument he ((Ranji) had had recently with Teddy'. As Sussex had won the toss and elected to bat with Ranjitsinhji 129 not out overnight, the contretemps must have happened on day two (Friday 23 July 1897) as Sussex went on to win by an innings and 176 runs.

Masterman refers to Wynyard coming in off the field and Ranjitsinhji getting changed, but as Teddy was not playing, he must either have been a substitute fielder or, more likely, practising in the nets. What is significant, however, is that Sussex were the home side and so, if hothouse grapes were waiting on the pavilion table, there was no obvious reason why Ranjitsinhji should expect them to be for a member of the visiting team who was not even playing.

Can Counsel on behalf of Teddy offer anything by way of mitigation for his outburst? He may well have been on edge with everything that was happening but his was such a disproportionate reaction that either it was the worst possible example of his short temper or there was a much more deep-rooted animosity towards Ranjitsinhji.

For many, the tirade was all the more inexplicable precisely because it was the Indian-born batsman who was the target. He was much loved, indeed revered, by the British public and his fellow cricketers not only for his cricketing artistry but also for being a generous and kind man. The awe in which he was held is illustrated by Gilbert Jessop, one of the fastest and best bowlers of his generation who said 'he drew crowds wherever he went and at the height of his cricket days, the shops in Brighton would empty if he passed along the street. Everyone wanted to see him.' Ranjitsinhji's obituary in *Wisden* opined that, 'he was to become and to remain from 1895 until 1912, with two breaks of four years each, the most talked of man in cricket.'

His cricketing statistics spoke for themselves, but Jessop was equally lavish in his praise about Ranjitsinhji as a person, extolling that he 'never heard him say an ill word of any player, whether on his own or on his opponent's side. That's a fine epitaph for a cricketer.' Ranjitsinhji's great friend, CB Fry, described him as 'mellow, kind, no one has a keener eye for what is good in other people' and referred to his genial ways.

By contrast Gilbert Jessop said of Wynyard that he was a man of 'many and varied enthusiasms in life, whose occasional dark moods often took the form of a violent tirade which left those who witnessed it, or heard it from afar, shaken and exhausted'.

Wynyard was one player who clearly did not share the praise bestowed upon the Indian maestro. Simon Wilde asserted, 'Ranji's straightforwardly attractive public persona was complemented by a less well known and altogether less acceptable side.' Indeed the book reveals many aspects concerning Ranjitsinhji's background and behaviour with which his adoring public would have been largely, if not totally, ignorant.

He had been born and brought up in humble surroundings and his claim to be a Prince was based upon initially being chosen as the heir by the then ruling Jam Sahib, Vibhaji, when he exiled his own son. Vibhaji then changed his mind but agreed to fund Ranjitsinhji's education and pay him an allowance.

At the age of sixteen he travelled to England and was educated at Cambridge where he lived the lavish lifestyle of a prince, but only by running up debts to local tradesmen and having to borrow from friends to stave off bankruptcy. Later in life he employed Archie MacLaren as his secretary, part of which job was to fend off Ranjitsinhji's creditors.

On 14 August 1906, the incumbent Jam Sahib, Jassaji, died amid unsubstantiated rumours of foul play at the hands of Ranjitsinhji's supporters. There followed a dispute over who should be the successor. The decision fell to Percy Fitzgerald, who was the political officer with responsibility for dealing with relations between British India and the princely states, and Ranjitsinhji was duly chosen. It did not bring about a significant change in his financial circumstances but did enable him to run the defence, when he was sued, that he was exempt from the jurisdiction of the English courts because he was a ruling sovereign of an independent state. This even prompted questions in the House of Commons along the lines 'does His Highness claim to be above the jurisdiction of British Law and was there any way a creditor could obtain repayment?'

In spite of Ranjitsinhji's determination during his life to maintain his public image and reputation, after his death on 2 April 1933, a more critical view was taken. *The Times* said 'he could be ruthless in the pursuit of his aims and was uncannily adroit'.

Wynyard viewed himself as an excellent judge of a man and may well have seen through Ranjitsinhji's superficial veneer and espied the true character beneath. Teddy may well have had very good reason, therefore, 'to think rather less of KS Ranjitsinhji than some of the public do'. It would be remiss, though, not to consider in the context of their relationship the very delicate issue of prejudice. When FS Jackson presented Ranjitsinhji with his Blue at Cambridge University in 1893, quite a controversial award at the time, he admitted he did not possess a 'sympathetic interest for Indians'. Racial prejudice was never far away and Wilde says that, in the beginning, Ranjitsinhji was 'ignored by other members of the team and sometimes sat alone and friendless in the pavilion'. MCC had not selected him for the previous year's Lord's Test.

Ranjitsinhji confronted these attitudes in two pioneering speeches. At Cambridge in 1893, when just twenty years of age, he expressed the aspirational opinion that 'I don't think Indians are foreigners in England, that distinction has passed away long, long, ago and I think that in time to come we shall look upon each other as absolutely the same subjects under Her Majesty the Queen'. Three years later he continued in a similar vein saying 'I trust that the wrongs done in the past by Her Majesty's Indian subjects and the injustice, if any, which they have suffered in days gone by, will be forgotten and that England and India may in future form one united country'.

When making these comments he must have had the Indian Mutiny in mind, and Wynyard's father had been in the thick of the action. Teddy knew the sub-continent and its people well and may even have been returning there to work and this may all have influenced how well disposed he felt towards the, then, self-styled Indian Prince.

Whether Wynyard had good reason or less commendable motives for his attitude towards Ranjitsinhji, no excuse can be proffered for his tirade over a mere bunch of grapes. Those who witnessed it must indeed have been left shaken and exhausted, not least Ranjitsinhji, who was very sensitive to criticism. Even though he was the innocent party, he remained eager to please and still made his gift of the *Jubilee Book* to Wynyard. Precisely how Teddy responded upon its receipt must remain tantalisingly a matter of speculation!

After creating mayhem without even playing in the defeat by Sussex, Wynyard returned to captain Hampshire five days later on 29 July 1897 at Old Trafford, but his side lost badly. He did then manage two half-centuries in a win away at Derby (52) and in an innings victory over Leicester at Grace Road (58).

The next match was at The Oval and was a much severer test at the hands of Surrey. The home side won the toss and made the very substantial total of 579. The two openers Abel and Brockwell made the record first-wicket stand at the time of 379, with Abel scoring 173 before being stumped by Steele off Wynyard's bowling, and Brockwell making 225. Teddy tried everything at his disposal to make inroads and took the almost unique step of putting every player in the team on to bowl – including the three wicketkeepers who were used; Robson, Steele and himself.

Hampshire replied and were all out for 149 with Teddy making 3 and Richardson taking four for 85. Following on Teddy scored 4 and Richardson again was the major protagonist with five for 35 as Surrey were easy victors by an innings and 303 runs.

The next day, 12 August, Warwickshire visited Southampton and yet again the openers put on a massive opening stand registering 288 before Wynyard stumped Captain Bainbridge off Baldwin's bowling, for 162. For the second time in a week, every member of the Hampshire side bowled and *The Times* described these as 'anything but pleasant experiences'. Wynyard took two wickets, a catch and made two stumpings. He opened the batting and was fourth out, playing admirably for 67 in an hour and three quarters but his side was dismissed for 137. Following on, he again opened and made 37 in a much better batting performance by his side and a draw was secured.

Wynyard's decision to bowl all his players in two successive games warrants a closer look at his approach to captaincy. It probably reflected a measure of desperation but, in its own way, was an example of innovative leadership, demonstrating a touch of flair by someone not prepared to be hidebound by convention.

In one sense, Teddy was a man ahead of his time with his thinking on cricket tactics. He wrote an article in *The Idler* in 1899 suggesting 'two or three stout hitters in a team, who are prepared to take all risks for the purpose of forcing the game and "putting off" the deadly bowlers would … be of infinitely more value to the side than correct players.' He added that the cricket loving public would 'delight in seeing merry, lively cricket and, better than that, are exhilarated to boiling point by a daring, dashing, slashing smiter' – a perfect description of the modern day limited-overs and T20 cricketer.

Masterman played under Teddy's captaincy after the First World War and had this to say:

> As a captain the word martinet is far too weak to express his dominant personality. Woe-betide the young cricketer who was heard to murmur that his best place in the batting order was three or four. In his firm hand, Teddy would write his name in the scorebook number eleven. Once in a match between I Zingari and the Lords and Commons (played, I think, on the Hampstead ground) a strong wind was blowing down the ground. I Zingari had two opening fast bowlers in the side and they were engaged in a friendly discussion as to which deserved to have the wind to help him. The side went onto the field and Teddy opened the bowling himself with lobs and with the wind behind him. I wish I could finish that story by saying that he immediately took a wicket; I cannot, but it is true that he nearly, very nearly bowled Lord Aberdare in his first over.

Wynyard made it clear to Masterman that he expected all the members of his side to behave themselves off the field as well as on. He also expressed the opinion that 'captains are sometimes a bit too clever' and disapproved strongly of any form of gamesmanship.

Lieutenant Colonel the Hon Gerald French DSO (1883-1970) wrote *The Corner Stone of English Cricket* and played under Teddy's captaincy. He told a similar story to Masterman observing that:

> When captaining a side Wynyard was a tremendous autocrat, and as ready with the rough of his tongue as a Master whose hounds have been outrageously pressed by overzealous followers. With his rather fiery temperament, he seems to have found it as difficult to overlook mistakes as to suffer annoyances impassively.

This is a particularly significant character assessment because French, who was the younger brother of Field Marshal Sir John French (later Earl of Ypres), went on to become Deputy Governor of Dartmoor and Governor of Newcastle prisons and had a reputation himself for being 'peppery'.

Whatever Wynyard's tactical capabilities may have been, it is very clear he was not a man prone to consult the dressing room nor one to rule by committee. His word was law!

Wynyard returned as captain at Southampton on 26 August when Leicestershire were the opposition in a match badly affected by rain, but Hampshire were the victors, thanks in no small part to Teddy returning his best first-class bowling figures to date of four for 47, and then making 43 with the bat in the second innings. Hampshire's final Championship game of the season was away to Somerset at Taunton and again the weather intervened although Wynyard scored 42 in a drawn game.

At the season's end Lancashire were the Champions with Hampshire finishing ninth of the fourteen counties. Teddy played in ten out of eighteen games, but these included all four victories – the other six were equally split between draws and losses. *The Times* summarized by saying 'Capt. Wynyard, if not so brilliant as in former seasons, played consistently well and his sound defence and hard hitting on the treacherous wickets recently experienced were invaluable.' In eighteen Championship innings he scored 594 runs, top scoring with 80 at an average of 33.

After the season was over, in September, Stoddart and eleven members of his squad (Ranjitsinhji joined at Naples) boarded the Orient Line steamer *Ormuz* and their tour to Australia was under way. The change of heart by the War Office meant Wynyard was not on board and their decision denied him the one opportunity, when he was at the peak of his powers, to test his cricketing ability on the ultimate stage – in an Ashes series in Australia. To make the disappointment all the more poignant, Teddy did not after all go with his regiment to India, nor did he become the Chief Constable for the Oudh district, but stayed in England.

If there is any silver lining to this story for Wynyard, Stoddart's tour turned out to be an unhappy one. The decision to take only thirteen players proved to be a mistake and the team lost 4-1. There was much talk of dissension among the players and in Frith's biography of the England captain he wrote 'in truth Wynyard's absence may have been a blessing, for he was a cantankerous individual'.

Cantankerous he may have been, but might his playing ability have improved the chances of returning with the Ashes? We will never know!

Frith then went on to quote the comments of one unnamed, but clearly exasperated, professional on the tour that 'Ranji's airs and graces had become intolerable'. Perhaps, after all, Stoddart had offered a silent prayer of thanks to the gods of the War Office for Wynyard being at Davos in January 1898 to time Edgington's attempt at the distance skating record, rather than sharing the amateurs' dressing room in Australia with Prince, or no Prince, Ranjitsinhji!

WG Grace leads the Gentlemen
on the occasion of his famous jubilee.
Back: CK Kortright, JR Mason, AC MacLaren,
JA Dixon, AJ West (umpire).
Middle: SMJ Woods, AE Stoddart, WG Grace (captain),
CL Townsend, FS Jackson.
Front: EG Wynyard, G MacGregor.

10

EG Attends WG's Birthday Party 1898

1898 saw the debut of another military cricketer for Hampshire, Major (later Brigadier General) Robert M Poore, who was to have one glorious season the following year that earned him the accolade of being one of the Wisden Cricketers of the Year, an honour never attained by his fellow soldier, Captain Wynyard.

The spring and early summer weather was not good and it rained heavily at Southampton on the morning of Hampshire's opening match against the new champions, Lancashire, on 13 May 1898. The visitors were all out for 153 by 4.30 pm. Poore did not play but Wynyard and Barton made 37 together in twenty minutes and by the close, the score was 62 for three with Wynyard on 41 not out. *The Times* said he 'was seen at his very best – his defence and hitting being equally fine'. He went on to make 47 and bowled 4.3 overs in Lancashire's second innings, taking the three wickets of Briggs, Hornby and Mold for 13 runs, but so much time had been taken out of the game that the only possible result was a draw.

Instead of playing cricket, towards the end of May, both Wynyard and Poore were competing in the Royal Military Tournament at the Agricultural Hall in Upper Street, Islington. The Tournament was the world's largest military tattoo and was a major public attraction with tickets on sale for up to ten shillings each. Wednesday 1 June saw the opening of the officer competitions and the fencing contests began at 9 am. Wynyard fought Captain Walter Edgeworth-Johnstone in the first round of the sabre-versus-sabre event and, in a closely fought encounter, just came off second best, largely because his opponent adopted modern techniques deployed in Italy. The consolation for Teddy was that the man who beat him went on to win first prize. Edgeworth-Johnstone was in the Royal Irish Regiment and, like Teddy, was also an accomplished boxer. He was Amateur Boxing Association Heavyweight Champion of England in 1895 and 1896. In 1915 he became the Chief Commissioner of the Dublin Metropolitan Police and was instrumental in crushing the Easter Rising a year later.

Major Bertie Poore of the 7th Hussars progressed to the third round of the sabre before being eliminated, but his performances overall meant he was named Best Man at Arms. When reporting back to Hampshire he held the bragging rights in the dressing room, but Wynyard and Poore were to play only one Championship match together in 1898, and that was not for over another fortnight.

Wynyard was selected for the Gentlemen against the Players at The Oval starting on 13 June. He opened with Grace but was bowled by Lockwood for 18. The Gentlemen were all out for 301 with Billy Murdoch making 57. The Players had reached 11 for two by the close with Teddy taking one catch.

Tuesday saw a keen wind blowing from the north-east and no sign of the sun. The Players batted for nearly the whole day making 352, to leave them 51 ahead. One of the highlights of the day was Wynyard's fielding. He made an excellent catch at short slip to remove Brockwell and took two further catches to dismiss Chatterton and Marlow, making it four in the innings. He also bowled four overs for 16 runs. There was time for the Gentlemen to bat that evening and Wynyard, opening again with Grace, was swiftly out for 1. The Players eventually won comfortably by eight wickets.

Wynyard returned to Hampshire's ranks on 16 June as both captain and wicketkeeper at Southampton, where Leicestershire were the opposition. In their second innings Hampshire scored 291, nearly half of the runs being made by Wynyard with a magnificent 140. When he reached 114 he passed 3,000 runs in first-class cricket. His score was made in under three hours and included twenty-four fours. Leicestershire needed 386 to win, and in spite of 65 by Albert Knight, Hampshire secured their first victory of the season by 145 runs. Teddy took two for 44 in the process with his lobs.

In later life, Leicestershire's Knight wrote some pen portraits of his playing contemporaries, and in 1906 he described Wynyard 'as the greatest of all military players'. He continued:

> No English cricketer possessed more character and was more greatly gifted in the matter of strokes. In the quicker rhythm, the fiercer energy which distinguished him, whether humming a tune and whistling an air, he flashed his bat like a sword from which runs glinted, or raced in mad career from boundary to boundary, one instinctively realized the presence of most brilliant capabilities. He had a wonderful stroke high and hard over cover and a superb pull drive to the on side from a ball a foot outside the off stump. This utter fearlessness, carried to a vicious excess, possessed him with an inordinate desire to achieve the virtually impossible.

Purple prose, but indisputably capturing the essence of the man. Fascinating to learn that he hummed a tune and whistled an air whilst at the crease or in the field!

On 22 June, Teddy played for Old Carthusians against the Staff College at Camberley and retired on 205. The next day he was back at Southampton for the county game against Essex. In response to 252 by the visitors Wynyard and Poore opened the batting but both openers were out cheaply for 4 and 16 and Essex went on to win by 126 runs. During the match Wynyard reached 2,000 Championship runs, but it was his last county game for Hampshire that year.

One game dominated the 1898 season. MCC had agreed to defer their showpiece Gentlemen versus Players fixture at Lord's until 18 July so that it would coincide exactly with the fiftieth birthday of the 'Great Cricketer', Doctor WG Grace. By common consent the counties had also not arranged any contests to start on that day so the strongest possible sides could be selected to play. Selection was

a great honour and to mark the occasion MCC and WG presented medallions that had been especially struck with the individual
player's name on the back for all those who played. Much later in
life, on 25 October 1935, BBC Radio broadcast an interview with
Archie MacLaren in which he said that, of all his cricket mementos,
the medal given to him for that game was the one he prized most.

The significance of this match can perhaps be judged by the fact
that social and cricketing historian, David Kynaston, has devoted an
entire book to it: *WG's Birthday Party*.

With Grace obviously captaining the Gentlemen, the honour of
selection alongside him fell upon Stoddart, Jackson, Townsend, MacLaren, Mason, Dixon, Woods, MacGregor, Kortright and Teddy
Wynyard. The Players comprised Shrewsbury (captain), Abel, William Gunn, Storer, Tunnicliffe, Brockwell, Alec Hearne, Dick Lilley,
Lockwood, Haigh and Jack (JT) Hearne with Wilfred Rhodes on
standby if the weather changed.

There was criticism of these choices. *The Daily Telegraph* said
'one hardly thought he [Wynyard] would be chosen. No doubt his
exceptionally good fielding has told in his favour.' Teddy had only
played five first-class matches all season but he had been selected to
play for the Gentlemen in the fixture against the Players five weeks
earlier at The Oval and taken four catches. One possible reason for
Wynyard being preferred was that the MCC Committee wanted as
many captains to play as possible. As it happened, eight out of the
eleven in the Gentlemen's team captained their counties.

On the Monday morning gates opened at 10.30 for a midday
start. It was 6d (2.5p) admission and by 11.30 all the seats were
occupied with 17,423 paying customers which, with the members
and their guests filling the pavilion, brought the crowd to around
20,000.

It was a hot July morning and Grace arrived with his wife and
daughter just before 11 o'clock so there was no time for him to join
his teammates, including Wynyard, who were practising in the nets
at the Nursery End. They were being watched by an appreciable
crowd, especially those who had paid for admission but not been
able to gain a vantage point on the ground.

Shrewsbury won the toss and made the obvious decision to bat on a fast and true wicket. Just after midday, WG emerged from the pavilion door to a rapturous reception. His fellow Gentlemen followed at a respectable distance, not wanting to encroach on his special moment. Shrewsbury and Abel entered by the separate side gate for the professionals, their dressing room being what is now the Bowler's Bar.

WG decided to open the bowling with Charles Kortright from the Pavilion End, although there had been a major spat between them only a fortnight earlier. Wicketkeeper MacGregor stood twelve yards back accompanied by no fewer than four slips (Wynyard, Mason, Stoddart and MacLaren). Jackson came on from the Nursery End but, when the score was on 11, WG limped off the field suffering with a bruised heel and Stoddart assumed the captaincy. After an hour the score was 29 for two with Storer at the crease but he was missed at slip by, of all people, Teddy Wynyard.

The score had progressed to 85 for two when a leisurely one-hour luncheon interval was taken between 2 and 3 pm. This was to allow time for photographs to be taken of both teams in the garden of the house occupied by MCC's Assistant Secretary located behind the Grand Stand. The cricketers then paired up and, led by the two captains Grace and Shrewsbury, walked from the garden in a procession that was recorded in rare moving picture footage that can still be seen to this day. There are fifty-nine seconds of sheer delight and nostalgia on You Tube under the heading 'WG celebrates his Jubilee', albeit the fifty feet of British Movietone film has been printed the wrong way around! When stepping back in time, therefore, do not forget that Grace was actually on Shrewsbury's right and not his left.

Whilst most of the cricketers studiously avoided looking directly at the camera, the mischievous side of WG's character took over and he simply could not resist impishly raising his peaked cap for the benefit of future generations of cricket lovers. The pairings made for some interesting comparisons. Stoddart, pipe in hand, was with Gunn followed by Woods and Lilley. Fourth in line was six foot one inch Teddy Wynyard swinging his arms in parade ground style alongside five foot four inch Bobby Abel – a contrast not just in terms of height but in style as well – the cavalier Captain and the pragmatic professional! Behind them were Jackson and JT Hearne, then MacGregor with Brockwell, Dixon and Tunnicliffe, MacLaren alongside Lockwood with Townsend and Haigh behind. Kortright, the only Gentleman not to be wearing a jacket in the team photograph, had found one in time for the movie cameras. With nonchalantly turned up collar and smoking a cigarette, he broke ranks to walk alongside Mason, so they were four in line with Alec Hearne and Storer. This just left the twelfth man for the Players, Wilfred Rhodes, on his own bringing up the rear, before members of the crowd managed to get into shot and achieve their own immortality.

By the time these ceremonial activities had been completed the weather had changed. Storer, who had been dropped earlier by Wynyard, went on to make an important 59 in just under two hours before being caught by Woods off Mason. Tea was taken at 5.10 pm with the Players on 240 for four. 1898 was the first year the idea of a tea break, which originated in Australia, was introduced into this country. The Players progressed stutteringly to 328 for nine by the close.

The scorecard recorded that play would go on to seven o'clock but in fact stumps were drawn at 6.30 almost certainly because MCC had arranged a private banquet in honour of WG that evening.

Between 7 and 8 am next day, there was heavy rainfall and the state of the wicket was dramatically changed. The turf was soft on the surface but hard underneath causing the ball to kick badly. The Players were all out for 335 and at midday Grace and Stoddart walked down the pavilion steps. WG took guard at the Nursery End to face JT Hearne. His heel injury prevented him from running freely and then he was hit on the hand by a fierce delivery from Haigh which caused him to drop his bat. He was out for 43 and when lunch was taken at 2 o'clock, the Gentlemen had progressed to 99 for three.

The wicket was starting to improve but wickets continued to fall and, on 226 for seven, Teddy came into bat at number nine. This was surprisingly low in the order for him and despite one aggressive strike to the square leg scoreboard, he never really settled. When he had scored 12, he skied a delivery from JT Hearne, bowling from the Pavilion End, down to third man where Brockwell easily took the catch. It was now 4.35. Fifty minutes later the Gentlemen were all out for 303, just 32 runs behind.

The Players were left with fifty minutes to bat in bad light facing the fast attack of Kortright and Sammy Woods. They lost two wickets (Abel and Shrewsbury) and had reached 42 for two by the close.

That evening just a few miles across London in St James's Square, the Sports Club had arranged a dinner for WG with a large attendance of members and friends including Teddy Wynyard. Sir Richard Webster proposed the toast to WG and the Doctor then responded. Grace did not enjoy public speaking and said he would as soon 'make a duck as a speech'. He was brief and expressed pride for being captain 'of the lot we have got here tonight' and said 'getting 300 on that wicket today was better than we expected'.

Wednesday morning saw no more rain with a forecast of better weather. When play started at 11.30 there was a chill wind blowing and doubtless this deterred some spectators from attending, especially as the game was generally viewed as drifting towards a draw.

When Lockwood came in, he skied a Kortright delivery towards long leg where Wynyard made a 'gallant but unavailing attempt to catch it on the run'. The Surrey bowler only made 6 and a last wicket stand of 26 left the Players all out on 263 at 3.45 pm. 296 runs were needed with the official scorecard saying stumps would be drawn at 6.30 pm.

Play resumed at 4 o'clock and WG did not open because of his injuries, but clearly he had not given up hope of a successful run chase because he now moved his hitters up the order. When the score was 55 for three, Wynyard came in at number five. Kynaston described Teddy as having 'the reputation of being a shaky starter' and this was evidenced by his failure to last out Hearne's over being bowled off his pads, without scoring, trying to glance the ball to leg.

At 5.37 pm, with the score on 77 for seven, WG made his entry into the fray, but Dixon was immediately out and just three runs later wicketkeeper MacGregor followed him back to the pavilion. There was still three-quarters of an hour to play and it was down to

Charles Kortright to try and save the day for Grace in his special jubilee match. Although they had not been speaking at the start of the game there were reports now of a brief exchange out in the middle. It did not extend though to Grace telling Kortright, who started walking off at 6.30 pm, that he had agreed with Shrewsbury an extra half an hour would be played if a result was likely.

The hands on the racquet court clock were about to reach 7 o'clock and there were just three deliveries left with Lockwood bowling, although for the first time from the Pavilion End. Kortright was on 46 and he simply could not resist a slower one just outside off stump. Haigh, running back at cover point, took the catch. 158 all out – the Players had won by 137 runs, with Jack Hearne taking eleven for 152 in the match. *The Sportsman* described the game as 'one of the most memorable matches witnessed on the historic Lord's ground'.

But it was not a very memorable match for Teddy: just 12 runs in two innings and, unusually for him, two dropped catches. He played only two more first-class matches that season, both at the Scarborough Festival. On Monday 29 August he turned out again for the Gentlemen against the Players at North Marine Road. Lord Hawke captained the Gentlemen with William Gunn taking over from Arthur Shrewsbury, who had played his last ever match for the Players back at Lord's. Wynyard, batting at number seven, made an impressive 49 not out towards a total of 208 (Wilfred Rhodes four for 72), hitting vigorously in a last-wicket stand of 71. In the second innings the Players struggled to 169 and lost by eight wickets. Teddy had been moved up to number four and was 32 not out at the end, partnering Jackson who finished with the same score.

On 1 September Wynyard captained CI Thornton's Eleven in a drawn match against Yorkshire led by Lord Hawke, who went onto become the 1898 county champions. Hampshire dropped down to twelfth out of the fourteen teams, winning only two of their eighteen matches, drawing and losing eight apiece. *The Times* concluded:

> No county has shown more disappointing form this season than Hampshire. With their captain assisting very little they only managed to win two matches and one of them by the bare margin of 9 runs. Capt EG

Wynyard though playing three times only for Hampshire took part in many other matches and in this way rather failed to carry out the duties involved when he accepted the captaincy.

A stinging rebuke which perhaps prompted Harry Altham to write, as a partial defence, that 'Wynyard, only found himself able to play in three games, thereby incurring a good deal of criticism from those who failed to recognize the prior claims of his military duties'. Warsop, however, was a little less sympathetic, commenting, 'Wynyard was accustomed to playing a lot of service cricket early in the season but his commitment to Army matches in 1898 sparked criticism of his frequent absences from the Hampshire team of which he was still the official captain.'

Wynyard's cricket had always been forced to come second to his military career and these obligations restricted his ability to play for his county. Nevertheless there seems to be legitimacy in the view that at least some of his absences were as a result of his choice to play service cricket or for other teams. Three games out of eighteen is a very poor ratio, so why indeed accept the county captaincy?

How would the members react at the AGM scheduled for 16 November in Southampton? *The Times*, as well as criticizing Wynyard, also said that 'a first-rate wicketkeeper was still sadly needed'. In spite of their comments, Wynyard was re-elected as captain and the position of vice-captain was formalized and given to wicketkeeper Charles Robson. In fairness to Robson, he had started his career with Middlesex as an attacking opening batsman and change bowler. It was only when he joined Hampshire that he was persuaded to don the gloves. Robson was, though, viewed as a superb captain, being ahead of his time in field placing and in his strategies to secure the dismissals of individual batsmen.

Wynyard's re-election and his acceptance of the post may have been facilitated by the news reported on 22 September that he had been selected for the Adjutancy of the 1st (Oxford University) Voluntary Battalion of the Oxfordshire Light Infantry.

It might just mean Teddy would have more time for cricket in 1899.

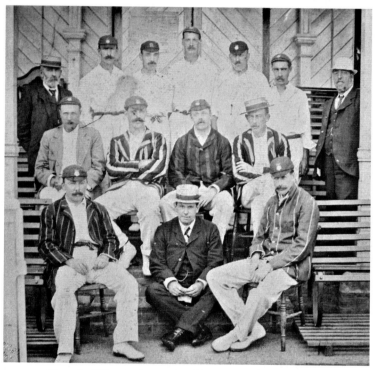

Captain Wynyard captains his county against Essex.
Back: Webb, Gravett, Soar, Baldwin, Barton.
Middle: Robson, Poore, Wynyard, Quinton.
Front: English, Bencraft (secretary), Heseltine.

11

THE CAPTAIN AND THE MAJOR

1899

Wynyard's Adjutancy at the start of 1899 meant his duties coincided with Oxford University's term time, so he should have been able to play regularly after the third week in June.

As that time approached, *The Times* reported on the first visit to Oxford of the Duke and Duchess of York. On 19 June they stepped off the train from Paddington, and the streets were thronged both with local residents and students. At Christ Church they were met by a guard of honour made up of 100 Oxford volunteers organised by Teddy Wynyard. The Royal salute was given and the band played the National Anthem. Afterwards the Duke of York called Teddy over and complimented him upon the smartness of the guard. The Duke and Duchess entered the Deanery and in the evening there was a Commemoration Ball given by members of the College with 400 to 500 in attendance.

It was a smooth military operation, courtesy of the organisational skills of the adjutant judging by *The Times* account, but all was not quite what it seemed. Many years later Wynyard related the behind the scenes story to Masterman. Let Teddy tell what really happened in his own words:

The volunteers were not, when I arrived, a very warlike or efficient body of men and the work was not onerous, but it did bring me into one awkward predicament. I received information that the Volunteers would be inspected by the Duke of York and that I was to arrange things accordingly. How was I to put on a respectable show with only a small and motley band of partially trained undergraduates at my disposal? In such situations Oxford always plays up. I explained my trouble to the OUDS [Oxford University Dramatic Society] and the Society produced an excellent band of enthusiastic actors whom I disguised as soldiers and who did not let me down. There was, however, a last-moment hitch. I had inquired at the War Office if it would be right to call for three cheers for the Duke at the end of the day's proceedings and received the answer that we were considered a military exercise and that, in consequence, cheers would be most improper. In the evening there was a ball in Christ Church Hall and before it began I was summoned to be presented to the Duke. 'A very smart parade, Captain Wynyard; a good display of military efficiency-but I was surprised that you did not call for cheers for me at the close.' I apologized as best I could for my omission and, of course, did not give away my superiors. My apologies were accepted with good nature. 'Very well we will forget it. Now you may dance with the Duchess.' I was worse than an indifferent dancer, but protocol demanded that no one else should dance until the Duchess and I had circumnavigated the Hall. What an infernally big Hall it is!

This interesting tale shows a much lighter and softer side to Wynyard's character as opposed to the general perception of him as an autocratic disciplinarian. Here was a classic example of a man displaying not only initiative and innovation but also a real sense of fun on what was both a formal and regal occasion.

Meanwhile, the 1899 cricket season was to see another Australian tour and *The Times* expressed the view this was their 'strongest side ever'.

For the first time this was to be a five-Test series in England with the MCC and county committees taking over the selection of the English team. Also there was to be a pooling of the host county's share of gate receipts for division among the clubs. Worcestershire had now been added to the Championship ranks for the first time and they could call upon the services of the Foster brothers, earning them the nickname 'Fostershire'.

The season began for Hampshire at Old Trafford on 15 May but Teddy was playing in another first-class match, although this was forgivable since it was in Oxford where he was working, against the University at The Parks. He captained AJ Webbe's Eleven in the absence of Webbe through illness. He won the toss and batted but, for once, must have questioned his own judgment when he opened the batting and was stumped for a duck with his team being dismissed in under an hour for 43. Webbe's side included GW Beldam, making his first-class debut, although he is better known today as one of the pioneers in sporting action photography. His capture of Trumper leaping out to cover drive at The Oval later in the season is probably one of the most enduring and iconic cricket photographs of all time. The University had Tip Foster and BJ Bosanquet in their side and won comfortably by an innings and 85 runs.

Teddy was able to secure his availability for the MCC side to play Australia at Lord's on 5 June. He was lbw to Jones without scoring in the first innings and was caught and bowled by Monty Noble for 17 in the second. Australia comfortably progressed to 125 for two to win by eight wickets with Teddy getting on for three overs at a cost of 21 runs.

On 8 June, Wynyard was also able to make his championship debut for the season, at Leyton against Essex, but it was in a lost cause. With the Duke of York's imminent visit to Oxford, Teddy was unavailable for the next two matches at Portsmouth and Southampton against Somerset (match drawn) and Lancashire (lost by 71 runs). Major Poore did play in both matches and very successfully too. He scored 104 and 119 not out in the first match, followed up by 111 and then 40, so he narrowly failed to create a record by scoring four consecutive centuries.

With term time over and the students on vacation, Wynyard was free to take up his duties as captain and led a strong Hampshire side in a drawn game against Essex. He was then at the United Services Ground in Portsmouth for the visit of Surrey who made 200, with Hampshire responding by the close of the first day with 88 for four.

Poore, going in at number three, was 42 not out accompanied by Teddy, batting at number six, on 6 not out. The following morning Wynyard played well and helped Poore put on 103 before being bowled by Stoner for 26. There was nothing stopping the Major though, and he scored an outstanding 175 in five and a half hours. Rain interrupted the match and with ninety minutes remaining on the last day, Hampshire needed 94 to win. Wynyard chose to lead by example and opened the batting. He made 10 before being caught by Hayes off Lockwood. Poore was first wicket down and steered the side home with 39 not out to secure victory by six wickets. He scored 214 runs in the match and had now passed 1,500 championship runs. Hampshire was the first county to beat Surrey that season.

It was a great morale booster for Wynyard and his men but they failed to follow up, losing a match they were in a position to win against Sussex at Hove.

Wynyard was back at Lord's on 17 July for the MCC fixture against Worcestershire. The highlight of the first day was his opening partnership with Murdoch and they put on 152 in over two hours, with Teddy playing very attractively and hitting fifteen fours in his score of 89. After that formidable start MCC must have been disappointed only to reach 309. Worcestershire had three Foster brothers playing for them (Harry, Tip and Bill) but a promising start was not maintained and they were all out for 204 (Wynyard one catch and no wicket for 20). On going in a second time Teddy's 81 was the best batting of the day. He made his runs in over one and half hours and hit another fifteen fours before being caught by Tip Foster. Overnight MCC were 327 for eight but only made a further 11 runs. Their score though was largely academic because Albert Trott took seven for 33 as Worcestershire crashed to 111 all out.

The next match was one that remains in the record books to this day, with the Major and the Captain playing the key roles. There were many similarities between Bertie and Teddy. Poore was a six foot, four inch Army officer who was also awarded the DSO. He did not suffer fools gladly and had a great sense of humour. As a cricketer he was a nervous starter and at his most vulnerable against the new ball. He was also a superb all-round sportsman playing golf, tennis, polo and racquets, as well as being named Best Man at Arms in 1899 at the Royal Military Tournament for the second year running.

In 1895 Poore had travelled to South Africa with the 7th Hussars where he displayed his cricketing talent. It was the *Natal Mercury* who called him 'the Grace of the Army', which was adapted by Jeremy Lonsdale for the title of his excellent biography *The Army's Grace: The Life of Brigadier General RM Poore*. Lord Hawke was touring South Africa and invited Poore to play in the Tests but he declined and offered to play for the home side instead. This was controversially accepted because he was not South African by birth, but he played in all three Tests with a top score of only 20.

Poore's family frequently visited the Douglas-Hamiltons and on 29 September 1898 Bertie married Flora, the sister of the thirteenth Duke of Hamilton. In 1901, to keep matters within the family, Poore's sister, Nina, married the Duke to become the Duchess of Hamilton. In the 1920s the Duke moved to Dungavel House, where by the time of the Second World War, there was an airstrip.

On 10 May 1941, a parachutist bailed out of a burning Messerschmitt 110 and declared in English 'I have an important message for the Duke of Hamilton'. He was, of course, Rudolf Hess, Deputy Fuhrer to Adolf Hitler whose aim had been to land at the airstrip and contact the fourteenth Duke (Poore's nephew by marriage, Air Commodore Douglas Douglas-Hamilton) in the hope of persuading him to broker a peace deal with Churchill.

Newly married, just promoted, four Championship centuries already to his name for the season as well as selection for the Gentlemen against the Players, Poore must have been on a crest of a wave as he left the Castle Hotel to travel to the County Ground at Taunton on 20 July for the away fixture against Somerset. Before the game started the Hampshire professionals presented him with an engraved matchbox in recognition of his batting to date.

The home side had one of the weakest bowling attacks in the Championship. For this match they were also without Sammy Woods following the death of his sister. Somerset batted first and made a respectable 315, with Wynyard taking the two wickets of his opposing captain, Newton, and the Reverend Archdale Wickham for 20 runs. At 5.25 pm, Hampshire began their innings and, twenty minutes later, when Victor Barton was lbw to Tyler, Poore marched to the crease with the score on 26 for one. He had made 4 when dropped by the Reverend Wickham behind the stumps, and as the following day unfolded, the wicketkeeper must have been asking his God what he had done to offend him in such a terrible way. There was nothing, however, to indicate how the game was going to develop because three more wickets fell that evening with the visitors closing on 65 for four (Poore 24, Soar 2 not out).

Play began on the following day at 11 o'clock, half an hour earlier than usual so that the game could finish thirty minutes earlier on the Saturday. By 12.15, after seventy-five minutes, Poore had cut and driven his way to a century. Two runs later he was again dropped, this time by Ernest Robson in the slips. By 12.30, Hampshire had reached 200 and Soar fell five runs short of a well deserved century, hitting fifteen fours in the process, to make it 258 for five. Having dropped down the order to number seven, Teddy was the next man in and the new pairing put on another 48 runs together before lunch was taken at 1.20 pm. In the morning session Hampshire had scored 241 runs for the loss of one wicket. When Teddy scored 2, he passed 3,500 Championship runs.

Play began again at 2.20 pm and Poore brought up his 150 in the first over after the resumption. He and Teddy reached their 100 partnership when they had been together for eighty minutes and, shortly afterwards, Wynyard made 50. Poore then passed his previous highest score of 175 when he cut Cranfield to the boundary. It was Teddy though who was particularly severe on the bowler, cutting him and then hitting him to leg onto the roofs of the cottages adjoining the ground. Full of confidence, he then attempted a back stroke off a delivery from Tyler – another illustration of his innovation and how suited he would have been to modern day, white ball cricket.

By tea, Hampshire had reached 461 for five with Poore on 216 and Wynyard 106. There was a quarter of an hour break but by 5.20 pm the score had reached 500. Whilst Wynyard progressed from 97 to 132, Poore took a breather and added 10 runs. When he was on 146, Teddy gave his first chance to Barnard in the deep but was reprieved. He was given another life when he had made 158 with the long-suffering Cranfield failing to take a caught and bowled chance. Poore then passed 250 as Hampshire reached 550, but out of the next 40 runs Wynyard scored 39 of them. At 6.25 pm Teddy was caught by Bernard off Tyler for 225. His partnership with Poore had lasted four hours and twenty minutes and they had put on 411 runs together. Wynyard had given three chances, hit two fives and thirty-six fours. *The Times* described it as a 'truly wonderful display' and 'an extraordinary display of batting by Major Poore and Captain Wynyard'.

At the time of writing, 411 remains the record Championship partnership for the sixth wicket and the third-highest of all time in first-class cricket worldwide.

The score was now 669 for six but, as so often happens following a big stand, Poore was out one run later in the same over. The Reverend wicketkeeper finally had his prayers answered when he stumped Bertie off Tyler for Hampshire's then record individual highest first-class score of 304, beating Wynyard's 268 against Yorkshire three years earlier. The innings lasted six hours and fifty minutes and included forty-five fours. He, too, had given three chances. This was an amazing feat of endurance (as was that of Wynyard) given it was a swelteringly hot, July, day. It is now the second highest score for Hampshire having been beaten by RH ('Dick') Moore's 316 against Warwickshire at Dean Park in July 1937.

At the close Hampshire were 672 for seven and the spectators had witnessed 607 runs in a day for the fall of three wickets. 154 five-ball overs had been bowled, equating to 129 six-ball overs. When was the last time that could be said of a modern-day Championship game?

Not surprisingly, Wynyard declared overnight. All the stuffing had been knocked out of the home side, who were all out by 3.15 pm for 206 to lose by an innings and 151 runs. Wynyard bowled ten overs taking three for 18, and so in addition to his 225 runs had taken five wickets in this memorable victory.

Cricket magazine ran a poem ending:

Then let us fill a bumper,
And drink a health to those,

Who made their runs by hundreds,
Against the Western pros,
May Captain and may Major,
Improve with future years,
With a tow-row-row-row-row-row,
Like the British *Officiers*.

Hampshire travelled up to Edgbaston for the match against Warwickshire starting on Monday 24 July and Wynyard again impressed with 89 in a rain-affected drawn game. Teddy did not play at Worcester where Poore scored yet another century (122) but Bill Foster scored 140 and 172 not out with his brother, Tip, making 134 and 101 to become the first pair of brothers to score two separate centuries each in the same first-class match. It remains unique in county cricket, although it is a feat emulated by Australians Ian and Greg Chappell in the 1974 Adelaide Test against New Zealand.

Wynyard and Poore also played against the touring Australians at Southampton. On a perfect wicket and in fine weather, Teddy won the toss, batted and kept his opponents in the field for the whole five and a quarter hours of play. He was also back opening the batting and in one hour and twenty minutes, 96 was added for the first wicket before Hill was out for 60. Poore came in to join Wynyard and they added 59 in forty-five minutes so that by lunch the total was an impressive 151 for one. Poore (29) and Bradford (0) were then out in quick succession. When Teddy had scored only 6, he ought to have been caught by wicketkeeper Kelly, off Ernie Jones, but this was his only mistake in two hours and forty minutes. He was fourth out with the score on 180 for his side's top score of 79. *The Times* described how clever placing to leg was the chief feature of his play and his score comprised a seven (four for an overthrow), and ten fours. The match ended in a draw.

Poore and Wynyard again put on 89 together for the fourth wicket in sixty-five minutes at Derby. Wynyard, batting at number five, gave a couple of chances in his 57 but when he had made 30 he passed 4,000 runs in first-class cricket. Poore made 79 and Hampshire won comfortably.

Hampshire then travelled to Grace Road, Leicester where Wynyard won the toss and Hampshire batted on an excellent wicket making 331, with Poore contributing 157 before being bowled by a full toss. Teddy, going in at number four, assisted him to put on 119 runs for the third wicket in one and three-quarter hours, before being caught by Geeson, off Pougher, for 46. By the close Leicestershire were 32 for two with Wynyard bowling the opener Gustavus Fowke for 16. Next morning, the home side rallied to 379 to secure a lead of 48. Bradford opened the bowling but was no-balled again during his thirty-six overs, having previously been called in the match against the Australians. Why had his captain put him on for such a long spell, or at all? Only Wynyard knows the answer to that question, but perhaps he had a perverse streak? It was Teddy who was the star of Hampshire's attack, though, with figures of 35.4 overs, twelve maidens, six for 63. Five of the wickets were bowled with the sixth being a stumping by wicketkeeper Charles Kendle.

This was Teddy's best ever first-class bowling performance. His lobs had been profitably employed for Old Carthusians but he had only taken nineteen wickets for Hampshire in the four seasons until then, although *Baily's Magazine* had stated in 1897 that he had 'a scientific style of lob bowling – as good as it is successful'.

Over the course of the nineteenth century, lobs had gradually been replaced by round and overarm bowling although Digby 'The Lobster' Jephson was practising his art for Surrey and took over 300 wickets for them. The last great lob bowler was George Simpson-Hayward who played in all five Tests against South Africa in 1909-10, taking twenty-three wickets at 18 runs apiece. Jack Hobbs said of him that 'he used to spin the ball as if it belonged to the billiard table; I believe it was by manipulating a billiard ball that he learnt his job. You could hear the click of his fingers as he let the ball loose.'

Lob bowling was the inspiration for Sir Arthur Conan Doyle's *The Story of Spedegue's Dropper* but in reality rather than fiction, the Reverend Canon E Lyttleton was not a believer and wrote in *Cricket* that 'it is quite certain that most of the wickets which even a really good lob bowler gets are got by the folly of the batsman, more than by the skill of the bowler. Very rarely is a decent player beaten by a lob.'

The Leicestershire match was drawn but, in spite of Poore's prolific run-making, he was not selected for The Oval Test. As it happens he would not have been able to play in any event because he was recalled to military duties with war against the Boers now imminent.

Wynyard, though, was available for the match against 1898 champions Yorkshire at Bradford starting on 14 August. Yorkshire were all out for 456 with Wynyard again bowling well, taking three for 54 (including Hirst) and he also took two catches. Play was shortened by wet weather but Teddy opened the batting and played brilliantly for a top score of 77. On the final day Hampshire were forced to follow on. Wynyard again opened and it was his second-wicket partnership with Webb that saved his side from defeat.

Teddy was back at Southampton on 24 August for the visit of Worcestershire. He opened and made 26 but it was the visitors who had a 49-run lead on first innings. When Hampshire went back in they were soon 106 for six, but Teddy had dropped himself down to number eight and, by the time he was last man out, had made 108. He was only at the crease for eighty-five minutes and hit twenty-one fours. It was a remarkable performance on a day when temperatures touched ninety degrees Fahrenheit in the shade. Worcestershire failed to make the 204 they were set to win and lost by 52 runs.

Teddy's last Championship match of his last season as captain was an innings defeat by Sussex in which Ranjitsinhji took five wickets with his slow right-arm deliveries. Hampshire had one more fixture to fulfil but they lost badly at The Oval to Surrey. Rather than play in that game, Wynyard chose instead to travel up to Scarborough for the festival where he was selected for CI Thornton's Eleven for the games against the Australians and Yorkshire.

The weather was fine for the tourists and there was a record attendance of 8,000 to see them bat on the first day. Trumper went in at number three but made only 14 before falling victim to Rhodes. Again Teddy's bowling proved successful, taking four for 30 including the wickets of Darling (caught and bowled) and Frank Iredale as the Australians were dismissed for 233. Thornton's side, captained by FS Jackson, progressed to 54 for three. The following day Wynyard, going in at number six, was one of Hugh Trumble's six victims when caught by Joe Darling for 10 towards a total of 185.

In the second innings, Wilfred Rhodes then struck taking nine for 24 including seven wickets in twenty-four balls to dismiss the Australians for 83. Thornton's team needed 132 to win but the wicket was a difficult one to bat on. Wynyard was promoted to open and was dismissed for 1. Soon the side were struggling on 37 for six, only for Hirst to stage a recovery. The score had progressed to 81 for seven when rain intervened and prevented a result in a very close match.

The Scarborough Festival continued with Wynyard taking over as captain of Thornton's Eleven for the match against Yorkshire, but it was Lord Hawke's men who ran out victors by 51 runs.

The last cricket season of the nineteenth century came to a close with Surrey as champions. Australia had won the Test series, Grace played his last Test but, in the same game at Trent Bridge, both Wilfred Rhodes and Victor Trumper made their Test debuts. Archie MacLaren took over from Grace as the England captain in what turned out to be a good summer for batsmen. Bertie Poore topped the county averages with 116.58, amassing 1,399 runs from eighteen innings. Only Walter Hammond with 126.25 in 1934 has a higher average for a Championship season. In all first-class matches Teddy took twenty-seven wickets and scored 1,281 runs at 41.32, which was more than respectable but, for once, his performances had been eclipsed. Indeed, it was Poore and not Wynyard who had been talked about in terms of playing for England and was selected to represent the Gentlemen in their matches that season against the Players. Nevertheless, their combined achievements did mean that the county had fared marginally better, finishing tenth of the fifteen counties with four victories and eight matches apiece lost and drawn.

Poore and Wynyard had their record partnership of 411 at the crease, but what was their personal relationship off the field? Both of them continued playing well into their sixties and in later life Wynyard spoke about cricket at the turn of the twentieth century. He said, 'those were the days and I am pleased to see my old colleague Poore is still doing great things with the willow'. Warm and friendly words, but Bertie is said to have confided to his wife that he found Teddy 'an impossible man to deal with'. An enlightening observation bearing in mind they appeared to have had so much in common!

Whilst Poore set sail with his regiment, the troubles in Africa also prompted the announcement in *The Times* on 25 December that 'Capt EG Wynyard DSO Welsh Regiment, Adjutant of the Oxford University Volunteers has been selected for Instructor in Military Engineering at the Royal Military College.'

The news of Teddy's return to Sandhurst coincided with the Christmas and New Year festivities. How many of the multitude gathered to celebrate the dawn of a new century, could have predicted that, within barely a score of years, the world they had known would be changed forever and the values that had been their bedrock would be replaced by disillusion?

Teddy alongside I Zingari teammates, one of several amateur
touring sides he was invited to represent, in a match against
Northern Nomads in July 1900.
Back: GF Vernon, EC Morduant, JA Turner, AG Archer,
GJM Atkins. Front: EG Wynyard, HW Forster, FE Lacey,
JHJ Hornsby, HT Hewitt, AR Don-Wauchope.

12

TAKING FRESH GUARD

1900-03

As the hands of Big Ben ticked past midnight into the twentieth century, Britain was at war in the second Anglo-Boer conflict.

There was an urgent need for more officers to travel to South Africa and a short emergency course was introduced at Sandhurst whereby 360 cadets in residence were swiftly commissioned. Amongst this batch were Wavell and Dill who both progressed to become eminent generals of the Second World War. It was clearly important that the education of the fresh intake be accelerated, and this required experienced instructors, which is why Wynyard was recalled on a temporary basis to teach Military Engineering and Fortification.

The Royal Military College was very much in the spotlight at this time for all the wrong reasons. There was criticism of the curriculum, feeling it was not sufficiently attuned to modern-day warfare. The war had begun badly with a number of shocking defeats revealing shortcomings in the officer corps, which, in turn, reflected on the quality of their training.

During these challenging times for both the Army and the College, not surprisingly, there was little time for Wynyard to play county cricket, but he did manage to fit in four first-class matches during 1900. From this year onwards the game changed to the six-ball overs we know today. Before donning his whites though, on 11 May, he participated in the second day of the Royal Military College athletics meeting. A large crowd visited the cricket ground in front of the gymnasium, with Lady Markham, wife of the Governor, presenting the prizes and Captain W Edgeworth-Johnstone (Teddy's opponent at the 1898 Royal Military Tournament) amongst the judges. Wynyard won the 100 yards handicap for officers.

On 24 May, he travelled to Bath to play against Somerset, although there was no play on the first day. Robson captained Hampshire, won the toss and elected to bat. Teddy went in at number three and top scored with 38 as the side crashed to a total of 81 all out. Batting at number ten was Hesketh Vernon Hesketh-Prichard, who was 0 not out. Sir Arthur Conan Doyle had recommended him to Teddy as a prospective Hampshire player and he went on to become one of Teddy's closest friends. He was a fast right-hand bowler who could move the ball both ways off the pitch, as well as bowl with swerve, and took three for 34 as Somerset reached 249 by the close. On the Saturday Wynyard tried very hard to save his side from defeat, resisting the Somerset bowlers for two hours. He was dropped on 31 but went on to score 107 out of 209. The home side easily knocked off 44 runs for the loss of just three wickets, although Hesketh-Prichard was able to take the prize scalp of Lionel Palairet for 8.

Teddy played at the United Services Ground in Portsmouth when Yorkshire were the visitors on 12 July. He went in at number three and top scored with 54 out of 202, being caught by Taylor off George Hirst, but Yorkshire ran out easy winners by six wickets. He also turned out for I Zingari against Northern Nomads on 25 and 26 July before travelling on 6 August to play for his county away against Derbyshire in a drawn, rain-affected game.

On 13 September, Teddy was back at Lord's for the season finale as part of a strong South side playing against the North in a match for the benefit of pavilion attendant, Philip Need. The South batted from midday until 5.30 pm and reached 431 for seven with

Grace making 126 in three hours. Gilbert Jessop hit with vigour including four fours in one over off Hirst, and made 77. At 319 for seven, Wynyard and Albert Trott came together and punished the tired bowlers. Their partnership lasted for one hour and made 112 so that, by the close, Teddy was on 80 and Trott 48 not out. Next morning Teddy was dismissed for 85 and Trott made 75 towards a total of 474. Teddy then dropped Briggs in the deep early on and the Lancastrian eventually contributed 38 as the North totalled 405. Time was at a premium and the match was abandoned as a draw at 5.30 pm on the third day with Lord Hawke's side standing on 130 for seven, needing 213 to win.

In his four first-class matches Teddy had made 310 runs with a top score of 107 at a more-than-respectable average of 51.66. The extent to which Hampshire missed Wynyard can be gauged by the fact they finished bottom of the Championship, not winning any of their twenty-two matches.

Elsewhere, one of the most famous incidents of the second Boer War was the Relief of Mafeking, where the British garrison was under the command of Teddy's old school and footballing compatriot, Colonel Robert Baden-Powell. The October 1900 edition of *The Carthusian* reported that Frederic Girdlestone intended to erect a cloister on the south side of the Charterhouse Chapel to commemorate old boys who had served in the war, and he requested donations towards the cost of £3,000. Teddy was one of the first to donate two guineas and was on the executive committee for a dinner to honour Baden-Powell and other Old Carthusians who had been in South Africa. The event was to be held at the Hotel Cecil with tickets costing twenty-five shillings.

There was a major change at the start of the new century that had a deep effect on the entire country. On 22 January 1901, Queen Victoria, aged eighty-one, died at Osborne House on the Isle of Wight to bring the Victorian age to an end and usher in the Edwardian era. For Teddy there was a much more personal bereavement when his step-mother, Isabella, who had been living at Wrenthorpe, Southsea, died on 9 March 1901, in her sixty-first year, leaving an estate worth £3,964, fourteen shillings and sixpence (£384,400 in today's money). This was to be administered by her son, Teddy's half brother, Henry Buckley William Wynyard.

With the Boer War at a critical point, sporting opportunities continued to be limited for Wynyard in 1901. His first-class season began playing for MCC against the champions Yorkshire at Lord's on 6 May. He opened and made 9 before falling victim to Rhodes and 29 in the second innings batting at number four. Yorkshire lost four wickets in making 57 for victory with Bosanquet taking a fine catch deep on the offside and Wynyard taking another at forward short leg. George Hirst was the hero of the match, making over 100 runs for once out, fielding well and taking eleven for 83.

On 6 June, Wynyard played one of only two games that season for Hampshire, against Kent at Dean Park, Bournemouth. Teddy took two for 36 and in so doing reached fifty wickets in first-class matches. He scored 31 towards Hampshire's total of 342. In the second innings a draw looked increasingly possible but Kent's last six wickets only produced another 48 and Hampshire were left 131 to win. In just fifteen minutes they stood at 12 for three but Wynyard, who had opened the batting, then received help from Llewellyn (38) and Webb (31), enabling Hampshire to win comfortably with four wickets to spare. Teddy's 59 was described by *The Times* as 'an example of dogged self restraint combined with power of scoring'.

He played for MCC during Military Week, then against Bedfordshire, and on 1 August travelled down to Southampton for his only other match that season for Hampshire, against Surrey. The match was drawn with Wynyard opening the batting and scoring 52. Instead of playing for his county, Teddy then turned out alongside Arthur Conan Doyle for MCC in a losing cause against Wiltshire. He moved on to Ireland for the I Zingari cricket week beginning on Monday 19 August, where he was the guest at Viceregal Lodge, Dublin for a dinner hosted by the Lord Lieutenant and Lady Cadogan.

Wynyard ran sides for I Zingari for many years, and Gerald French told a story of when he first played under Teddy against Sandhurst at around this time. He wrote in *The Cornerstone of Cricket* that he:

...was unlucky enough to fall foul of the rather awe-inspiring Teddy Wynyard before the match had even begun. It being my first appearance as a Zingaro, and not having had time to provide myself with the colours, I foolishly wore the blazer of another club. The effect on my captain was much the same as a red rag is said to have on a bull. The mere sight of my offending coat caused an immediate outburst, and I was peremptorily told, inter alia, to 'go and take that damned thing off.' This I hurriedly did, reflecting somewhat ruefully the while on my unfortunate introduction to this notorious disciplinarian ... and that was not all, for, going in first, Wynyard soon returned to the pavilion after being out lbw by the Sandhurst umpire. Dissatisfaction with the decision added fuel to the flames already kindled by my unwitting self, and at no time during the rest of that morning would it have been wise, or indeed anything but foolhardy, to have approached the captain with even the most trivial request. Probably much of this great player's irascibility was due to remarkable enthusiasm, causing him to inveigh against those guilty of error, negligence, or faulty judgment, affecting the game that, above all others he loved so well.

An example of how Wynyard was respected to the point of reverence, in spite of his cantankerous behaviour.

The Times in their summary of the 1901 season again expressed 'the regret of the county that Captain Wynyard should have found such little time for his side'. He topped the averages for them but only played three innings, totalling 142 with a top score of 59 and an average of 47.33. Hampshire played eighteen matches; winning six, losing six and drawing six. They improved their position considerably to seventh out of fifteen in the Championship, which was won again by Yorkshire.

In one of the many tributes to Wynyard after his death, Colonel RF Pearson, who had been a Company Commander at the Royal Military College, had a story to tell dating back to their days together at Sandhurst in 1901. Teddy was in charge of cricket there and amongst the fixtures was one against WG Grace's Eleven, but two days before the match Grace wrote to say he could not personally now attend. Wynyard was considerably annoyed and, in talking about the match with the cadets, he discovered that none of them had seen the Doctor play, whereupon he made up his mind that he should make him appear. On the Saturday morning Pearson lent his rooms to Teddy, who sat in a chair whilst his friend, who was an assistant to Willy Clarkson – the leading wig maker and theatrical costumier of the time – started work on him.

After one hour, Doctor WG Grace was ready. Pearson accompanied him, carrying the cricket bag across the college grounds to the cricket pavilion. 'Grace' batted, making several runs, and then deliberately allowed himself to be hit on the hand so that he retired hurt. At lunchtime when, both teams were assembled, Wynyard appeared – still in disguise except for the cap and wig – and announced 'I think I have spoofed you all this time!' Pearson observed that the make-up and Wynyard's actions were so good that no one spotted the difference. It is said the Governor and Commandant, Lieutenant General Markham, was not best pleased at being duped in this way.

The story is interesting for two reasons. First, it reinforces the impression created by the earlier incident with the Duke of York's parade of a mischievous, freethinking, slightly rebellious character with a great sense of fun – quite contrary to the image normally portrayed of a hot-tempered autocrat. Secondly it is a great testimony, not just to his acting skills, but also to his cricketing prowess that he was able to imitate the batting of the greatest cricketer of his day without anyone suspecting anything.

Simon Rae's biography of Grace told a story of another attempt at impersonation seven years later. In 1908 the Doctor was due to unveil a granite obelisk to the Hambledon Club on Broad Halfpenny Down, but he did not turn up. A certain Henry Warren of West Byfleet looked upon himself as Grace's double and duly boarded the train en route to the ceremony. At the station he was ushered by the railway porter into the only vehicle going to the unveiling, but the deception was foiled because the other cricketers attending, including Teddy as it happens, quickly realized it was not the Doctor. WG was amused when he heard the story and gave Warren a signed photograph when they eventually met.

It is not known what Grace thought of Wynyard's impersonation but the 'beard, voice, batting style and all' fooled all those at Sandhurst who thought they could boast to their grandchildren that they had played against the Great Cricketer in the summer of 1901.

Pearson, when writing his tribute, said that by this time Teddy was a company commander of cadets. There were six companies each commanded by an officer who lived and messed with the company. All company commanders in infantry battalions were still mounted on horseback and the officer had responsibility for discipline as well as the cadet's welfare, including their finances.

At this time there was considerable unrest at Sandhurst. Discipline, especially relating to drunkenness amongst the cadets, was a real problem for both the college and its company commanders, including Teddy. Hugh Thomas in his *Story of Sandhurst* observed that the college 'remained a violent, ruthless and cruel place although at the same time free and exciting'. He commented that to anyone who had been to a tough public school it was reasonably pleasant, but if a cadet had bad manners at mess he was court-martialled. The normal punishment was an ink bath. The victim then had to run the gauntlet, naked and dripping with ink, between lines of fellow cadets who would flick him with wet towels. Officers kept well out of the way of the activities of cadets when off duty.

The most publicised incidents of bad behaviour occurred during the spring and early summer of 1902. There were four fires in five weeks, all apparently started by igniting debris in wastepaper bins. The Commander-in-Chief of the Army, Lord Roberts, intervened and ordered 'all leave will be stopped until the culprit or culprits are discovered'. This created a burning sense of grievance and, on 11 June, a body of cadets went to the Governor's house and serenaded him with some choice Sandhurst songs. They then made their way to the local Camberley Fair, bending lampposts and rolling some of the Royal Military College's guns into the lake along the way. Rumour then started to spread that a patrol of officers and senior corporals were on their way to round up the miscreants. They escaped, but on reaching the College, the Duty Orderly was waiting to take their names. Twenty-nine cadets were identified and ordered to leave.

The next morning the press wrote about 'Mutiny at Sandhurst'. Roberts then interviewed all the cadets personally and, when they signed affidavits to the effect they knew nothing about the fires, were exonerated. They were allowed to return at the beginning of the following term and, remarkably, could count the exams of the previous term as passed!

The Boer War ended on 31 May 1902. Over 20,000 British troops had died in the conflict with another 22,829 wounded. Given the criticism of the officers during the campaign, Sandhurst was already under the microscope and these hijinks, for want of a better description, increased the tensions still further. Teddy really had been brought back into a hotbed of unrest. The need for change was clear and a committee was set up under the Right Honourable Aretas Akers-Douglas to advise on necessary reforms.

The first specific term of reference was to consider what should be changed in the training of candidates for the Army at public schools and universities. This was a topic that Teddy was uniquely placed to comment upon, having been both Charterhouse-educated and the recent Adjutant of the Oxford University Volunteers. Indeed, a letter had already been written to the editor of *The Times*, on 23 February 1900, by G Herbert Morrell that explained the importance of the University Volunteers in training officers ready to command and go to South Africa. He put this success down to the ability of the Adjutants and made specific mention of Wynyard.

When Akers-Douglas issued his report, the recommendation was that both Woolwich and Sandhurst should be retained, but the Royal Military College came in for particular criticism with a finding that the general standard and system of education was far from satisfactory. The cadets had no incentive to work and, in turn, the instructors had no inducements to teach.

Perhaps the most telling of the findings was 'that economy appeared to have been sought without sufficient regard to efficiency'. How often has that mistake been made in all walks of commerce and administration through to the present day? The report went on to recommend that the teaching staff must be chosen with the greatest care, and senior instructors should be selected Staff College graduates, a requirement that Teddy did not meet.

As the Boer War was over and as part of the changes taking place, Wynyard left Sandhurst on 17 September 1902. College records state that on this date he was 'struck off strength' but that is purely an administrative remark and the way the Army indicated that an individual had officially ceased to be the Royal Military College's responsibility.

Indeed, there had been an earlier announcement in the *London Gazette*, on 8 August 1902, that 'Supernumerary Captain EG Wynyard DSO was to be Captain in succession to Major TLW Lucas who holds an extra regimental appointment'. Supernumerary meant he had no assigned job but would take the place of someone else if and when they moved for whatever reason.

By late summer 1902, therefore, Teddy was back with his regiment but after twelve years without a further promotion, he must have started to think seriously about what the future held for him in the Army. On 22 May 1903 the *London Gazette* carried the following notice: 'The Welsh Regiment. Captain EG Wynyard DSO retires on retired pay.'

The time had come to take fresh guard!

Teddy wears his I Zingari cap in this impressive
1905 Chevallier Tayler print

13

WYNYARD'S WORLDWIDE
WANDERINGS 1903-05

Whilst it appears a military career had been mapped out for Wynyard from his earliest years, there is no evidence to suggest he would have chosen anything other than the Army for himself. Indeed all the indications are that he was ideally suited for this way of life. Now at the age of forty-two, for the first time since his school days, he was a civilian and had to decide what he wanted for his future.

He chose to embark upon a worldwide tour and over the next decade visited Newfoundland, West Indies (twice), South Africa (twice), New Zealand, North America and Egypt, predominantly to play cricket. This was a remarkable traveller's log by any standard, but even more so when one considers there was no air travel at this time.

What is interesting is that, following his retirement from the Army and his continued desire to play cricket, he did not commit himself to Hampshire. In spite of his age he played first-class cricket until 1912 but, during the next nine years, he only turned out for his county eleven times. Wynyard wrote of his close friend, HV Hesketh-Prichard, whom he referred to as HP (also nicknamed 'Hex') that he, 'made no secret of the fact that the most enjoyable years of his cricket came after his ambition to take part in representative cricket had been realised. He was a member of the three great clubs MCC, I Zingari and Free Foresters.' It sounds like Wynyard was also speaking for himself.

He did not play any first-class cricket during 1902 but the following season appeared at Lord's, on 18 May 1903, for MCC against Grace's London County. No play was possible on the first two days but, quite incredibly, there was time for four innings on the last to produce a win for Marylebone by nine wickets. Wynyard opened and played well, scoring 28. Albert Trott (seven for 37) then bowled out London County for 87 after they had been dismissed for 72 in their first innings. MCC needed only 10 to win, with Teddy not having to bat.

On Saturday 6 June he was back at his old school playing for MCC who were the victors yet again by nine wickets. He opened the batting and played a fine innings of 111, giving only one very difficult chance in one hour and forty minutes.

The following Monday he was at Lord's for MCC's match against Leicestershire, making 38 and 2 in his two innings. When he reached 15 he passed 5,000 runs in first-class cricket. On 17 July, military week began at Lord's and Teddy played for the Gentlemen of Marylebone Cricket Club in their three games, none of which was first-class, scoring 136 against the Navy and 91 against the Brigade as well as taking five wickets and a catch in that match.

As the season drew to a close, Wynyard played three successive home matches for Hampshire, beginning against Essex on 24 August. In a drawn game he batted well for over two and a half hours before being bowled by Mead for 72, and scored 17 not out in the second innings. The team then moved along the south coast to Dean Park, Bournemouth, for the visit of Kent who won by an innings and 17 runs in two days. Wynyard opened but was stumped by Huish off Colin Blythe's slow left-arm bowling for 22, second time round he was run out for 27, but that was by some way the top score as the side was 74 all out with Blythe taking ten for 120 in the match.

The next fixture was also at Bournemouth, starting on 31 August against Somerset. In another remarkably low scoring game, Wynyard opened the batting and again made the top score of 68. He then took three for 47 in Somerset's second innings and Hampshire were set 217 to win. Wynyard opened and, after twenty-five minutes, was run out for 8. After his departure the side collapsed to 107 all out, losing in two days for the second match running.

This was the end of Hampshire's Championship season and they had only one victory from their eighteen matches to finish fourteenth of the fifteen teams competing. The Championship was won, for the first time, by Middlesex.

During the winter of 1903-04, Plum Warner led an England team in Australia, the first time MCC had assumed responsibility for sponsoring and arranging an overseas tour, which was won 3-2. A victorious Warner arrived back at Victoria station on 17 April 1904, just after 6 pm. A large crowd was waiting for him, including Teddy, as part of MCC's welcoming committee. Just over a month later, on 30 May, a dinner was arranged in honour of Warner by the members of the Authors Club at their base in Whitehall Court, London. In the chair was JM Barrie, the creator of Peter Pan and founder of his own amateur cricket team of celebrity authors called the Allahakbarries. Amongst the dignitaries present were Teddy Wynyard, his friend Hesketh-Prichard (also a well-known author of his day), Sir Arthur Conan Doyle and EW Hornung (Doyle's brother-in-law who created the gentleman thief and cricketer, AJ Raffles). In his address Barrie described Warner as one 'of the gayest and gallantest captains that ever led a team of heroes across the seas ... They had entrusted to his hands the reputation of the game of cricket for honesty, manliness, fair play and courtesy and he brought that back to England unsullied.' Who remembered those words when Warner returned as manager of Jardine's team nearly thirty years later, after the Bodyline Tour of 1932/33?

At this time Teddy was helping out at Lord's and so was playing for MCC rather than Hampshire. He took responsibility for organising and captaining MCC teams with a particular interest in the development of public school cricket.

He began his cricketing season on 2 May 1904, playing for MCC and again Grace's London County were the opponents at Lord's. In the second innings he was at the crease with Arthur Conan Doyle and their respective scores of 75 and 31 were the two highest, accounting for well over half of MCC's 186. In spite of Teddy catching both Grace and Murdoch in the run chase, London County secured an easy seven wickets win. The Wynyard/Conan Doyle combination teamed up again in a very strong MCC team, including four South African tourists plus Albert Trott, JT Hearne and HV Hesketh-Prichard, in a 33-run defeat of Kent in the game beginning on 16 May.

A fortnight later, Teddy then played in two of the biggest matches of the season at Lord's. The first was for MCC against the South Africans in the opening fixture of their tour, and then for I Zingari against the Gentlemen of England.

Frank Mitchell was the captain of South Africa but he played international rugby for England, having been born in Yorkshire and educated at Cambridge University. He had volunteered for the Boer War and went back to Johannesburg where he worked for diamond mogul, financier and politician , who became a key figure in the development of South African cricket and was a close ally of Cecil Rhodes. Bailey's deep pockets enabled him not only to recruit Frank Mitchell as his personal secretary, but also George Lohmann as a coach and, a few years later, Teddy Wynyard as South Africa's cricket representative in England.

Bailey underwrote Australia's tour of South Africa in 1902 and this tour in 1904. He was a daring mining speculator and nationalist who had been jailed for his support of the Jameson raid. Whilst he advanced the case of Wynyard's Hampshire teammate, Charles Llewellyn, who was of mixed race, he openly made deeply offensive, racist comments, the like of which were tragically to dictate the course of South African politics for decades to come. From 1912, Bailey increasingly lived in England at properties in Bryanston Square and Surrey. Winston Churchill was a frequent visitor and his daughter, Diana, was briefly married to Bailey's son, John, from

1932 to 1935. Bailey's second wife was the famous aviatrix, Mary Westenra.

In the opening fixture of the 1904 tour, Frank Mitchell won the toss and elected to bat. Tancred and Shalders opened and progressed comfortably to 32 when Grace brought Bosanquet on to bowl. South Africa slumped to 194 all out and Bosanquet had taken nine for 107 with only Llewellyn seeming to know how to play him, ending on 68 not out. Bosanquet is widely credited as being the first person to master the googly and in its infancy the delivery was named a 'bosie' after him.

Kotze was one of the fastest around and MCC slumped to 94 for six. Wynyard and George Thompson then came together and advanced the score to 156 before Teddy was very unluckily out, caught by Schwarz, off a ball from Kotze that rose quickly and hit the shoulder of his bat. He had been missed early but played attractively and top scored for his side with 52. *The Times* commented that he always seemed at his best on a wicket of about this pace. MCC finished on 196 for eight, but no play was possible on either of the next two days and so the match was drawn.

Nine years earlier, Teddy had played for I Zingari in their jubilee match against the Gentlemen of England, and now, on 6 June 1904, he was back for a repeat of the fixture at Lord's. In March the surviving founder, Sir Spencer Ponsonby-Fane, had reached his eightieth birthday. To mark the event I Zingari entertained him to dinner at Prince's Restaurant in Piccadilly on the opening day of the game. This was also the first and last time since the 1895 fixture that I Zingari played a first-class match.

The two sides were not quite as strong this time but it proved to be Wynyard's best performance of the summer. The Gentlemen won the toss and batted. Middlesex's Leonard Moon opened and nearly carried his bat, being eighth out for 162. Bosanquet took seven for 83 (with Teddy taking one catch). Wynyard opened in reply to a score of 267, but three wickets were soon down for just 18 when Lord Hawke marched out to join him. They took the score to 95 before they were separated, but then three more wickets fell leaving I Zingari on 146 for seven at the close. They were facing a bowling attack comprising Charles Kortright, HV Hesketh-Prichard and George Beldam, although it was Somerset's Hugh Montgomery who had taken Teddy's wicket with the help of a catch from Moon, for a top score of 45. Lord Hawke made 43.

The following morning, I Zingari were dismissed for 175, leaving them 92 behind. The Gentlemen had the better of what turned out to be an unusual but memorable second day. Play had started early because the match was suspended between 1.30 pm and 3.50 pm to enable several members of both elevens, as well as groundsmen and spectators if they so wished, to attend the wedding of Pelham Warner to Miss Agnes Blyth at nearby St Marylebone Parish Church. Lord Hawke was the best man, with the reception at the home of the bride's mother in Portland Place, but there was still cricket to be played back at nearby Lord's. Quite remarkably, 365 runs were still scored in the day. There was time for the Gentlemen to make 319 in their second innings (Bosanquet four for 68), setting I Zingari the formidable target of 412 to win.

Although I Zingari had been second best up to that point, it was their batsmen who held the upper hand throughout the last day to pull off a surprising and brilliant victory. After Lucas was out with the score on 27, Wynyard walked out to join Ernest Steel and they were not separated until after lunch having put on 201 together. Steel made 111 and, following his dismissal, Teddy received valuable help from AJL Hill (38) and Bosanquet (68 not out) before he was fourth out, bowled by Key, for a magnificent 147. The score had now reached 385 and the final 27 runs were quickly polished off with Lord Hawke at the crease for a win by six wickets.

Wisden said that Wynyard 'was batting over three and a quarter hours and scarcely made a mistake'. RL Arrowsmith recounts, however, that Teddy was 'so dissatisfied with his own form in the morning that, summoning the three best pro bowlers available, he kept them bowling at him through the luncheon interval and when play restarted, he emerged from the practice ground to join his partner at the wicket.' The clearest possible example of the high standards he set for himself and then expected of others.

After MCC were comprehensively beaten by Leicestershire (Wynyard 0 and 18), Cambridge University were the next visitors to St John's Wood and they set a target of 277 to win. Wynyard and Ranjitsinhji made such a brilliant start that 237 had been scored in two hours and twenty minutes before Teddy was out just two short of his century. Their partnership must have helped relieve any strain that may still have existed in their relationship. Whilst Teddy was known as a fast scoring batsman, it is remarkable to record that Ranjitsinhji, in much the same time, had hit all around the wicket, barely making a mistake, and finished on 166 not out. *The Times* described MCC's performance as a 'brilliant nine-wicket victory'.

On 29 August, at the same time as the Scarborough Festival was taking place in Yorkshire, the Bournemouth Festival was being played in the south. Wynyard decided to participate in his second and only other match for Hampshire that season at Dean Park against Somerset. He scored just 1 in a drawn match badly affected by heavy rain. Hampshire won only two of their eighteen Championship matches in the season and finished last of the fifteen counties. Lancashire were convincing champions, going undefeated and winning sixteen out of twenty-six games.

Teddy's last first-class game of 1904 was representing the Gentlemen of England, captained by Grace, against the Players of the South. This was the third match of the Bournemouth Festival and he was run out for 20 then bowled by Hampshire teammate Llewellyn for 8 in a 94-run win for his side.

Wynyard had played eleven first-class matches and batted twenty times with an aggregate of 642 runs, achieved a highest score of 147 and an average of 32.10. During the last game at Bournemouth, Hesketh-Prichard had reached 100 first-class wickets for what was to be his best season. In addition to playing alongside Teddy for MCC, in the autumn they embarked upon a hunting expedition together to Canada.

In 1924, Eric Parker published a memoir crediting Hesketh-Prichard in the title with the description *Hunter: Explorer: Naturalist: Cricketer: Author: Soldier* which included an appreciation by Teddy of his friend, 'HP.'

HP had also been born in the Uttar Pradesh region of India but in 1876, and so was fifteen years younger than Wynyard. He had travelled to South America in 1898 to see the construction work for the Panama Canal but had been forced to return when he contracted malaria. He then explored the uncharted interior of Haiti and travelled to Patagonia in search of the Giant Sloth which was thought to be (and indeed proved to be) extinct.

HP then set about exploring Newfoundland and Labrador in Canada and corresponded with Theodore Roosevelt (the US President between 1901 and 1910) who confided that he would not have been able to cope with the 'infernal mosquitos'. HP was fascinated by the fact there were relatively uncharted areas and expressed the view it was a great pity that such 'a terra incogniti should continue to exist under the British flag'.

As a crack shot he visited the region for the first time on a hunting trip in 1903 with the assistance of Jack Wells, who was one of the best local guides, and returned the following year with Wynyard for the same purpose. He knew from this earlier trip what lay before him, both in terms of the equipment he needed and the kind of man he must choose as a companion. It must be someone he could trust in the most extreme conditions. By day, they trekked across rough terrain and crawled on their stomachs through wet swamps in order to hunt their prey. By night, they lived in tents and ate over campfires in isolated, lonely locations. Parker described Hesketh-Prichard as one who 'was to lead and not to follow'. He and Wynyard were indeed kindred spirits!

On 1 October 1904, Hesketh-Prichard, his mother Kate and Teddy boarded the Allan Line ship, SS *Carthaginian*, in Liverpool, bound initially for St John's where the three of them disembarked. Mrs Hesketh-Prichard remained in lodgings there, having been welcomed by Judge Prowse, author of the *History of Newfoundland*. The previous year he had wandered into Hex's camp at 10 pm, soaked to the skin and hungry. He was provided with fresh clothes, warmth from the fire and a cooked meal of trout and bacon. The judge was keen to repay the hospitality.

Hesketh-Prichard and Wynyard boarded the Newfoundland express on 14 October and travelled the 170 miles north-west to Terra Nova. Unfortunately the weather was rainy and they saw fewer stags than HP had witnessed the previous year and missed the main stream of migrating caribou, who did not pass through the Terra Nova district this time. They had a licence from the Newfoundland Government to hunt but it stipulated the number of kills they could make. It was not until 29 October that Hex killed his first stag from a distance of 200 yards, but Teddy had to wait until 7 November, when he killed two good stags. Parker commented 'on the whole the 1904 trip was a disappointment'.

It is a clear sign of the change in social attitude to compare Parker's fulsome description of the kills and a picture of HP kneeling beside a shot Canadian caribou, with the public outcry that accompanied the publication of a photograph in 2008 depicting Australian fast bowler, Glenn McGrath, gun in hand, alongside a 'kill'. The picture was withdrawn and McGrath apologised for his participation in the Zimbabwean safari which he said was 'legal but in hindsight highly inappropriate'.

In fairness to Hesketh-Prichard, whilst he may have been a hunter, he also campaigned for animal protection. He was successful in lobbying for the passing in 1914 of the Grey Seals (Protection) Act and also argued for the protection of birds from being killed for their plumage to be used in hat making. In the First World War, he was awarded the DSO and credited with saving as many as 3,500 lives by measures he introduced in the British trenches to protect the men from German snipers and by improving the strength of the armour-plated defences.

Their hunting trip over, Wynyard and HP had another journey to make together. They were part of Lord Brackley's team touring the Caribbean to play cricket at the beginning of the New Year.

Brackley's side was the fifth to tour the West Indies, but for the first time two professionals, Ernie Hayes of Surrey and George Thompson of Northants, were included and considerably strengthened the team. In addition to Brackley, Wynyard and Hesketh-Prichard, of the remaining eleven amateur players, the most notable amongst them were Worcestershire's lob bowler, George Simpson-Hayward, and Sussex's wicketkeeper, Arthur Somerset, who was now fifty years old but still a more than useful batsman.

Twenty matches had been arranged between January and April 1905, of which ten were regarded as first-class including two against representative West Indian teams. *The Times* referred to these games as 'Tests' but they were never officially recognized as such.

The opening game of the tour was a first-class fixture at Sabina Park, Kingston starting on 12 January. Jamaica's batting was weak and they were dismissed for 143 but Teddy, opening the batting, was out for a duck and Brackley's side were all out for just 121. On the second and last day of the match Jamaica scored 248, setting the visitors 271 to win. Wynyard fared much better second time around, top scoring with 38 before being trapped lbw by Morrison. The match was drawn but the result clearly showed the home side had been in the ascendancy.

At the same venue, on the following day, the twelve members of Lord Brackley's side now in Jamaica (Hesketh-Prichard joined up later) played Eighteen of Jamaica Colts (none of whom had played in the opening contest). The fixture was not first-class and Wynyard, batting at number five, retired when he had made 103 in another drawn game.

The second first-class match and the last on this leg of the tour began on 19 January. Brackley opened with Wynyard and they put on 129 for the first wicket and then, when Hayes (76) replaced his captain, there was a second wicket stand of 135. Teddy eventually scored 157 in three and a half hours hitting one six, a five and fifteen fours before being bowled by Morrison. The total of 484 for eight declared was the highest of the tour and enough to secure victory by an innings and 169 runs.

From Jamaica the side moved on to Barbados, stopping at Trinidad for five to six hours on the way. Four matches had been arranged, three of which were first-class, all to be played at Kensington Oval, Bridgetown. The ground was nicely situated with a plentiful grass covering (not always the case in the Caribbean at that and subsequent times). The wicket was a good one but could be unplayable when there were heavy downpours of rain.

Hesketh-Prichard had now joined up with the rest of the team. Barbados had strength in both the batting and bowling departments. Fitz Hinds opened the bowling and, like Percy Goodman, had been on the tour to England in 1900 led by Aucher Warner (Plum's brother). *Cricket* said 'a big, finely-built man, Goodman perhaps carries a little more flesh than a cricketer would elect to bear in a hot climate'! The Barbados captain was Harold Austin, who became a very influential figure in securing Test match status for the West Indies. Wynyard scored 75 before being stumped off Austin's bowling in the second innings for another comfortable victory, this time by 177 runs.

The first of the unofficial Tests against a combined West Indian side began on 6 February, although it was by no means their strongest team, especially as Trinidad's best bowler, Sydney Smith, was unable to play. Austin was the captain and he did have Goodman as well as Hinds in the side plus the services of William Shepherd, a fast right-arm bowler, along with Richard Ollivierre, one of three cricketing brothers and one of the best black all-rounders of his generation.

Brackley won the toss and he, along with Wynyard, opened the innings on a perfect wicket but the captain was soon out. Hayes joined Teddy and the tally rose slowly with both batsmen playing with great caution until Hayes was well caught in the deep by Hinds for 28. Teddy had progressed to 51 by lunch and in the afternoon he pressed ahead more quickly. He had just completed his century and was on 101 when he was caught behind off a ball from Shepherd that lifted sharply. *The Times* said 'his innings had been quite faultless and most attractive to watch and the delight of the crowd at his dismissal was very emphatic'. The tourists were all out for 353, but the West Indies were dismissed for 107 and 229 to lose by an innings and 17 runs.

The next match was a repeat of the first-class fixture against Barbados, beginning on 9 February. Hayes and Hesketh-Prichard were absent, which greatly reduced the strength of both the bowling and the batting. Brackley won the toss and batted, but his side was all out for 220 with Wynyard making 32 before being bowled by Hinds, who took five for 41. Barbados replied with 295 (Goodman 103) and they pressed home their advantage. Teddy went in at number three and had made 13 before becoming one of Shepherd's five victims as the tourists were skittled out for 95. Barbados easily made 21 to win by ten wickets. Brackley had suffered his first defeat and his side had been outplayed throughout the game.

It was then time for the team to move on to St Lucia, but Somerset and Simpson-Hayward stayed behind. On the third leg of their tour the tourists had matters very much their own way. None of the games were treated as first-class. The ground at Victoria Park, Castries was very pretty, surrounded by hills and covered with trees of every colour and description. Unfortunately the turf wicket there was dangerous and so for the last two of the three matches, Brackley asked for matting to be put down. All three fixtures were won easily with Wynyard scoring 108 in the first match.

The team then left Castries and stopped off back at Barbados en route to British Guiana (Guyana) on the north-east coast of the South American mainland. On 27 February, there was time to play a one-day match against the Barbados Garrison. In the absence of Hesketh-Prichard and Thompson, Brackley opened with his two lob bowlers, Wynyard and Simpson-Hayward, who took two for 49 and five for 46 respectively, but the game ended in a draw with Wynyard not batting.

It was a return to first-class cricket when the tourists played their two games against British Guiana at the Bourda Georgetown ground in the county of Demerara. This was a delightful setting with beautiful turf everywhere, and had it not been for the heavy showers of rain, the wicket would have been perfect. Brackley's side won both matches and Teddy's 80 in the second innings of the last game prompted *Wisden* to comment that 'Captain Wynyard played one of his best innings during the tour'.

The fifth leg of the trip saw two matches, neither first-class, in St Vincent. The Arnos Vale Playing Field in Kingstown was a very small ground, and the wicket was made up of matting. St Vincent, along with St Lucia, Grenada and Dominica was part of the Windward Islands and home to the cricketing Ollivierre brothers. Both matches were drawn, with Teddy scoring only 12 and 1.

The tourists then moved on via Barbados to Trinidad where four matches had been arranged, including the second unofficial Test against a representative West Indian side. All the teams faced were strong especially in the bowling department with the slow left arm of Sydney Smith taking centre stage. Trinidad's batting was also good, with the likes of Sarel, Learmond and Harragin, but arguably the best Trinidadian was Lebrun Constantine.

Constantine was the grandchild of slaves (slavery being abolished in 1835) and became the overseer on a cocoa estate in Cascade. His wife, Anaise Pascall, was the child of slaves too, and her brother, Victor, was a Trinidad and West Indian first-class cricketer. Lebrun toured England twice and made his last first-class appearance on 28 September 1922 for Trinidad against Barbados at the age of forty-eight, playing alongside his son, Learie, who went on to become one of the most famous of all West Indian cricketers. As Lord Constantine of Nelson, he was the first black peer to sit in the House of Lords, and two years earlier had been a driving force behind the introduction of the Race Relations Act in 1965.

Young Learie was just four years old when his father prepared to face Lord Brackley's team in Trinidad on the sixth and final leg of their tour. Temperatures were very high on the island, at one point registering thirty-two degrees Centigrade before play had even begun.

Constantine did not play in the opening game, for Queen's Park at the club's Oval ground in the St Clair district of the Port of Spain. It was not first-class and the poor state of the wickets meant matting had to be used. Wynyard scored 46 as Brackley's side won by an innings and 14 runs.

The team then played an All Trinidad side in a first-class fixture at the Queen's Park Oval on Saturday 25 March. Home captain, Alfred Harragin, won the toss and elected to bat. Lebrun Constantine, who was also the wicketkeeper, contributed 11 towards a total of 149, with Thompson and Hesketh-Prichard taking five wickets apiece.

Wynyard made 9 and 1 as Brackley's side suffered their second defeat of the tour by 120 runs. *Wisden* recorded that 'the wicket was very difficult and Cumberbatch, right hand medium pace, bowled with extraordinary success'. He took Teddy's wicket twice and ended with figures of thirteen for 57 in the match.

Wynyard had played in every one of the eighteen matches on the tour to date, but in this game against All Trinidad he sustained a bad injury to his leg which prevented him from participating in the last two fixtures, both of which were designated first-class.

Sadly it meant he missed the second unofficial Test against a representative West Indies side, which *Wisden* recorded 'as by far and away the most exciting match of the tour with Brackley's men winning after a great finish by four runs'. The final match was against All Trinidad and Constantine played exceptionally well, steering the side to a five wickets victory with 47 not out.

The tour had been a considerable success. Of the twenty matches played, eleven had been won, six drawn and three lost. The three outstanding players were Wynyard as a batsman, Thompson in the bowling department and Hayes as an all-rounder. In first-class matches, Wynyard was top of all the trees with the highest aggregate (562), highest score (157) and average (40.14). In all the matches Wynyard had an average of 41.27 and an aggregate total of 908 runs. *Wisden* observed, 'it was quite a triumph for Capt Wynyard, at nearly 45 years of age, to head the batting averages. He made four scores of over one hundred and Hayes three.'

The Times was also very complimentary in its tour review, saying 'he was in grand form and delighted both spectators and his opponents whom he kept in the field so long by his hitting and his strokes on the leg side'. The overall standard of the fielding was good, with special praise for Wynyard, Simpson-Hayward and Hayes, but the paper went on to make a particularly significant observation, with future tours in mind, that Wynyard and Hayes had their best performances on the fast turf wickets and the matting did not suit Teddy's style of play.

Unfortunately it is also necessary to record a blot on the tour. In *Cricket: A History of its Growth and Development throughout the*

World, Rowland Bowen said that, 'Lord Brackley took a team out in 1904-5 (following RA Bennett's) and during it occurred some disagreeable behaviour by some of the amateurs with the team: a forerunner of shemozzles of various kinds that have come to be associated with the visits of English teams to these islands.'

Wisden reported that 'some friction arose out of faulty umpiring at St Vincent, but otherwise the trip passed off in the pleasantest way'. *The Times* went further, complimenting all the islands for making the visit so enjoyable with 'picnics, concerts, dinners and dances arranged everywhere the team went. Great credit to Mr CP Foley in his management of the tour and Lord Brackley who captained with great keenness.'

Whilst Bowen did not give further and better particulars of the behaviour in question, it is difficult to read his comments without suspecting that he had in mind something more sinister than dubious umpiring. A year later the West Indies visited England in the summer of 1906 and *The Times* concluded its review of that Tour in the following way:

> The composition of the team did not appeal much to the average Englishman. There is an obvious interest felt in the colonial cricketer. A kind of peculiar interest may be felt in the cricket of the man who differs from him in race, colour, associations, training and temperament. But a team in which the attempt has been made to blend the two is of the nature of a compromise which does not convince. Combination, even at cricket, means something more than the appearance on the same field under the same leader of two totally different sets of men. Various parts of the British Empire have various customs. It is, however, safe to say that neither from the dependency of India nor from the colony of South Africa is there any likelihood of a mixed cricket team being sent to England. There is great enthusiasm about cricket in both countries but in the history of both countries important events have occurred and indeed continue to occur which makes other considerations paramount ... They are at least assured that in England the colonial cricketer, playing as a colonial cricketer, is always very welcome.

Words that tell their own story about Edwardian attitudes to race and class that may lie behind the conduct and 'shemozzles' referred to by Bowen.

In spite of the leg injury that forced Wynyard to miss the last two matches of the tour, he was back in England and fit enough to play for MCC in a team that included seven members who played in the West Indies, against Nottinghamshire on 3 May. The visitors, captained by AO Jones, won the toss, batted and were dismissed for 47 in an hour and a quarter, with Thompson maintaining his form, taking seven for 14. Wynyard renewed his opening Caribbean partnership with Brackley and made 37 out of 155. *Wisden* commented that he 'showed unwonted caution' taking an hour and a half to make his runs, but MCC won comfortably by ten wickets, an hour and a half into the second day, without Teddy needing to bat again.

Sussex were the next visitors to Lord's and their captain, CB Fry, scored 156 and 106 to register, for the fourth time, two hundreds in the same game. Until then he was the only player to have achieved that feat and so it must have been particularly galling for CB to end up on the wrong end of a seven-wicket defeat, largely brought about by Plum Warner's outstanding 204 in MCC's first innings. Wynyard scored 10 and 40 in the match.

The Australians were in England in the summer of 1905 and, Test matches apart, their game against the Gentlemen of England at Lord's, starting on Thursday 18 May, was the most interesting of their tour. Gilbert Jessop was unable to play and so Teddy Wynyard took his place against a strong touring side captained by Joe Darling that included Syd Gregory, Victor Trumper, Warwick Armstrong, Monty Noble and Tibby Cotter. The Gentlemen won the toss and batted with only Warner (85) and Wynyard (61) making significant contributions, although *The Times* said Teddy was 'decidedly lucky. As a rule he makes his runs so quickly and well that his display yesterday was particularly disappointing. He deserves great credit for his innings played at a time when things were not going very well for his side, but he gave more than one chance and he did not seem at home to several of the bowlers, Mr. Armstrong, in particular often leaving him in difficulties.'

In response to a score of 300, the Australians lost their first four wickets for 94 including Trumper bowled by Brearley for 6, but it was the performance of Warwick 'the Big Ship' Armstrong aided by

Joe Darling that dominated the day. The two of them then put on 276 in two hours and forty minutes. Armstrong made what was at the time the third-highest score in a first-class fixture at Lord's of 248 not out, with runs coming all around the wicket. Darling cut and drove to make 117 not out, declaring his side's total on 555 for six. Rain fell during the night and next day the Gentlemen slumped to 57 for six. Teddy then strode on to the Lord's pitch, but he was not to be the saviour on this occasion, being caught in the slips by Howell off Laver for 3. The Gentlemen were all out just before 1 o'clock for 66, losing by an innings and 189 runs.

In June, Teddy played two matches that were not first-class at Lord's. The first was a victory for the Gentlemen of Marylebone against the Royal Navy when he retired having made 151 with Arthur Conan Doyle in the side. They also played together for MCC in an innings and 16 run win over Wiltshire, beginning on 23 June, with Wynyard taking four for 20.

It was then the time of year for the MCC matches against the Varsities. Teddy opened against Cambridge and scored another century (115) in less than two hours hitting nineteen fours. He also bowled five overs, taking one for 15, and secured two catches in a four-wicket victory. Oxford fared very much better, making 459 in their first innings, and their top scorer was opener, Mr WHB Evans, who made 139 not out. It should be recorded that he made the runs and then retired because he had an examination to take and returned when his side were nine wickets down! In the end Wynyard only scored 17 and 1 as MCC were lucky to escape with a draw.

For his final three first-class matches of the 1905 season, Wynyard returned to play for Hampshire. On 17 July the eventual champions for the year, Yorkshire, were the visitors at Dean Park, Bournemouth, and as the home side were destined to finish bottom of the table, the game proved to be a fair reflection of their respective positions. Hampshire were dismissed twice for 172 and 152 to lose by an innings and 167 runs. Wynyard opened in both innings making 34 and 19.

Worcestershire were the next opponents at Dean Park. Teddy was caught for 44 as Hampshire progressed to 449 all out. The country was experiencing a heat wave, which clearly benefited the batsmen as the visitors reached 434. The final day was to prove one of the most exciting of the season. Wynyard opened and batted well for his 55. Hampshire's captain, Edward Sprot declared on 261 for six, leaving free hitting Worcestershire to chase 277 in two hours and twenty-five minutes. The winning hit was made with just one minute to go and five wickets in hand. Wynyard took one for 36 during the run chase; 1,424 runs had been scored over the three days.

Hampshire then moved back to the County Ground at Southampton for the visit of Somerset on 24 July. Sammy Woods won the toss, batted and his side made 374 with Wynyard taking three for 45. Hampshire responded with 350 but Teddy was out for a duck. In the second innings he opened with AJL Hill and they safely progressed to 150 to secure a comfortable draw. Hill made 118 and the normally attacking Wynyard just 18! *The Times* commented that the Hampshire openers 'batted with nothing but a draw in view [and] they batted cautiously' – Teddy a little more so than Hill, they might have added.

In his ten first-class matches of the 1905 domestic season Teddy had played eighteen innings (once not out), aggregated 583 runs with a top score of 115 at an average of 34.29. Good, but not spectacular, and it was really only in the game against the Australians that he had faced high-class opposition before the middle of July.

For the winter of 1905-6, MCC were organizing a tour of South Africa to include five Test matches and, during June, Wynyard had agreed to participate. One imagines, he had felt the need, therefore, to hone his skills before the season's end in the more competitive forum of the County Championship, with the added benefit of enjoying the social atmosphere surrounding the Bournemouth Festival. As a couple of the match reports had described him as exercising a degree more caution than was normally the case – was this his way of preparing for the Test matches that lay ahead?

From PF Warner, *The MCC in South Africa*

The MCC team for the second Test against South Africa.
Back: Blythe, Denton, Hayes, Lees, Board.
Front: Crawford, Fane, Warner (captain), Haigh, Moon, Wynyard.

14

TESTING TIMES WITH PLUM
1905/06

Since South Africa's very first Test match at Port Elizabeth against an England touring team led by Charles Aubrey Smith in 1889, they had played a further ten Tests, all at home, and never won. Whilst there had been four previous tours, this was the first under the official auspices of MCC, but finding a team had not been an easy process, and by mid-September 1905, arrangements had still not been finalised. From the nineteen players who had played during the Ashes series that summer only three (the professionals Haigh, Denton and Blythe) were selected and/or able to tour.

As the Hon FS Jackson was unavailable, it meant a new captain had to be found. Lord Hawke also declined, so who should lead the side? In *Test of Time*, John Lazenby tells a fascinating story about his grandfather, Jack Mason, and the cricketing politics of the day. Mason had been on Stoddart's tour to Australia in 1896/7, from which Wynyard had withdrawn, had played alongside Teddy in Grace's jubilee match for the Gentlemen, but in 1902 had relinquished the Kent captaincy to become a full-time solicitor. He then played each August only when he took his summer holidays, but Lazenby unearthed two letters, now owned by collector Roger Mann, which he described as 'dynamite'. The first was from Pelham Warner, dated 27 June 1905, which said he had been asked to take a team to South Africa. Teddy Wynyard and Fane had already agreed to go and he invited Mason to join the party. A week later Mason received a second letter, this time from the Secretary of MCC, Francis Lacey, dated 4 July. It stated that, at a committee meeting the previous day, it had been agreed to ask him to captain the side.

Lazenby and Mann discussed the implications of this correspondence. Warner subsequently wrote in connection with the tour that Mason was unavailable but made no mention of the captaincy issue, and it seems likely Warner was never aware of the offer made by Lacey. Lazenby and Mann concluded the truth might lie in some duplicity on the part of the Marylebone Club. This tour would require not just a cricketing leader, but also an ambassador for the game. Warner was a safe pair of hands and, having secured his services, MCC felt they could look around to see if there was anyone else who was better suited to the role. If Mason had accepted then, as an establishment man, MCC felt they could rely on Warner's innate sense of loyalty to do as he was bid, but Mason declined and to his eternal credit never revealed the offer that was made to him.

When the touring party was finally announced there were fourteen names comprising seven amateurs: captain 'Plum' Warner (Middlesex), Teddy Wynyard, FL Fane (Essex), Jack Crawford (Surrey), LJ Moon (Middlesex), JC Hartley (Sussex) and HDG Leveson Gower (Surrey). Seven professionals joined them: David Denton, Schofield Haigh (both Yorkshire), Ernie Hayes, Walter Lees (both Surrey), Colin Blythe (Kent), Albert Relf (Sussex) and wicketkeeper Jack Board (Gloucestershire). Hayes had, of course, been on the Caribbean tour with Wynyard the previous winter.

The South African press expressed disappointment with the composition of the MCC side, having hoped to see the likes of Bosanquet and Tom Hayward amongst others, and this was not surprising bearing in mind their cricket association had agreed to be responsible for the cost of the tour. Warner's men were not playing in Rhodesia because the necessary guarantee could not be raised there.

There were also three very significant factors that had to be taken into account when considering MCC's chances; the climate, a gruelling itinerary and the matting wickets. On one occasion at Kimberley, Warner spoke of 'walking about on hot bricks' with temperatures exceeding ninety degrees Fahrenheit in the shade. Originally twenty-five matches had been arranged (although ultimately twenty-six were played), starting at the beginning of December in Cape Town and, after travelling all over the country, ending back there at the end of March. It was a schedule that makes the maligned modern-day cricket administrator look like a paragon of virtue. Perhaps the most significant factor was that all the wickets were made up of matting, a surface with which the South African players were highly familiar and well suited to their spin attack.

In addition to overcoming these obstacles on the pitch, Warner would have to be at his most diplomatic off it. The tour came just three years after the end of the Second Boer War and sensitivities remained acute. Furthermore, the use of Chinese workers in the Rand gold mines had led to disturbances, resulting in the execution of twelve Chinese labourers. This became a hot political issue at home and was felt to be one of the factors in the subsequent landslide victory by the Liberals, led by Henry Campbell-Bannerman, in the 1906 General Election. Whilst the purpose of Warner and his team was to play cricket, it is clear a significant and subsidiary aim was to heal some wounds and see if a few bridges could be built along the way.

This was the backdrop, therefore, as all the team, barring Wynyard, met at Waterloo station on Saturday 11 November 1905 to catch the 11.30 am train bound for Southampton. Teddy had travelled down earlier to meet up with his younger half brother, 25-year-old Henry Buckley Wynyard, who was travelling with him on board ship.

Union Castle ran a Royal Mail steam packet from Southampton to the Cape and Natal via Madeira every Saturday, and RMS *Kinfauns Castle* left port at 5 o'clock. The usual travel arrangements had been made, with the seven amateurs plus Mrs Warner, her maid and

Teddy's brother, travelling first-class and the seven professionals in the second-class accommodation.

This tour was very well reported. Warner wrote a book based on letters he sent back to the *Westminster Gazette*. It was also an MCC custom that the youngest member of the team be given the task of writing the press reports for the newspapers at home, and so this honour was bestowed upon nineteen-year-old Jack Crawford. Meanwhile the oldest member of the side, 44-year-old Teddy Wynyard, also wrote home chronicling the tour. His and Crawford's accounts were kept by Colin Blythe and have been relied upon by John Blythe Smart in his biography *The Real Colin Blythe*.

The first news item was that the weather in the Bay of Biscay sorted out the sailors from the landlubbers. Waves swept high over the boat, bulwarks were stove in and the storm shattered the windows of the smoking room and cabins. Wynyard fared better than most with the conditions, but umpire Jim Phillips was the envy of all as he sat at the meal table and tucked into his menu choices.

There was time to enjoy a break at Madeira where there was a stop to take on board more coal. After leaving the island a committee was formed, which included Teddy, to organise deck games and pastimes to keep the cricketers occupied. There was a deck cricket match between the first- and second-class passengers that the professionals won comfortably thanks to the bowling of Denton. Cricket could not really be played because of the narrowness of the decks, but the opportunity was taken for some slip catching practice. The stumps were then used for deck hockey at which Wynyard excelled with his forward play.

As dawn broke at 6 o'clock on 28 November, seventeen days after leaving home, RMS *Kinfauns Castle* steamed into Table Bay, overlooked by Cape Town and dominated by the flat-topped Table Mountain. The team were greeted by the President of the Western Province Cricket Union, Mr MV Simkins, and after breakfast and a formal lunch at the Town Hall, the team took the train for the six-mile journey through gorgeous countryside to Newlands for their first session in the nets. Warner referred to the rustiness of the players and Wynyard observed that their efforts revealed a large degree of practice was needed. He was granted his wish as the next two days were spent with the team honing their skills before travelling to Simon's Town on Friday 1 December to have lunch on the flagship HMS *Crescent*.

Next day saw the opening fixture of the tour, a first-class match at Newlands against a strong Western Province bowling attack captained by Murray Bisset. Rain had freshened up the pitch, but when Warner won the toss he opted to bat and opened with Wynyard. Unfortunately, when the score had reached 15, Teddy was run out having scored just 6. Nevertheless, the rest of the top order all made runs, with Denton top scoring on 78 out of a total of 365 (Whitehead six for 100). The Western Province batting was weak though and they were dismissed for 96 and 142 (Wynyard one catch) to lose by an innings and 127 runs.

The second fixture was an odds match located seventy miles away at Worcester. Wynyard stood down but reported on the game. Dirk Miering entertained the team on the last evening at his typical Dutch farmhouse named Vitylught, where a band played under trees adorned with Chinese lanterns. Liquid hospitality was in abundance and this made for an eventful return journey in four muled wagons along a track bordered by a barbed-wire fence on one side and a spruit (a small stream) on the other. It was sufficiently bumpy for a bandsman to be parted from his double bass, which was last seen somersaulting down the path back towards whence it came. Nevertheless, Teddy and the rest of the team did eventually board the 1.30 am train to Cape Town where MCC were scheduled to play the return first-class fixture against Western Province.

Wynyard came back into the side to open alongside Warner. The home side won the toss and elected to bat, but there had been a storm the previous evening and the ball turned so sharply that by 3.15 pm they were all out for 81. MCC started badly, with Wynyard caught by Rowe off Whitehead's bowling for 2, but they recovered to make 272. In their second innings Snooke, who opened, batted particularly well for 80, but Wynyard and Warner quickly polished off the runs needed, scoring 27 and 15 respectively, to produce a ten wicket victory by 2 o'clock on the third day.

After the first three games Warner expressed the opinion that the results achieved so far filled him with confidence but he was 'fully convinced' that a combined South African team would take a lot of beating. *The Times* also carried a review of the tour up to this point in time. The paper expressed the opinion that the majority of the team had acclimatised well to the cricket conditions including the heat and bright dazzling sunlight. Warner had set an example with his defensive cricket but 'Captain Wynyard has not at present found his true form' although 'in his last innings there were glimpses of it'.

On Wednesday 13 December at 11.20 am, the side departed on the Rhodesian Deluxe Express, which left at the same time each week, arriving at Bulawayo the following Saturday. MCC's destination was Kimberley and the means of transport was very much to Warner's liking as he described the train as rivalling the best Europe could offer. The bathroom allowed him 'to rid oneself of the dust which is ever the lot of the traveller in South Africa'.

The journey was 647 miles long and took the tourists past Matjiesfontein, which had been developed by Scottish-born James Logan into a renowned health resort that had attracted Surrey and England bowler George Lohmann to the area. Dean Allen's biography of Logan, *Empire, War and Cricket in South Africa*, describes Logan's role in developing South African cricket. Just south of Matjiesfontein in the local cemetery is the elaborate memorial to Lohmann that was paid for by Logan and Surrey County Cricket Club. One wonders what Wynyard must have been thinking on this journey because Lohmann had always caused him trouble, dismissing him five times on the occasions they had opposed one another in all classes of cricket, together with him being one of the players making a pay demand immediately before his Test debut nearly ten years earlier.

By Thursday morning, the train had reached the large De Aar railway junction and passed through some of the key battlefields of the early part of the Boer War. The cricketers would have seen the large cross on the top of the kopje (a small hill) that served as a memorial to those in the Highland Brigade who lost their lives on 11 December 1899 at Magersfontein. Ten miles north of the Modder River, the train was brought almost to a halt by a swarm of locusts which infested the rails to such an extent that the train struggled to gain traction on the slippery surface. Cometh the hour, cometh the man! Wynyard sprang into action and, assisted by Moon and Crawford, they braved the locusts to shovel sand onto the rails in an attempt to provide a better grip for the wheels. The train could only crawl for the next four to five miles but, after a thirty-hour journey, arrived in Kimberley only half an hour late.

Kimberley was the diamond centre of South Africa, if not the world, at that time. On 12 March 1888, De Beers Consolidated Mines Limited was established with Cecil Rhodes, the founding Chairman, paying the astonishing sum of £5,338,050 to the liquidators of Barney Barnato's company. There followed massive migration to the area as De Beers needed labour to mine the diamonds.

During their stay the team had plenty of time to explore and visited the offices of De Beers as well as the Kimberley mine. By special permit, they were allowed to touch the most valuable stones, saw the cheque for £5,338,050 and a model of the Cullinan diamond from the rival Premier mine. They also went underground to inspect the mine, and Warner described the scene as:

> All was dirt and grime and half naked men bathed in perspiration were hammering, shovelling, picking, and keeping up a chant which here, echoing about the bowels of the earth, sounded weird and even awe inspiring. And all this strenuous labour, organization and expenditure just for a few stones to deck my lady's finger! ... [the visit to the mine] did not appeal to some of us who thought the whole thing rather unedifying and the kind of spectacle that one does not care to see twice. Hundreds of creatures were yelling and shouting around us as if they were mad and later on they gave us a war dance which was not really amusing and only raised the dust.

It seems Warner's encounter with the miners had offended his sensibilities rather than stirred any deep feeling of moral outrage in him about the conditions under which they were working.

Two odds matches had been arranged for the stay in Kimberley against Fifteen of Griqualand, with MCC playing twelve. The first game was at the Eclectic Ground where locusts were hopping about on the practice matting and temperatures were extreme. Board and

Wynyard opened the batting, but Board, Warner and Denton were all dismissed cheaply. Teddy, after taking a little time to settle down, then played sound and attractive cricket making excellent use of the hook stroke for 82 towards a total of 374. On the Saturday, the opposition were dismissed for 174 and then 207. By 3.30 pm the grey-red gravel of the outfield had become unbearably hot and like a road underfoot, which was not surprising given the drought conditions with only one and a half inches of rain having fallen in eight months. It must have been a relief that MCC only needed a handful of runs for their eleven-wicket victory, with Wynyard contributing 6 not out.

The second match was a three-day game played at Pirates Cricket Club ground against the same opposition. The home team batted and scored 233. MCC responded with 432 for eight declared with Crawford (98), Fane (62), Denton (64) and Wynyard accounting for most of the runs. Teddy was especially strong on the leg side and, batting at number eight, had made 62 not out when the innings was closed. Blythe took six wickets in the match as the home side lost by an innings and 12 runs. Warner did not play in this game but travelled ahead to Johannesburg with his wife and her maid.

As the direct rail route from Kimberley to Johannesburg was not scheduled to open until April 1906, the team had to travel south back to the De Aar junction and then further southeast to Naauwpoort, before proceeding north on to Johannesburg. It was Christmas time, the trains were very crowded and for the first part of the journey to Bloemfontein there was no dining car. The cricketers had to eat at the station dining rooms en route, where there were too few waiters on hand and tinned tongue was the order of the day. The team arrived on Christmas Eve and their next match was a first-class fixture at the Old Wanderers ground against Transvaal starting on Boxing Day. The whole team had time to visit local townships as well as swimming at a local pool and visiting the racetrack whilst in Johannesburg.

It was widely thought that the balance of cricketing power had shifted from the Cape to Transvaal and so this was going to be the stiffest fixture so far. In pleasant weather the home side won the toss and batted on a fast wicket, but the brand-new matting made the ball jump and they were swiftly dismissed for 135, with Lees taking five for 34 and Blythe three for 41. In reply, Wynyard, batting at number four, was caught by Aubrey Faulkner off Schwarz for only 7. MCC were all out for 265 thanks largely to Yorkshire professional, David Denton, carrying his bat for 132.

In their second innings Transvaal batted steadily and set a target of 175. What then followed was, in Warner's words, 'a fiasco', with only Fane escaping criticism. Relf was singled out for batting 'very badly indeed', 'the pull stroke getting more than one of us into trouble'. In fact Wynyard was brilliantly caught low down at leg by wicketkeeper Sherwell off Schwarz for 1. The bowler ended with figures of five for 34. He turned the ball sharply, pitching outside off stump with the ball missing leg and spinning off the matting at great pace as well as rising sharply. Faulkner, who took three for 62, had shown himself to be a fine bat and field but his great attribute was that off a short two or three yard run he could break the ball both ways, like Bosanquet, making it very difficult for the batsman to read the delivery. Schwarz and Faulkner made an ideal combination on the matting wicket, and MCC were all out for 115 to lose, for the first time on the tour, by 60 runs.

On Tuesday 2 January 1906, the first Test match began at the Old Wanderers ground. All five Tests were scheduled to be four-day matches. In batting order the MCC side was Warner, Fane, Denton, Wynyard, Hayes, Crawford, Relf, Haigh, Board, Lees and Blythe. Teddy, who had opened at the start of the tour, was now to go in second wicket down. He was approaching forty-five years of age but, at just nineteen years and thirty-two days old, Jack Crawford became the youngest cricketer to play for England. He held the record for forty-three years and still remains second behind Brian Close.

As for South Africa, eight of the side who had represented Transvaal a week earlier were in the Test team: Louis Tancred, William Shalders, Christopher 'Maitland' Hathorn, Gordon White, Jimmy Sinclair, George 'Aubrey' Faulkner, Reggie Schwarz and Percy Sherwell (captain). The other three players were Albert 'Ernie' Vogler (Eastern Province), Sibley 'Tip' Snooke who had played in the opening game for Western Province, and Arthur Nourse (Natal). It was a side growing in experience that batted down to the last man, their captain, and could call upon as many as nine bowlers if necessary. Given the result against Transvaal just after Christmas, this looked like being an interesting and close series.

In glorious weather and on a good pitch before 7,000 spectators, Warner won the toss and batted. In Schwarz's second over the captain was dismissed for 6. Denton came to the crease and was promptly out first ball to the same bowler for a duck. Captain EG Wynyard then strode to the wicket with his side in the perilous position of being 6 for two and Schwarz on a hat-trick! Thirty-five Test matches had been played and exactly nine years, four months and twenty-three days elapsed since Teddy's debut at The Oval, but there was one constant factor – Jim Phillips was again the umpire.

Wynyard joined fellow Old Carthusian, Frederick Fane, who was fourteen years his junior, but their partnership had only progressed the score to 15 when Schwarz caught Fane, off Faulkner, for 1. Hayes was next man in and, after fifty minutes, 53 runs had been accumulated when the Surrey professional was caught and bowled by Vogler for 20. It was now the turn of debutant Jack Crawford to join Wynyard, who was 23 not out having been missed when on 18. They steadied the ship, adding another 23 together when Sherwell stumped Teddy, off Schwarz's bowling, for a useful 29 that included three fours.

Relf was then out for 8, and at lunch MCC were in the unpromising position of being 105 for six. In the afternoon the crowd increased to 10,000 and was so large that they were sitting five to six deep around the cycle track and also encroaching on to the perimeters of the pitch, hampering the fieldsmen. Crawford continued to play superbly for the top score of 44, but MCC were all out for 184.

Warner's bowlers immediately struck back with Lees and Blyth reducing South Africa to 44 for seven. Ernie Vogler came in to bat and on-drove Colin Blythe over the green hedge opposite the pavilion. Jack Crawford then replaced Blythe, and with his very first ball in Test cricket, knocked over Vogler's leg stump for 14. At 6 o'clock, when play finished for the day, the score was 71 for eight with Nourse partnering Schwarz at the wicket.

Rain fell during the night and play resumed in cool clear weather on the following morning, when South Africa were only able to progress to a total of 91. MCC had a first innings lead of 93, but again did not start well, with Fane being bowled by Snooke for 3. There was then a good partnership between Warner and Denton before the Yorkshireman was bowled for 34 by a ball from Faulkner, which pitched outside off and hit his middle stump. The score was 55 for two and the tourists were ahead by 148 with eight wickets in hand when Teddy Wynyard walked out to bat. Unfortunately he was soon bowled by a quick leg break from Ernie Vogler without scoring.

The weather was threatening and the attendance was down to 3,000, but the play was enthralling. Schwarz smartly caught Hayes in the slips, off Snooke, and then Warner, who was well set, played on to Vogler for 51. Crawford hit freely, especially through the covers, but from 166 for five the tail capitulated to 190 all out with Relf out to what Warner described as a 'wretched stroke'.

The fourth-innings target was a very challenging 284 to win and Louis Tancred, with his crouching batting style who had arguably been the best batsman on the 1904 tour, was quickly out, caught by Warner bowled Blythe for 10. Crawford then caught Hathorn in the slips, off Lees, but Shalders (38 not out) and White (16 not out) stayed until the close and with the score now on 68 for two, another 216 runs were still needed for victory.

On the third day, MCC were handicapped by the loss of Schofield Haigh who bowled only one over in the match. He had succumbed to a mild attack of dysentery and could hear the noise of the crowd from his hotel bed a quarter of a mile away. Leveson Gower fielded in his place. Blythe was also feeling ill, but ended up bowling 28 overs in the second innings.

The tourists made a good start on the third morning as Shalders was run out without any addition to the overnight score. Snooke was then trapped lbw to Lees for 9, Sinclair splendidly caught by Fane at long on, again off Lees for 5, and when wicketkeeper Board threw down the wicket to run out Faulkner for 6, the tide had surely turned in MCC's favour. South Africa were reeling on 105 for six and their target was 179 runs away with just four wickets standing. Nourse then came in to join Gordon White and, when he had made 11, gave an extremely difficult chance high and wide to the left of extra slip. The opportunity was not taken and in two hours and a quarter they added 121 runs together as home hopes started to rise again. Warner tried everything to break the partnership and turned to Wynyard's lobs but his three overs cost 15 valuable runs. Nevertheless, over thirty years later when writing Wynyard's obituary for *The Cricketer*, Warner wrote that Teddy 'was very unfortunate to have an lbw appeal given against him. At this distance in time, there is no harm in stating that the late GC White considered himself very lucky indeed to have been given "not-out" off one of Wynyard's lobs.' Relf eventually bowled White, with a fine delivery, for 81, after four hours batting. 226 for seven quickly became 230 for eight when Vogler was clean bowled by Hayes for 2 and the game was back in the balance once again.

Directly after the tea interval the ball kicked up awkwardly and Schwarz gave Relf a return catch for just 2. The score was now 239 for nine and with the last man now in, 45 runs were still needed. Warner must have been confident of success. The man walking to the crease was South Africa's captain, Percy Sherwell, but he was no ordinary number eleven as he demonstrated when he promptly hit his first delivery for four. Lees and Crawford replaced Relf and Hayes, but to no avail. All the bowlers were tiring in the extreme heat and on the hard, grassless ground. Haigh was sorely missed, especially as he always bowled well to left-handers like Nourse. The score was creeping towards the target and Crawford was proving inaccurate in this second innings. Relf came on from the opposite end to where he had previously operated and, with just 8 still needed, Crawford sent down a very fast delivery that Sherwell edged, but the ball went between Relf and Hayes down to the boundary. Nourse then made 3 on the leg side from Relf's bowling and the scores were tied.

Warner brought all his fielders up around the bat and Relf duly bowled three deliveries to Sherwell who played two and left one alone. Let MCC's captain describe in his own words what happened next:

> Relf sent down the slowest and easiest of full pitches on the leg side and Sherwell seized the opportunity and hit it for four to square leg. Relf! Relf! What were you about that at the crisis you should have presented Sherwell with a four, you, who had up till then bowled with so much determination and life, and with such accuracy of length?

Nourse said he simply heard Warner utter 'Good God, Bert!'

South Africa had won a Test match for the first time in their history, and it was on their home soil against England. Nourse had batted magnificently for 93 in three hours and forty minutes, and had been superbly supported by his captain, Sherwell, who it should be noted ended on 22 not out, almost exactly half the final number of runs needed when he came to the wicket.

There were descriptions of men in the crowd shrieking hysterically, throwing their hats and sticks in the air and carrying the two not-out batsmen shoulder high in to the pavilion. Thousands lingered afterwards and the entire South African side were made to appear on to the balcony of the Committee Room. Wynyard had only played in two Tests but both had finished with similar scenes, only on this occasion he was on the losing side.

Abe Bailey asked Warner to address the crowd. He complimented the victors, saying he had never seen a side fight a better rearguard action. He observed later that he thought this was the greatest match he ever played in. He wrote 'and so we were beaten, but defeat in such a struggle was glorious, for the first Test match will be talked of in South Africa as long as cricket is played there'. He also said that few of his batsmen had shown any aptitude to overcome the difficulties of facing leg-break bowling on unfamiliar matting wickets.

One interesting footnote to the story is that apparently Mohandas Gandhi (the honorific 'Mahatma' was not applied to him until 1914) and the Transvaal Indian Cricket Union wanted to see this Test but were unable to gain admission.

The next examination of the tourists' technique was forty-five miles north in the city of Pretoria. During their stay the team were able to visit the botanical gardens, zoo and the cemetery where ex-President Kruger was buried. On their first evening they attended a banquet held in their honour and chaired by the mayor, who had fought for the British in 1881 but for the Boers in the last conflict.

Warner objected to the local side turning out with fifteen players and eventually the game was played as a conventional eleven-a-side fixture, albeit it was still not treated as first-class. The venue was Berea Park, a ground that belonged to the Central South African Railway Company and had the potential to be one of the best in the country, although at that time the wicket was bumpy and the outfield not as true as it should have been.

It was a tight schedule. The first Test had only finished on the Thursday and by Saturday 6 January MCC were playing again in glorious weather in front of a crowd that included Sir Richard Solomon (Attorney General of the Transvaal) his wife and Sir Godfrey Lagden (a friend of the author Rider Haggard, and chairman of the South African Native Affairs Commission). Warner was staying with Lagden in his 'palace of all the comforts'.

By lunch the tourists had reached 86 for three. Shortly after the resumption Denton was bowled for 41 and Wynyard came out to the wicket. Hartley batted faultlessly for two and a half hours to score 77 but *The Times* thought Wynyard's contribution of 39 was lucky. The side made 338, with Fane and Warner going in at ten and eleven.

When Pretoria batted they were dismissed for just 87. Crawford, who came on as second change, had the remarkable figures of 6.1 overs, three maidens, five wickets for 6 runs. Warner had actually opened with Relf (four for 48) and Wynyard's lobs (one for 2 off four overs). Teddy's wicket was the opener, Zulch, stumped by Moon who had taken over the gloves from Board for this game. He did not bowl in the second innings although Warner put himself on, but the home side was still all out for 171 to lose by an innings and 80 runs.

Wynyard then took a three-week break away from his teammates in order to travel up through Southern Rhodesia to see Victoria Falls. This was not an easy journey to make because there was no direct route there by train from Pretoria. He would have to retrace the steps he had taken and pick up the once a week Cape-Bulawayo Express at De Aar junction. He could possibly change on to the Zambezi Express at Kimberley and go straight through, or stop at Bulawayo and take the train to the waterfalls from there. Either way it was a long detour, but there was another option of cutting across country by stagecoach from Pretoria to Mafeking and picking up a train from there.

It was the dream of Cecil Rhodes to have a railway that ran from the Cape all the way through to Cairo. Whilst this aspiration was never achieved, a new railway line had been completed on 24 August 1904 through to Victoria Falls and crossing the Zambezi River by way of a bridge below the waterfalls. The bridge was officially declared open on 12 September 1905, only four months before Wynyard's visit. It was and still is an incredible engineering feat, 650 feet long and 350 feet above the water, which at that time was the highest (above water level) anywhere in the world. The opening of the bridge then facilitated the extension of the railway on towards Lake Tanganyika.

In order to accommodate those working on these projects, the Victoria Falls Hotel was built. It was a simple building of wood with a corrugated iron roof and was raised from the ground to afford ventilation and freedom from damp and pests. It subsequently housed the growing tourist trade and very quickly an extension comprising two locomotion sheds was added. The hotel was capable of hosting twenty guests with twelve single and four double rooms, there was also a dining room, bar and office facilities. The cost was twenty-one shillings a night.

At this time the train went straight past the front of the hotel and then on to Victoria Falls railway station. This is where Wynyard alighted and made his way back to the hotel. It is remarkable to think that it was barely fifty years beforehand that David Livingstone, recovering from malaria, had set out from Linyanti and followed the Zambezi River downstream in search of a great waterfall about which he had heard much talk. Even by 1895 it is likely that no more than thirty white men had visited this spot, so Wynyard was one of the earliest Europeans to travel there by railway, stay at the hotel and be able to see Victoria Falls from the vantage point of the bridge. Rhodes and Sir Charles Metcalfe, who had actually chosen the site, were determined that passengers going over the bridge should have a very good view of the waterfalls from downstream and even feel the spray of water in their faces. The enterprising railway company allowed visitors to walk across if they paid a toll of one shilling.

Wynyard was also fortunate in the timing of his visit. The water was at its lowest in August and September, but by January and February when he arrived, there were huge masses of liquid. It virtually covered the whole width of the lip, which would only be visible in glimpses as the spray shifted about. The hotel was about a mile from the principal viewpoints and there were paths that allowed Teddy and the other visitors to approach every key sightseeing location and enjoy the scenery, including the bridge which, it was felt, only served to improve the overall view. If he wanted, he could also have been taken in a canoe to Livingstone Island to see the waterfalls from the same spot that the explorer had first witnessed them.

Wynyard had already travelled extensively but now experienced what is listed as one of the seven natural wonders of the world – the largest sheet of falling water anywhere to be seen. Unfortunately he contracted a fever during the course of the trip and it was to plague him for the rest of the tour. Quite what the other MCC cricketers thought of Wynyard's sightseeing diversion is not reported in Warner's chronicle, but for those who remained there were a number of journeys to undertake and three more matches to play.

After beating the Army in Pretoria, the team had a twenty-six hour train journey to Durban for one game, then on to Pietermaritzburg for another, before returning to Durban and enduring a rough sea passage to East London for the third fixture. The next match was a three-hour train journey away at King William's Town, a prosperous little town and a renowned centre for wool. There were rail links from De Aar to both East London and King William's Town, and Wynyard was back in the team for the contest beginning on Friday 2 February.

Denton and Fane had both scored centuries and the innings was well set by the time Wynyard came in at number six, but he was bowled when he had made 14. The tourists reached 415 for eight declared but a fine rain fell throughout Saturday making cricket impossible, although Warner and Moon were able to go to a rifle range whilst other members of the team played golf. When play resumed on the Monday, King William's Town were dismissed for 75 and 44, with Wynyard taking one for 9 in the second innings. Warner was left to ponder why he had ever been 'asked to play such an appallingly weak team'. Indeed, the next four games were all odds matches as well, so these fixtures were presumably seen as flag-flying exercises for the Empire rather than any meaningful cricket practice.

From King William's Town the team had an overnight railway journey to Queenstown, although the journey was interrupted by a two to three hour wait at Blaney Junction, which enabled everyone to appreciate the glorious night sky.

Queenstown was the centre of the Border district and the Sandringham cricket ground was one of the best in Southern Africa, with pleasant views of the hills all around. Crawford opened with Warner in another twelve-man side and carried his bat for a remarkable 212 not out towards a total of 400 for eight declared. Wynyard went in second wicket down and was bowled for 6 by Barnes, who had an action that Warner likened to Warwick Armstrong. The Queenstown Eighteen made just 111 (Blythe nine for 16) and 113 with Blythe taking the final wicket with his first ball of the last over of the match. It was here that Mr Harry Luff presented each member of the MCC party with a courtesy copy of the 1906 *Wisden* containing a full account of Teddy's tour with Lord Brackley to the Caribbean the previous winter.

From Queenstown the team journeyed to the centre of the wool and ostrich district at Cradock. The team slept in the saloon at the station overnight because it was an early 6.30 am start and they did not arrive at their destination until 9.30 pm. Whilst Queenstown was 'very English', Cradock was 'very Dutch' and, although the two towns were only fifty miles apart, there was no direct rail link between them. The tourists had to travel by train via Stormmead and Rosmead.

At the Standard CC Ground in Cradock, MCC played a Midlands Twenty-Two who batted first making 256. Wynyard reverted to the opener's slot alongside Warner and scored 47. The captain made 65 and Fane 67 towards a total of 413 for eight. A terrific thunderstorm left the ground underwater and the match was drawn. Despite the climatic conditions at the time of this visit, Cradock was much favoured by those suffering from lung problems and a sanatorium was being built on a site with warm springs.

There was then another all-night train journey to Grahamstown where the opponents were an Albany Eighteen at the City Lords ground beginning on 14 February. Wynyard took one catch in Albany's innings but he was absent when it was his turn to bat, presumably suffering from a recurrence of the fever contracted at Victoria Falls. A thunderstorm brought the game to an abrupt conclusion and the match was another draw.

There was a meal at the Grand Hotel followed by yet another night's travel, this time to Port Elizabeth where they were to start their nineteenth match of the tour the very next morning. In the last eleven days MCC had been expected to undertake three overnight train journeys and six days of cricket, which emphasised the gruelling nature of the tour arranged for them. Warner was particularly glad to arrive and be able 'to settle down here in the delightfully comfortable Port Elizabeth Club' to be 'feasted in their festive halls'. In addition to the captain being fed well, there was an excellent banquet for the team at the Humewood Hotel.

The next two fixtures were both at St George's Park, but the ground was not a good one. The matting was stretched on grass and proved to be the most difficult surface faced on tour as the ball both broke and bounced unpredictably. Wynyard, going in second wicket down, batted excellently against an attack led by Ernie Vogler for 29 before being bowled by Quirk. Port Elizabeth lost by an innings and 77 runs.

During the interval between the two matches there was time to visit Uitenhage, a pretty town over one hundred years old and located at the foot of the Winterhoek mountains, but then it was back to the ground for a first-class fixture against Eastern Province. Vogler top scored with 29 towards a total of 132 and then struck with the ball, taking six for 56, as MCC were dismissed for 201. The fact they reached such a total was largely thanks to Crawford, who opened but still formed an important partnership with Wynyard who was down at number eight in the batting order. The Surrey man top scored with 64 but Teddy ran out of partners when on 54. He was back to his best, combining impenetrable defence with powerful driving and pulling. Large crowds and a record gate watched his innings on the second day but Eastern Province were quickly dismissed for 92 and Warner's men secured an easy victory by ten wickets.

MCC then had another long and tiring train journey from Port Elizabeth to Oudtshoorn where the local industries were ostrich farming and tobacco production linked to cigar manufacture. The town was approximately sixty miles from Mossel Bay on the southern coast. The team left at 7.40 pm and it took twenty four hours to travel the 277 miles in order to play an odds match against Twenty-Two of South West Districts at the Recreation Ground.

The fixture began on Saturday 24 February, and there was something of a sensation when the tourists were dismissed for just 60. Denton was ill and had stayed at Port Elizabeth while Warner, Blythe and Lees had travelled direct to Johannesburg. Leveson Gower stepped in to captain and manager Ivor Difford was drafted into the team. Wynyard, possibly still suffering from his fever, was last man in and was bowled by Rogers for a duck. Indeed, Rogers bowled his right-arm fast-medium unchanged throughout both innings, keeping a good length on off stump, and taking five for 24 and three for 55. MCC were so impressed that the whole team signed a bat and presented it to him after the match. The local side made only 77 with Wynyard taking two catches, and then the tourists declared their second innings on 152 for six with Teddy moving up the order to number eight and making 28 before falling lbw again to Rogers. The game finished in a draw.

On Sunday's rest day, the team took the twenty-mile drive to the Cango Caves and crawled around the galleries and passages guided only by the light of a candle or magnesium wire to see what had been described as the finest stalactites in the world. Whilst this was clearly an enjoyable day's relaxation, as soon as the match was over on the following day, they had to make another very long and tiring journey up to Johannesburg for the second Test match beginning in a week's time on 6 March. Oudtshoorn was just about as far away from Johannesburg as it was possible to be.

At 9 am on Tuesday 27 February the side began their journey north and did not arrive at their destination until 7.30 am on Friday 2 March. This was hardly ideal preparation for a Test match, leaving them only the rest of that day, the weekend and the following Monday to recover from the tiredness of their train journey and to re-familiarise themselves with the conditions at the Old Wanderers ground. To make matters worse, although Warner had travelled up earlier, he had caught a severe chill en route and been forced to stay in bed for three to four days. He did have the consolation of being a guest at the home of a local dignitary, Mr Julius Jeppe. Warner's propensity to report these social contacts in his chronicles back home did not pass unnoticed and had prompted a satirical article about him published in *Punch*.

The team practised hard and managed to fit in two sessions during which they batted in pairs with the others bowling and fielding, so as to replicate a match situation. By the end they had real confidence that they would level the series. For the second Test a photograph was taken of the MCC side. Wynyard cut a powerful, imposing and authoritative figure at the end of the front row. He, along with the other members of the team, looked resplendent in their new team blazers, caps and whites. At a meeting held at Lord's on 27 July 1903 it was agreed, for the first time, that an England team would have a recognisable uniform of a dark blue coat with a narrow MCC trimming and a design of St George and the dragon wired on the front. The touring sweater was faced with red and yellow and trimmed with thin dark blue.

There was a controversial start to the Test when Warner requested that the South African umpire, Walter Richards, be replaced. Abe Bailey agreed to the request as he 'did not wish that Mr Warner should go back to England and state that the reason he lost the second Test was through the umpire'. Warner made no mention of this incident in his own book.

A heavy thunderstorm on the Tuesday morning of the first day threatened play and the rain did not stop until 11.30 am but, as the Old Wanderers ground was sand based, it dried well, making it possible to start at 2 o'clock. The matting was dry since it was not laid until a few minutes before play commenced. Wynyard commented that the dry mat was stretched over an even, sandy soil, but as that was wet, the wicket was slower than during the first Test. Warner won the toss and, remembering how easily the wicket had played under similar weather conditions when he had been a member of Lord Hawke's tour, he elected to bat.

There was just one change in the two sides from the first Test with Moon playing instead of Hayes. It was Wynyard who was the lucky man – *The Times* reported the intention had been to leave him out for Moon, but when Hayes injured his finger Teddy was slotted back into the team. Warner also rejigged the batting order with Crawford being drafted in to open, Fane now going in at number four and Wynyard dropping down two places to number six.

England had a very bad start with Warner receiving a fast, lifting ball from Snooke to be well caught by White at short slip when he had made just 6. Denton, who had been ill, did not last long as he was caught and bowled by Sinclair for 1 to make the score 13 for two. Fane played well until he was magnificently caught and bowled low down to his right by Faulkner. Crawford who had batted carefully for eighty-two minutes and made 23, then mishit Schwarz into the deep where he was caught by Faulkner.

At 62 for four, MCC were struggling again as Wynyard walked out to the wicket. Unfortunately, six minutes later, without having opened his account and only four runs having been added to the total, Vogler sent down a delivery that pitched on leg and knocked back Teddy's off stump.

Moon and Relf both struggled but managed to push the score past 100, but MCC crashed to 148 all out. It was a sign of the strength of the South African side that six bowlers had been used. *The Times* concluded 'the South African bowling and fielding was brilliant while the Englishmen were over anxious and too cautious'. At the close of the first day, South Africa had made 4 runs without loss.

The next morning Lees and Blythe opened the bowling and both Shalders and Tancred were missed in the slips. Warner felt that, since the first Test, Crawford had been pitching the ball too short and so did not bring him on until the score had reached 70, whereupon he immediately struck, bowling both openers in his first over. From 133 for five in the early afternoon, South Africa rallied to 277 by the end of the day for a lead of 129 runs.

MCC dropped three catches and were now facing an uphill battle as play began on the third day. Heavy rain had again fallen during the night and the weather was threatening and windy, which kept the crowds away, although the wicket was in perfectly good order. Warner then floridly described how 'the Goddess who presides over cricket loves to upset our calculations'. In his case this meant he was bowled very first ball off his pads by Snooke! The same bowler had Denton caught at the wicket by Sherwell, following which Crawford was dismissed by the same combination when he tried to hit a short, quick rising ball. The wicketkeeper also caught Moon, low down, off Sinclair, for a duck. 25 for four, 104 runs behind – yet again Wynyard was walking to the wicket in a Test match with a crisis facing his country!

The two Old Carthusians, Teddy and Fane, were batting together once more. In Warner's words, 'right gallantly did they fight.' The bowling and fielding was good. Fane excelled with his drives past extra cover and Wynyard hit well to leg, also making one 'splendid chop shot' off Faulkner. Lunch was approaching and hopes were beginning to rise. Both batsmen looked well set when Vogler was brought on and, with his third ball, caught and bowled Teddy for 30. Warner commented, 'Wynyard had played admirably and his loss at that moment meant a great deal to us.' It was his highest Test score so far and he had batted for seventy minutes, but Vogler had now been the perpetrator of his dismissal in each of his last three Test innings.

The score was 97 for five and Relf came in to join Fane. They progressed the score without further loss to 113 at lunch. In the afternoon, once Fane was dismissed for 65, MCC resistance faded and they were all out for 160. South Africa made 34 for the loss of Shalders and it was a comfortable victory by nine wickets achieved in three days. They were now 2-0 up in the series. Warner openly admitted that the batting of his side had failed lamentably and he, Denton, Board and Haigh had scored only 12 runs between them in the whole match.

The third Test was due to start immediately after the second but, as this had finished a day early, there was time to visit the Simmer and Jack Mine, the second-largest gold mine in the world (the biggest being in Australia). They employed 4,269 Chinese migrant workers who had become the subject of controversy back home in the General Election campaign. Warner visited the compound and whilst conceding their conditions 'would not appeal to you and me' saw 'not a vestige of slavery and those who oppose Chinese labour on this ground spoil their case'. One might have felt more reassured by this opinion if he had not referred in an earlier paragraph to the Chinese worker as 'the heathen'. Furthermore it should be noted that the President and Chairman of Consolidated Goldfields was Lord Harris, who had been highly critical back in England of those who had objected to the use of Chinese labour. Warner was aware of these views and, ever the establishment man, would not have wanted to speak out of turn.

Not surprisingly, South Africa remained unchanged for the third Test starting the following day, but for MCC Hayes was now fit. Whilst Warner had felt the Surrey professional had not really been at his best during this tour, he had originally been selected for the last game. Wynyard, who replaced him, had impressed in the second innings when all around him were failing and so was likely to keep his place. The decision was taken for Hayes to replace wicketkeeper Board. Moon, already in the side as a batsman, would take over the gloves. Teddy then had to withdraw because he had not shaken off the fever contracted at Victoria Falls. It was decided he should return to England the following week, meaning he missed the last four fixtures. Unfortunately, because of the imbalance of the programme, this included three of the Test matches. JC Hartley was drafted in to the team in his place.

MCC lost by 243 runs and South Africa had won the series comfortably, but there were still two more rubbers to play. MCC won the fourth Test in Cape Town by four wickets and Warner put this change of fortune down to the fact that the South African side was heavily dominated by Transvaal players who were more at home on the Johannesburg wicket than at Newlands.

South Africa were unchanged for the last Test but spare a thought for Henry ('Shrimp') Leveson Gower, the stand-in captain of the team when Plum was absent. Even though this was a dead rubber and the team was down to only twelve fit men, he still did not receive the nod and was the only member of the touring party not to play in any of the Tests. MCC were 146 behind after the first innings and although they reached 90 for three, collapsed to 130 all out losing their last five wickets in half an hour. It was a humbling defeat in only three days by an innings and 16 runs. South Africa had triumphed in the series 4-1.

MCC had been greeted with friendliness and hospitality everywhere they went and so, at least on the flag-flying front, the tour had been a great success, but what about the cricket? The side had played twenty-six matches in all, won seventeen, lost five (four Test matches and the game against Transvaal) and drawn four.

In his book, Warner wrote a detailed review and was very complimentary about his opponents. Their bowling attack was strong and varied with pace from Snooke and Sinclair (who could also bowl deceptively flighted leg-breaks), the orthodox left-arm spin of Nourse, allied to Schwarz's googlies and the leg-breaks and googlies of Faulkner, White and Wynyard's nemesis, Vogler. No two bowlers were alike and they were particularly suited to the matting wickets where the ball turned twice as quickly and broke twice as much as on grass.

Warner wrote that 'over and over again Vogler would pitch an inch or two outside the leg stump and miss the off stump by a foot; while Schwarz would do even more the other way'. This gives the impression that Schwarz, unlike the others, was an off-spinner. In fact the difference was that, whilst the other leg-break bowlers used the googly as their secret weapon, for Schwarz it was his stock delivery, often sent down at medium pace. Sydney Pardon wrote Schwarz's *Wisden* obituary and said the South African did not bowl a leg break at all.

Warner bemoaned the absence of 'a genuinely fast bowler and as many leg-break bowlers as can be found', a lament repeated by England skippers to the current day! Undoubtedly he had Bernard Bosanquet in mind. The irony was that the originator of the googly had played for Middlesex alongside Reggie Schwarz, who had been born and educated in England. They became such close friends that Bosanquet named his son Reginald – who went on to achieve fame in his own right as the much loved anchorman of the ITN *News at Ten* during the 1960s and 70s. Schwarz learned from his friend and passed the information on to his South African spin colleagues who had also seen for themselves the delivery, first known as the 'bosie', when they had toured England in 1904.

Warner's ultimate conclusion was that the batting and collapses by the tail had been the real difference between the two teams. He accepted that his own performance was a particular disappointment but the team had been handicapped by illness to key players, although he did not specifically mention Wynyard.

It is hard not to conclude that these illnesses had been brought about by the punishing schedule that had been arranged. Twenty-six matches and sixty-six days of cricket had been played between 2 December and 2 April, requiring 5,348 miles of railway travel plus a sea journey from Durban to East London. There had been twenty-two nights spent on a train and 'the constant application of the brake, jolting, shunting and none too comfortable sleeping accommodation' as Warner described it, had most definitely not been to his liking.

He also noted that exactly half of the fixtures played had been against the odds and 'nothing is more tiring or more detrimental to success against strong antagonists than match after match against inferior fifteens and eighteens'.

How to assess Teddy's tour and precisely what was his relationship with his captain?

Wynyard had played in fifteen out of the twenty-six matches, six of which were first-class, including two Test matches. In all games he aggregated 469 runs from twenty innings (four times not out) with a highest score of 82 (against Fifteen of Griqualand West in Kimberley) and an average of 29.31. In Test matches, he scored 59 runs from his four innings (all out) with a top score of 30 and an average of 14.75. Even so, he was still ahead of Hayes who had an average of 13.8, Warner with 8.9 and Hartley on 3.75. He bowled four overs for 17 runs but took no wickets and no catches. In all matches (including the Tests) he bowled a total of twelve overs, two maidens and took two wickets for 30 runs. He made seven catches, but only one in a first-class game – the opening fixture against Western Province.

This was always going to be a difficult tour for him. MCC were by no means a young side, having an average age of thirty-one years and six months, but Wynyard was forty-five by the end of the fifth Test and had not played competitive first-class cricket on a regular basis since the turn of the century. Admittedly he had performed well in the Caribbean the previous winter, but even there he had struggled on matting wickets and the South African bowlers were always going to be a much tougher challenge than their West Indian counterparts.

The letter Warner wrote to Mason in June 1905 made it clear that Wynyard was one of the first amateurs to be inked in for the tour. He was twelve years older than his captain and, given his experience, it is reasonable to assume that Plum would have been looking to him for some senior support both on and off the field. There is no evidence that Wynyard fulfilled this role if, indeed, it was expected of him. The statistics show that, from a cricketing viewpoint, his performances were disappointing. His decision to take a three-week break to visit Victoria Falls raises a question mark over the level of his commitment.

Life was very different a century ago, especially in the approach of the amateur to the game. The itinerary was not settled at the time when Teddy initially indicated his availability and originally there had been a suggestion of playing in Rhodesia. When the programme was finalised there was a two-month gap between the first and second Tests. Wynyard's decision to visit the waterfalls must have been agreed in advance with Warner and MCC. Given Wynyard's sense of adventure, it is easy to understand why travelling to see one of the natural wonders of the world was a preferred option to playing four cricket matches in a very punishing schedule, especially as he would be back in time for the remaining Tests. It showed Wynyard had a broader appreciation of what life had to offer, but the question must be asked: was Wynyard's decision to travel to Victoria Falls either sensible or fair?

It made a lot of sense for the oldest man in the side to take a break at some stage from the relentless train journeys, but Teddy did not spend his time relaxing on the beach. He was a man of action and chose to embark upon an even more exhausting journey through Rhodesia and back down to the Southern Cape, contracting a fever on the way that meant he missed the last three Tests. Furthermore, there were only fourteen cricketers on the tour and, as illness, injury and fatigue took its toll, Wynyard's absence by choice for three weeks greatly reduced Warner's flexibility in terms of providing any of his players with a much-needed rest.

Warner made no adverse comment in his book but, in truth, Wynyard received very little mention on any of the 233 pages. Given Teddy's seniority, one would have expected him to feature more prominently, but the captain was not really fulsome about anyone apart from Crawford and, to a lesser extent, Fane. The temperaments of Warner and Wynyard could not have been more different. Teddy was direct to the point of bluntness and not afraid if his views caused offence. Plum, on the other hand, preferred diplomacy to confrontation and was not a man to cause upset with his peers if he could possibly avoid it. Their relationship was probably based more on mutual respect than being a naturally comfortable and close one.

In his review, Warner merely said 'Wynyard did creditably in the second Test'. Was Teddy's subsequent illness another instance of opportunity thwarted? What is clear, is that by the time he left the tour he had not demonstrated any mastery over the South African leg spinners on matting, especially Vogler.

Time was running out for Teddy to prove himself at the highest level – but did that matter to him?

Pulling square after stepping back:
Teddy demonstrates his batting technique

15

MCC AND ICC
1906-08

Although Wynyard was forced to return early from South Africa, he had recovered sufficiently to play in the opening match of the season on 3 May 1906 for Hampshire at The Oval. Abel had retired from first-class cricket two years earlier and Jack Hobbs was now at the top of the Surrey batting order with the seasoned professional, Tom Hayward, as his partner. Hobbs was in fine form, driving well through the covers and pulling anything remotely short. He contributed 79 towards his side's 178. When Hampshire batted, only county captain Sprot and Wynyard (caught Hayward, bowled Knox for 14), made double figures and showed any ability to time the ball with precision as wickets fell fast all around them. They were all out for 68, and, the next day, Hobbs made more on his own, 69 not out, prompting *The Times* to profess 'he can play the greater game'. Hampshire barely fared any better second time round and were dismissed on the last day for 104 to lose by 337 runs. Teddy fell victim to his fellow South African tourists, being caught by Hayes off Crawford for 22.

On Monday 7 May, Wynyard moved north of the Thames to play for MCC at Lord's against the champion county, Yorkshire.

He batted at number six and made 41 not out in a total of 218. Respectability was achieved, though, only when Wynyard held the tail together with experience and skill as half the team were dismissed around him. *The Times* said he played a clever innings in bad light against a strong bowling attack that included Rhodes, Hirst and Haigh.

Ernie Vogler then proved how good a bowler he was away from matting and hot climes. Yorkshire could not cope with him as he took seven for 59 and they were all out for 132, with George Hirst scoring 61. When MCC batted, Hirst attempted to strike back with his relentless left-arm in swing and masterful control of line and length, but it was his partner, Wilfred Rhodes, who accounted for a cautious Wynyard after he had made 39. MCC ran out the eventual winners by 40 runs. A week later, it was England's other great left-arm bowler, Colin Blythe, who took Teddy's wicket for 33 when Kent lost to MCC by 69 runs.

On 17 May it was the return fixture between Hampshire and Surrey at the Officers Club Services Ground at Aldershot. It turned out be a similarly one-sided affair, with the visitors winning by ten wickets. These matches against Surrey were the only two Wynyard played for his county that season. Hampshire finished mid-division (seventh out of sixteen) in a Championship won for the first time by Kent.

Moving into June, Wynyard travelled up to Christ Church Ground in Oxford to play for a very strong Free Foresters side that included Tip Foster, Charles Kortright, Sammy Woods and Simpson-Hayward against the University. Wynyard opened and scored 105 before being bowled by Charterhouse-educated Wilfred Curwen as the Foresters made a mighty 518 in a convincing innings and 89-run win.

On 17 June, at Lord's, Teddy renewed his opening partnership with Lord Brackley in a side selected from the 1904/5 Caribbean tourists. Their opponents were the visiting West Indian team. Austin won the toss for the visitors and batted but his side fell victim to Simpson-Hayward's lobs as he took six for 37 from 16.5 overs. Richard Ollivierre top scored with 41, Constantine made 16 and Sydney

Smith 30, in a total of 158. Brackley's side responded with 213 and Wynyard top scored with 76. The tourists were in trouble at 95 for six when Smith (76) joined Harragin (86) and, together, they put on 149. The total of 298 set a challenging target of 244. Four wickets fell rapidly and the match was in the balance until Wynyard, with 70 not out, saw the team home to victory by two wickets.

There was criticism of Austin's tactical astuteness, especially in terms of the rather fixed field placings adopted when Wynyard was batting. The tourists knew he was a great master of the pull stroke but, even though he used it to great advantage, no one was put on the boundary to stop the flow of runs.

On 25 June, Teddy was back captaining MCC at Lord's for the match against Cambridge. The University batted first and made 185 but were fortunate when MCC replied because Wynyard chose to drop himself so low down the order that he was left stranded on 34 not out in a total of 268. Nevertheless, MCC had a comfortable victory with Teddy scoring 74 in the second innings, prompting *The Times* to comment about him that 'few batsmen are making more runs consistently this season'. During the match Wynyard passed 7,500 runs in first-class matches.

At the end of August, Wynyard made his traditional visit to Scarborough for their end-of-season festival. Like many amateurs he loved this event, not just for the cricket but for the cuisine, wine and companionship that were essential components of the week. It was a strong MCC side that won the toss against Yorkshire and batted, making 346, with Teddy going in at number six, being bowled by Hirst for 13. In the second innings Yorkshire were set what appeared to be a severe target of 287 to win, but it was reached with five wickets in hand thanks to 109 from Wilfred Rhodes who opened and 76 from his usual bowling partner, George Hirst, going in at number five.

Two powerful North and South sides met in the next festival match. The North won the toss and made the most of batting first, ending on 590 in spite of a strong South bowling attack comprising JWHT Douglas, Relf, Thompson, Hayes and Kent's Kenneth Hutchings. The South's batting was very disappointing, with Wynyard (7) opening with HK Foster (15), and they were forced to follow on. Although Teddy and Hutchings then scored 79 apiece it was not enough to prevent an innings defeat.

Wynyard's final match of the domestic season was for the Gentlemen against the Players at Scarborough, and it was a great success for him. The professionals, captained by Tunnicliffe, won the toss and batted. Denton made a magnificent 157 not out in a total of 324, but there was still time for the amateurs to bat, and they had made 70 for one (Teddy 27 not out) by the close. Hirst bowled HK Foster early next morning, bringing Fane to the wicket with the score on 83 for two. The two Old Carthusians stayed together for eighty minutes, in which time they put on 154 runs with the Essex batsman contributing 61. *The Times* said:

> Capt Wynyard drove with all his old power and accuracy in the last stages of his innings. He was rather stiff in his method to start with and it took him one hour and twenty minutes to make the first 50 runs but he then forced the pace so freely that forty minutes later his score had reached three figures. He was finally well caught at cover point by Tyldesley off Thompson for 137.

This was a very impressive performance bearing in mind he was facing a bowling attack of Hirst, Myers, Rhodes, Thompson and Haigh. His innings included one six and seventeen fours. His driving was said by his old school magazine to have been 'one of the finest batting performances of the festival'. In Warner's *Gentlemen v Players 1806-1949* he described Wynyard as a veteran 'who in his earlier days had been in the front rank as a batsman'. The Gentlemen reached 387 to achieve a first innings lead of 63.

Ernie Hayes raced to 122 not out and the Players declared on 374 for six, setting a target of 312 to win. In the two hours that remained there was no chance of the runs being made, although Spooner and Wynyard hit 50 in the first thirty minutes. They went on to record an opening partnership of 98 when Hayes caught Teddy, off Rhodes, for 42. The match was drawn with JWHT Douglas, in his first match for the Gentlemen, still at the crease on 35 not out by the close of play.

It had been a successful season for Teddy. In first-class matches he totalled 614 runs with a highest score of 137 in his last match. His average of 38.37 was his best since 1900. He had also found time to play alongside his old Hampshire teammate, Major Poore, in the Norwich cricket week.

The New Zealand Cricket Council had asked MCC to extend their Australian tour scheduled for that season to include New Zealand. MCC decided not to send a team Down Under because of the serious friction that had arisen between the Melbourne Cricket Club and the Australian Board of Control for International Cricket (ACB) that had been formed in 1905. Until that time tours by Australian teams had been organised privately or by the players themselves and the proceeds distributed amongst those who were involved. Just as MCC had taken over responsibility for running England's overseas tours, ACB decided to adopt this role in Australia, but the Board's structure did not include any player representation. The Melbourne Cricket Club wanted to control Australian cricket, and so secured the support of prominent players behind ACB's back. MCC felt that to send an England side before the dispute was settled would simply fan the flames and make the feud worse. Nevertheless, they did accept New Zealand's invitation, and agreed to send an all-amateur team for a separate tour to play sixteen matches there.

MCC asked Teddy Wynyard to be the captain of a party of fourteen cricketers. A number of those eventually selected had either played with or against him during the season. The three best players accompanying him were Charles de Trafford (whose wife was also making the trip), George Simpson-Hayward and JWHT (nicknamed 'Johnny Won't Hit Today') Douglas of Essex.

Douglas went on to captain England on his Test debut in 1911 and journalist/cricket historian Sir Home Gordon wrote 'Johnny felt contempt for any physical weakness or fatigue being himself as hard as iron and believing everybody could also be if he had grit. A weakness as a captain was his inability to grasp that others were not as he was himself.' England cricketer and captain, Arthur Carr, described Douglas as 'a determined, stand no nonsense chap. Some people did not take to him at first, but when you got to know him you discovered what was really in him.' There are very clear shades of Wynyard in those character assessments, and one imagines precisely the sort of man Teddy would want with him given the inexperience of the rest of his New Zealand touring party.

The composition of the team and the absence of any professional was an indication that Wynyard and MCC did not anticipate strong opposition when they reached their destination. The itinerary comprised seventeen games including a stopover match in South Africa. Eleven fixtures were first-class, including two matches against each of the four main provincial teams (Auckland, Wellington, Canterbury and Otago), a game against Hawke's Bay, and two unofficial Tests where the opponents would be the New Zealand national team.

On Thursday 18 October 1906 the team, barring Johnson, who was making his own way, left Tilbury on board SS *Corinthic*. The thirteen cricketers travelled first-class and doubtless Teddy was looking forward to his first visit to this part of the world, which would afford him the opportunity to meet up with the large branch of the Wynyard family in New Zealand. His half brother Henry was unable to accompany him, as he had done to South Africa, because he was studying for his Bar exams – on 12 January 1907 *The Times* recorded his Class III pass in the Constitutional Law and Legal History paper for the Inns of Court.

The ship stopped en route at Cape Town and a one-day match was played at Newlands on 10 November 1906. The Western Province side included Tip Snooke, his brother Stanley and JJ Kotze. Their captain, Murray Bisset, could not have been more accommodating to Wynyard, giving him the choice of batting or fielding. Teddy chose to bowl and the home side graciously declared on 129 for six. The target was reached with one wicket to spare, but MCC batted on for practice and were 133 all out. Teddy dropped himself down the order to number eight but was bowled by Kotze for 1.

SS *Corinthic* docked at Wellington at the southern tip of North Island on Thursday 6 December. The party then travelled north to Auckland for their opening, first-class game that began eight days later. The whole team practised from 11 o'clock until 1 and had lunch, with the match starting at 2 o'clock. The wicket comprised bulli soil imported from Sydney and was a good surface, but it had little life in it. Wynyard won the toss and batted but his side performed badly. MCC were all out for 172, although their total could have been greater if Teddy had not chosen to bat as low down as number nine, and he was left stranded on 11 not out.

Rugby was the main interest in the area, but cricket had just started to be taught in the schools and there was a large gate when play resumed at midday on Saturday. The weather was ideal for cricket, with bright sunshine and a cooling breeze, as Auckland progressed to 195 for a first innings lead of 23. *The Times* commented on MCC's fielding that 'with the exception of Captain Wynyard's [it] was never clean and smart' and 'the bowling owed a lot to Simpson-Hayward's six for 39'. The tourists began their second innings badly, but there was an important stand between Branston (73) and his captain that put on 120 for the eighth wicket. *The Times* commented 'Captain Wynyard contributed a faultless innings of 48 not out which was invaluable to his side and a lesson to all to watch'. Again he had been selfless as a captain by going in low down the order and giving the younger players their chance. The game ended in a draw.

The aim was to begin the matches on a Friday so that the maximum gate could be secured, and the next game was 275 miles south against a Wanganui Fifteen at Cook's Gardens, beginning on 21 December. There was time for the tourists to enjoy a picturesque trip down the Wanganui River and the cricket proved not to be very difficult for them. MCC played twelve but actually only batted eleven (Wynyard missing out), also fielding only eleven at any one time.

The next game was a first-class fixture at Basin Reserve against Wellington starting at 2 o'clock on a boiling-hot Christmas Day. Teddy won the toss and again decided to bat. Burns batted well for 51, but again it was down to the captain, coming in at number nine, to rally the tail. He ended on 27 not out as his side was dismissed for 204. Wellington were 26 for two at the close of play.

Boxing Day morning was not a happy one for the tourists. In just one hour they sustained three injuries. Douglas strained his side and Torrens injured a tendon in his knee that prevented him from bowling, although he could subsequently bat and field. Sandwiched in between these two incidents, however, MCC sustained the worst blow imaginable. Their captain, Teddy Wynyard, snapped a tendon in his knee and was carried from the field. He could take no further part in the tour and was invalided home. Although de Trafford was not playing in this game, doubtless enjoying Christmas festivities with his wife, he took over the captaincy for the remainder of the fixtures.

Earlier a team photograph had been taken and, whilst Teddy stood tall, he now appeared a tad portly, not portraying the powerful athletic image of his youth. His subsequent injury was further testimony that age was starting to catch up with him. He returned on board the same ship that had taken him out, SS *Corinthic*, docking in Tilbury on 18 February 1907. He had spent 100 days travelling to and from New Zealand only to be in the country for barely three weeks before he sustained a potentially career-threatening injury.

Fortunately the injury appears not to have been as serious as first thought because, on 25 March, Wynyard was back playing for Hampshire Hogs in a twelve-a-side game against Charterhouse. The weather was not good, but Teddy opened the batting and made 52, then played alongside Conan Doyle for MCC in a two-day fixture against Hampstead. His only two first-class matches of the domestic summer were for MCC, first against Cambridge, then Oxford University. His last match was at Lord's, on 5 August, against the Public Schools captained by Albert 'Guy' Pawson of Winchester. Wynyard opened the batting and retired when he had scored 109 towards his side's total of 303. The Schools lost by an innings and 24 runs.

He did not play at all that season for Hampshire, who finished twelfth of the sixteen counties in a Championship won by Nottinghamshire. For Teddy, the summer was of greater significance for events happening off the field.

On 11 July, along with many other dignitaries and staff from MCC, he was present at Paddington Cemetery in Kilburn for the funeral of JA Murdoch, the Assistant Secretary at Lord's from 1878 until his death. Since leaving Sandhurst in 1903, Teddy had been involved in running MCC cricket teams and had chosen to captain them rather than play on a regular basis for his county. He now succeeded Murdoch as Assistant Secretary at Marylebone and held the position until 1917, although it appears he operated only during the summer months.

In his new role he inherited the issue of a tour to Australia. After MCC had declined an invitation to tour in 1906/7, it was thought politically desirable to send a team the following winter. Jackson declined the captaincy and MCC offered the ultimate accolade to Wynyard. Sir John Masterman had this to say:

> In 1907 he was invited to captain the MCC (or England) side in Australia and was compelled to decline the honour for 'domestic reasons'. I do not know what these reasons were, but I have always thought that that tour might and ought to have been the crown of his career. Had he been able to go, and had he been in form, he would I think, be numbered among the cricket 'immortals'.

I have found no public explanation for the 'domestic reasons' that prevented his acceptance of this prestigious position. He was very close to his family, and on 17 January 1908, his younger sister Rose died at just forty-one years of age. She lived at St Peter's House in Kilburn but at the time of her death was in St Peter's Memorial Home at Woking. It could be the case, therefore, that he knew the seriousness of her illness and felt he could not be out of the country for such a long period of time.

The greatest commanders know when to engage the enemy and the times when discretion is the better part of valour. Wynyard was never one to shy away from a fight, but was he applying this military maxim to his cricketing career? A tour of Australia was the ultimate examination of a player's ability. Teddy had only played two first-class matches during the summer and was now forty-six years of age. He had struggled when playing Test cricket in South Africa and had suffered a serious injury the following winter. Could his body, not to mention his game, stand the challenges of an Ashes tour? I would like to think he realised that this was a Test too far for him. Or, perhaps, he just did not want the job at his age and had other interests to pursue?

Masterman did qualify his own assessment with the caveat 'had he been in form' and admittedly the hard, fast Australian wickets may have been more to his liking. Nevertheless, Wynyard's chance to become one of the immortals had really been ten years earlier when he was asked to travel with Stoddart's team, only for the War Office to intervene and scupper his dreams.

As events transpired, it is unlikely Teddy's reputation would have been enhanced had he accepted MCC's offer. The role was given to AO Jones who had just captained Nottinghamshire to their first County Championship title. He was taken seriously ill in Brisbane with consumption and missed the first three Tests, with a reluctant Fane taking over in his absence. It was a strong Australian side captained by Monty Noble and, although the final tally flattered them, they regained the Ashes comfortably 4-1.

MCC was not helped in their selection by the fact that some of the amateur cricketers preferred a much shorter tour to New York and Teddy Wynyard was one of them!

Cricket in North America was largely played in the corridor along the east coast between Philadelphia and New York. The four chief clubs were Philadelphia, Germantown, Merion and Belmont, with Bart King, George Patterson and John Lester as the country's best players.

The party selected to play four matches in the USA and one in Canada was to be captained by HV Hesketh-Prichard. In addition to Wynyard, the side included Johnny Douglas, George Simpson-Hayward and Test wicketkeeper Gregor MacGregor. On Saturday 7 September 1907, nine cricketers left Euston by the midday special for Liverpool, where they embarked on the Cunard liner SS *Lucania*, scheduled to arrive in New York on the following Saturday, 14 September. The other two members of the party were South Africans, Reggie Schwarz and Tip Snooke, but they were playing for their country at the Scarborough Festival and so were unavailable for the start of the tour.

It meant Hesketh-Pritchard had to draft two local players, Bohlen and Bonner, into MCC's team against All New York. MCC batted first and Wynyard opened with Douglas. JWHT made 63 and Teddy recorded 145, including one six and twenty-four fours in a drawn game.

The side then moved on to Germantown Cricket Club at Manheim for a three-day first-class fixture against the Gentlemen of Philadelphia beginning on 20 September. Snooke and Schwarz had caught up with the party and Bohlen switched allegiance to play for the opposition. The home side included John Barton 'Bart' King and Herbert 'Ranji' Hordern. King was one of the pioneers of swing bowling and Plum Warner described him 'as one of the finest bowlers of all time'. Hordern was born in Sydney and selected for Australia seven times. He was a leg break/googly bowler and, once again, this proved to be Wynyard's Achilles heel. He opened with Douglas and was bowled by Hordern for 13. MCC made 162, with Hordern taking five for 41. King bowled Teddy for only 4 in the second innings in a drawn game. MCC won the third game comfortably against Philadelphia Colts Eighteen, with Wynyard only scoring 2.

The return fixture against the Gentlemen of Philadelphia was at the Merion Cricket Club in Haverford. Wynyard fell victim in both innings to Hordern, scoring just 3 and 2. Philadelphia needed only 120 in their second innings for a famous victory but the captain, Hesketh-Prichard, stepped up to the plate taking seven for 20 leaving the home side clinging on for a draw at 60 for nine.

The final match of the tour saw MCC travel north of the border to Ottawa for a non-first-class fixture against Canada beginning on Wednesday 2 October. Wynyard opened and, freed from the leg breaks and googlies of Hordern allied to the menacing swing of Bart King, top scored with 49, but it was another disappointing total for the tourists of 119. The suspicion must be that the pitches were not of the highest quality because Canada were then dismissed for 94 in another drawn match.

Upon his return from America and having declined the captaincy for the tour to Australia, Teddy had his first free winter since his retirement from the Army and seized the opportunity to return to winter sports in Davos. *The Times* observed 'Davos may well claim to be the tobogganing resort par excellence'. It was time for fresh challenges though, and Teddy had taken up the sport of bandy, similar to ice hockey but played on a larger rink with a small ball and eleven players a side.

The bandy match between Davos and St Moritz had first been played in 1894 and the encounters alternated between the two resorts. In 1908 it was the turn of Davos to host the event, but it had been ten years since St Moritz had won there. On the day it snowed all morning and only stopped about half an hour before the game began. The Pawson brothers were unavailable and Wynyard substituted ably for Guy Pawson. The report on the match said, 'he played a wonderful game for a man of his years: despite his lack of pace he was the most dangerous forward on the Davos side.' Nevertheless the Davos forwards did not combine well together and the visitors won comfortably 3-0.

Wynyard's cricketing summer began on 28 May when MCC hosted the Royal Academy of Arts in a drawn game at Lord's, which was not treated as first-class. The visitors were dismissed for 177, with Arthur Conan Doyle opening the bowling and securing four for 45.

At the end of June, Oxford University came to St John's Wood. Wynyard opened the batting with Ranjitsinhji in a drawn match. An interesting one-day fixture had been arranged for Lord's on 10 July, when Egypt and Soudan were the visitors. Both Lord Brackley and Conan Doyle turned out again for MCC scoring 3 and 13 respectively with Wynyard putting himself in as last man. He contributed 5 towards a total of 179 and then took one for 15 as Egypt won on first innings by 45 runs.

August's bank holiday weekend saw the traditional fixture that was so close to Teddy's heart, MCC versus Public Schools. Teddy went in at third wicket down and just after lunch was dropped at mid off, but went on to make 33 before falling victim again to leg spin. MCC made 359, but the Public Schools were well in excess of 100 for the loss of only one wicket, with five minutes to go, when Bardsley, from Shrewsbury School, who had made 25 enterprising runs, hit one of Wynyard's lobs hard back down the ground only to be caught by the bowler. Next morning they progressed to an impressive 333 with Teddy ending with figures of two for 30 off eleven overs. Wynyard then declared on 161 for six, top scoring with 58 in the process, setting the opposition 188 for victory, but the game ended in a draw.

Thursday 6 August 1908 was Ladies Day during Canterbury Week and Wynyard had, until now, never played at the Kent festival. This was an omission he intended to rectify and he made himself available for selection by Hampshire against a Kent side that included 21-year-old Frank Woolley and Colin Blythe. Kent were all out for 203, with Teddy having a mixed day in the field, catching Arthur Day at the second attempt at short slip but then dropping Humphreys at long on. In reply, with the score on 113 for three, Wynyard walked to the wicket for his first County Championship innings in over two years. He was in for over an hour but seemed unable to judge the varying flights of Blythe's deliveries. The Kent bowler ended with figures of eight for 83 and lured nearly all of his victims forward only to beat them when they failed to reach the pitch of the ball. Wynyard fell in this way, edging a quickly turning delivery to Hurst at short slip for 13. Hampshire's innings closed just after lunch on 178, giving the home county a lead of 25. By close of play Kent stood at 185 for eight, with Teddy having caught opener Hardinge at slip for 2.

This was not just a festival of cricket but also a significant social occasion, with Friday evening being the Old Stagers review of current events. The Old Stagers was the amateur theatrical group founded in 1842 by Frederick Ponsonby to perform during Canterbury week and that year's production was entitled *L'entente cordiale*. *The Times* commented upon:

> ...the strong feeling of fellowship which underneath all the fooling and frolic of the Old Stagers exists among the cricketers and cricket lovers during the week. Mrs Alwyn Fellowes as the spirit of Zingari attended by Capt EG Wynyard and other Zingari, carries the audience with her when she says that she 'is sure you will agree that the hitting was free when the game was Kent versus Zingari'.

Teddy appears to have taken to the boards!

It was back to serious business on the Saturday morning with the match so finely poised. The weather kept fine but the tail rallied until Wynyard caught Blythe at second slip, leaving Day on 77 not out and Kent on 240. Hampshire needed 266 to win. In the afternoon, when Sprot was run out and with Hampshire on 86 for three, it was time for Wynyard to walk to the crease for what was to be his last Championship innings for his county. After reaching double figures he was smartly stumped by Huish, trying to attack Blythe, for 14. It was both poignant and appropriate that, as Wynyard walked back into the pavilion and the door closed on his Hampshire career, it was a young 21-year-old who opened the professionals' door to make his way out to the wicket. He was to go on to become one of the county's greatest ever servants and best loved players, Charles Phillip Mead.

The total reached 215 for nine and there was still 51 needed for victory but, with just four minutes left on the clock, Hampshire made their target to secure a memorable win.

It was a fitting end to Wynyard's Hampshire career that had begun nearly thirty years before, on 6 June 1878, at Lord's against MCC. It was not a formal decision to retire because a year later his name was listed as one of those available for selection for the same fixture. As events turned out, however, he did not play again.

Whilst his Championship playing days may have been over, he still continued to play first-class cricket. A month later there was another landmark game to be enjoyed. 10 September 1908 was the exact anniversary of the match played 130 years earlier between Hambledon and All England on Broad Halfpenny Down. To mark the event a grand granite obelisk had been built in front of the famous Bat and Ball Inn and it had been hoped the unveiling ceremony would be performed by WG Grace. Unfortunately he cried off, and this was the occasion when Henry Warren's attempt at his impersonation proved to be less successful than Wynyard's at Sandhurst seven years earlier.

The wicket was in fairly good condition, but the outfield was simply the turf of the Downs, untouched by a mowing machine or scythe, with outcrops of flint and chalk. From the little two-storey, four-windowed Bat and Ball Inn, the ground sloped down rapidly, making it very difficult for fielders in the deep. There were no boundaries except for half a dozen tents and a hedge that occupied half of the ground along with cars and carriages parked by the spectators. Indeed, *Cricket* magazine said there were as many as 200 cars, 400 carriages and 641 bicycles, although it was not clear precisely who counted them! It was a blustery day and the scene resembled Derby Day on the Downs, with parties lunching on the grass and minstrels playing along with a band from the Mercury Training Ship.

Two strong twelve-a-side teams had been assembled, and at 12.30 pm, later than had been scheduled, Hambledon, comprising two men from the village (Whalley-Tooker and Langridge) plus largely the Hampshire County side, took the field to the strains of 'Auld Lang Syne'. It proved a difficult wicket to bat on, and Newman took seven wickets before lunch.

Before play resumed in the afternoon, Edward Sprot, as the Hampshire County captain, stepped in to replace Grace and unveiled the obelisk that had been erected by public subscription to mark the site of the old Hambledon ground. Dr Fearon (Archdeacon of Winchester) said a few words about famous players 'and the influence of cricket on the national character'.

England were then dismissed for 124 after only one hour and forty-five minutes of play. At 3.45 pm the Hambledon innings was opened by Wynyard and CB Fry – but surely Fry was a Man of Sussex and not Hampshire?

There had been rumours of discord within the Sussex side, with Fry being viewed as not an easy man to befriend, but when he became Captain Superintendent of the Training Ship Mercury, a naval training establishment based at Hamble in Hampshire, he wrote to Sussex in March 1909 to say his appointment meant he had to resign the captaincy. He then offered his services to Hampshire and was swiftly accepted, playing for them until 1921.

Clearly all of this was in the offing as Fry had been instrumental in organising the Hambledon team. His opening partnership with Wynyard had reached 22 when Jack Hearne bowled CB for 17. Edward Sprot then joined Teddy and, according to *The Times*, 'the two went in for some real country hitting' until Sprot was caught on the boundary for 37. Llewellyn was then well taken in the slips by Trott for a duck, but a long stand followed between the Reverend WV Jephson and Wynyard. No fewer than six bowlers were tried against them but, when the score had reached 148, Wynyard was out, caught at long on by Hearne off Gloucestershire's Dennett for 59. The stand had put on 110 in seventy minutes, and at the close Hambledon were 182 for six with Jephson on 69 not out.

When play resumed next day, Jephson became the first player to score a century against overarm bowling on Broad Halfpenny Down. He ended on 114 not out towards a total of 277, giving Hambledon a lead of 153 runs. When England resumed their innings, Langridge, the local gardener, was given fourteen overs and took the wicket of Leach, who was caught in the slips by Wynyard for 80. Jessop was in an attacking frame of mind hitting 48 off thirty-two balls in just twenty minutes, and when stumps were drawn the score was 277 for five. *The Times* correspondent, seeking sympathy, observed 'playing cricket and looking on at it on the Hampshire Downs in September is uncommonly cold work after 4 o'clock.'

The following day the last five wickets produced only another 32 runs. Hambledon needed 157 runs to win. Fry opened with Llewellyn this time round, and he made 84 not out to see his side home to a five wicket victory, with Teddy batting with him at the end on 9 not out.

The cricketing summer of 1908 proved to be far more active for Wynyard off the field than on it. After the previous year's successful tour of England by South Africa, Abe Bailey had wanted to strike while the iron was hot to ensure the promotion of his country's cricketing cause. On 30 November 1907, on his way home, he wrote to Francis Lacey at MCC suggesting the formation of an Imperial Cricket Board whose function would be to formulate rules and regulations to govern international matches involving England, Australia and South Africa. He also wished to promote a triangular Test series for 1909.

Wynyard was present at Lord's on 10 December 1907 for the annual meeting of county cricket club secretaries when the cricket fixtures for the following season were arranged. On that occasion Bailey's letter was read out and it was agreed the proposals should be considered. On 30 December news came out of Johannesburg that the South African Cricket Association (SACA) had sent a cablegram to Wynyard offering him the appointment of being their representative on the Imperial Cricket Board when such a board was created. The message went on to stress how enthusiastic the SACA were about a triangular tournament in 1909, preferably in England, failing which in South Africa. They had 'great hopes of the Marylebone Cricket Club' and for their part the SACA would 'endeavour to arrange matters here'.

On January 3 1908, Bailey gave an interview in which he urged the formation of an Imperial Board of Control on which the colonies should have one representative each, and England one representative in addition to the Chairman. He confirmed that Teddy had accepted the appointment as South Africa's representative and went on to stress that it was not so much a question of making it a financial success, as of developing the sport and 'establishing a further tie between Great Britain and the Colonies'.

The addition of Wynyard to Bailey's payroll (for it was a paid position) made them interesting bedfellows. The self-made millionaire, Bailey, perhaps saw in the military Englishman the direct, no nonsense and fearless advocate he needed.

On 20 February MCC's cricket sub-committee met to discuss the proposed triangular Test tournament, with Leslie Poidevin attending on behalf of Australia and Wynyard looking after South Africa's interests. Clearly this was not going to be plain sailing. After what *The Times* described as 'a protracted meeting', Lacey on behalf of MCC stated 'there was nothing yet for publication'. Nevertheless, on 27 April it was decided to send invitations to South Africa and Australia to play in 1909.

On 17 June, Australia declined, whereupon the Advisory Committee of the Counties met on 3 July with Lord Harris in the chair. All of the counties were represented except for Derbyshire, and there were also three delegates for the Minor Counties. Whilst Teddy represented South Africa, regrettably Poidevin, who had been invited, was not present on behalf of Australia. Lord Harris referred to two cable messages and a letter from Bailey. Wynyard stressed the tournament was being suggested only as an experiment in 1909 and repudiated the idea that South Africa had acted in any underhand manner.

After debate, Fry (Sussex) proposed and Bencraft (Hampshire) seconded a resolution, carried by a large majority, 'that the representatives of the counties here are in favour of a triangular cricket contest'. A second resolution was also carried after the original wording was 'slightly altered' (according to *The Times*) and it read, 'that the MCC be asked to impress on the Australian Board of Control that the counties are so strongly in favour of the triangular contest that the MCC would not be in a position to invite any colonial eleven in 1909 except for that purpose.'

This stance immediately prompted a strong reaction from Australia and her supporters, as evidenced by correspondence addressed to The Editor of *The Times*. The first letter came from a particularly influential figure in both cricketing and political circles, FS Jackson. It seemed to him that MCC's second resolution was 'needlessly curt, not to say ungenerous' though he could not believe there was an intention to offend. He made the point that Australia would, in the ordinary course of events, have sent a team the following summer 'under the direction of the new Board of Control which has been formed largely in deference to our wishes'. He continued that the triangular tournament had been suggested shortly after the South African tour last year and, 'while received in a kindly spirit, it aroused no great amount of enthusiasm and that it was, indeed quietly hinted that its adoption depended entirely on whether or not the Australians would be prepared to take part in the tournament.' Australia had declined but interestingly, and not without significance, Jackson said, 'what their reasons may be for refusal I know not. They may think the time inopportune or want more time to consider the scheme in detail.' Their decision 'is surely no sufficient cause for their being peremptorily told that they must either join in the tournament or stay at home'. He wanted the original invitation reinstated for Australia to tour alone.

On 9 July, JH Carruthers, President of the New South Wales Cricket Association but writing in a personal capacity, weighed in strongly behind Jackson. There had been a serious misunderstanding as to the Australian point of view. The proposed tournament was 'entirely novel' and 'not of our seeking in Australia and to force it upon us is to place at risk' what Carruthers described as 'our mutual current of existence'. He asserted, 'it is due to us to be your visitors next year.' Australia held the Ashes and, 'if anyone dared to make a change and insist upon it, surely the right, if any, belongs to the holders of the championship. As the holders of the Ashes we propose no change.'

Before considering any triangular tournament, he wanted South Africa to tour Australia, which they had never done. He continued, 'as the holders of the cricket championship why should Australia risk losing what it has fought so long for by multiplying the test contests on strange grounds with two sets of competitors in a triangular contest in which there will be added to the stress and fatigue of long journeys the strain of just about double the test matches?' He added that Australia had to finance the undertaking and could not ignore this aspect and 'who can blame them for not taking risks?'

He concluded with the admission that, whilst the Board of Control now represented the associated cricketing clubs of Australia, the players 'still exhibit impatience at that control but recognize Australia need the Board in the same way MCC controls cricket well and wisely in England'. He pleaded for a review of the decision and quoted Burke 'change is a word of ill-omen to happy ears' and posed the question 'why not be satisfied with what has done so much for the national game?' Not concepts readily espoused by modern day management where the mantra is change or die!

There then came support from Gilbert Jessop, who had attended as Gloucestershire's representative at the Advisory Committee meeting, though he too stressed his view was a personal one. MCC had already sent an invitation to Australia and he threw light on what *The Times* had described as a 'slight alteration' to the wording of the second resolution. Originally he indicated it had read 'something to the effect that whether the Australians saw fit or not to join in the proposed triangular scheme it would not interfere with their arranged visit for 1909'. It seemed to him there had been a change in position (an understatement if ever there was one) and 'our good friends the Australians have been treated somewhat cavalierly. To hold a pistol to one's head is no slight ordeal to face. I only hope - in my private capacity again – that our brethren from the Southern Cross will dare the pistol to be snapped.'

The gauntlet had been thrown down and South Africa's representative in England had to respond. In, as far as I can determine, the only letter to the Editor of *The Times* published from Wynyard, he wrote in the following terms:

Sir,

On reading the letters of Messrs Jackson and Jessop one cannot refrain from asking if they were present respectively at the meetings of the MCC Committee and of the Advisory County Cricket Committee when the resolutions to which they took exception were passed, as I am sure their views would have been received with respect, even if they were not deemed to be conclusive.

It seems regrettable that they should attempt to complicate the relationships between England, Australia and South Africa, now that after careful consideration a decision has been arrived at, by suggesting to Australia that they have been intentionally slighted.

Looking at the reasonable interpretation of the resolutions, and of the cable message of the MCC they mean, if they mean anything at all, that the counties do not wish to play a series of matches in 1909 with Australia alone; and, having regard, to this expression of feeling, it would be futile for the MCC to invite them to England unless they could be certain to arrange an attractive list of fixtures in which they could take part.

The position of the MCC in these matters seems to be that of agent for the counties, with a right of veto in case their views do not coincide with the best traditions of cricket.

The MCC would obviously place the Australians and themselves in a false position if they invited the Australians to England against the wishes of the counties; and I do not think that such an invitation would be acceptable to the Australians.

The "pistol at the head" suggestion appears to me tactless as well as inopportune.

The position I have taken up, acting as agent for the South African Cricket Association, has not always been quite fairly represented.

The request of the South African Cricket Association had no definite reference to the future beyond 1909. It was, as I clearly pointed out at the meeting of the ACCC at Lord's an attempt to bring into operation an Imperial contest that year as an experiment. If it proved a failure it need not be repeated. The South African Cricket Association were prepared to guarantee the Australians against pecuniary loss, and were prepared, if necessary, to make sacrifices in order to effect this. They wished, moreover, to establish an Imperial conference, at which future contests between the three countries could be discussed and, if possible, satisfactorily mapped out.

Many hard things have been said about the South African Cricket Association and many hinted at the attitude taken up by them; but no one can honestly say that they have done anything beyond making an attempt to bring about a meeting of the three countries with the best motives, and in making the attempt they have done nothing they did not believe were in the best interests of the game.

There are let us hope, many years of cricket besides 1909 before England and Australian cricketers in which they can contest the "ashes" in friendly rivalry.

Believe me yours faithfully,
EG Wynyard, Captain, representing SACA.
Lord's Cricket Ground, London NW, July 10.

A forthright response, as was only to be expected because Teddy was never going to pull his punches, but how to unpick this political intrigue?

The letters from Jackson, Carruthers and Jessop all refer to Australia sending a team in 1909 in the ordinary course of events before South Africa made their triangular tournament proposal. There was no obligation upon Australia to agree to any change in arrangements and so it is easy to see why they would have been upset when they received notification of MCC's amended resolution. It may have been emotive for Jessop to talk in terms of a pistol being held to their head, but there was some legitimacy to the analogy drawn. It was also disingenuous of Wynyard to say Jackson and Jessop had inflamed the situation. The resolution had achieved that end before anyone else expressed an opinion. Furthermore, Wynyard's comments that the invitation could only be made with the blessing of the counties rather ignored the point the counties appeared happy for Australia to tour alone before Bailey came up with his idea.

Sympathy for the Australian stance must be tempered, though, by the absence of any clear and cogent reason for their refusal to participate in the triangular tournament. Carruthers referred to the need to be cautious about the financial risks of such a contest given Australia would be financing the undertaking. Indeed, the history section on the website for the current International Cricket Council says that Australia's rejection was 'probably on financial grounds – Australia had agreed to tour England in 1909 and was not keen to share the tour with South Africa'. Whilst it is true any profits would need to have been shared three ways rather than two, Wynyard's letter made it clear there was no financial risk to Australia because South Africa (for which read, Abe Bailey) was prepared to provide a guarantee against any pecuniary losses.

It seems more likely the real reason for Australia's attitude can be discerned from some of the other remarks made by Carruthers. The ACB had been formed recently and was still trying to establish its authority, not just within its own country, where the players were still exhibiting resistance against this control over them, but also on the wider cricketing stage given the pre-eminence of MCC, who were now issuing apparent ultimatums to them. The ACB could not afford to have its stature undermined by having an Ashes tour changed following a proposal from an emerging SACA. How else to interpret the observation by Carruthers that, 'if anyone dared to make a change it could only be the current holders of the Ashes?' This was a battle for power and jockeying for position given the other proposal for the formation of an Imperial Cricket Conference. The victim of this particular spat was the future development of world cricket – it does seem a triangular tournament in 1909 would have been an interesting experiment to make for the promotion of the game on a broader front.

When Australia refused 'to share the limelight and the gate', as cricket writer Gideon Haigh described it, Bailey's instructions to Wynyard were to urge the formation of an Imperial Board 'by all means within his power'.

The Australians carried the day and toured England alone in 1909, retaining the Ashes. The *quid pro quo* was the meeting on 15 June 1909, when representatives of all three countries met at Lord's under the chairmanship of the Earl of Chesterfield (President of MCC). It was agreed that a triangular tournament would be staged in the future. A month later, with Lord Harris in the chair this time, the Imperial Cricket Conference was up and running when rules were agreed to control Test cricket between the three nations.

The triangular tournament did take place in 1912 but no further meeting of the Conference happened until 1921. Five years later, a further meeting, presided over again by Lord Harris, agreed that membership should comprise the 'governing bodies of cricket within the Empire to which cricket teams are sent or which send teams to England'. This was unfortunate for the United States as they continued to be excluded, but the meeting effectively created three new Test nations. West Indies played their first Test in 1928, New Zealand in 1930, India made their debut in 1932.

In 1964, it was suggested the Conference be expanded to include non-Test playing countries, including those outside the old Empire. The following year saw a change of name to the International Cricket Conference and a new category of Associate membership was created. In 1984, a third category of Affiliate Member was introduced although in 2017 this was removed with all previous Affiliates becoming Associate Members. In 1989 there was another name change to the International Cricket Council, best known as the ICC. As of May 2018, there are 104 members.

From the small acorn of Abe Bailey's proposal and the arguments advanced on his behalf by Teddy Wynyard, has grown the mighty oak of the ICC that governs world cricket today.

From David Frith, *The Golden Age of Cricket 1890-1914*

In foreign climes again:
MCC returned to South Africa with Teddy in 1909.
Back: Thompson, Rhodes, Woolley, Hobbs, Strudwick.
Middle: Simpson-Hayward, Wynyard, Leveson Gower (captain),
Denton, Buckenham, Bird.
Front: Tufnell, Fane, Blythe.

16

SHRIMP IN SOUTH AFRICA

1909-10

After sowing the seeds for the formation of the ICC, Teddy was the guiding hand in the creation of the lesser-known Charterhouse Friars Cricket Club in October 1908. There were thirty-eight original members, including Wynyard and Parry, with GO Smith on the committee.

With all this committee work behind him, Wynyard abandoned the snowy slopes of Davos for a winter in the Caribbean sun. On 31 October 1908 he set sail on RMS *Port Kingston* bound for Jamaica, with Lord Kitchener of Khartoum as one of his fellow first-class passengers. He returned on board SS *Tagus* arriving at Southampton on 8 February 1909 in time for his next cricketing tour, to Egypt.

Egypt is even less associated with cricket than North America, but British residents had formed Alexandria Cricket Club as long ago as 1851. More clubs were established by the military and, by 1909, the game had become the main sporting and social activity of the British population.

The MCC tour party comprised twelve amateurs with Lord Hawke originally intended to be the skipper. On 19 February 1909 the team left Tilbury Docks on board SS *Omrah*, but Wynyard and the captain, now George Simpson-Hayward, chose to avoid the journey through the Bay of Biscay and joined the ship at Marseilles a week later.

There were a total of eight scheduled non first-class matches, with three fixtures against All Egypt. MCC won seven but All Egypt secured a memorable victory in the last game of the tour at the Gezira Sporting Ground in Cairo – a wonderful setting located on the island in the middle of the River Nile. Wynyard's aggregate total for eleven innings was 187 with a top score of 50 not out (retired) in the game against the Civilians. In the first of the games against All Egypt, he probably changed the course of the game with his fielding, as he just managed to secure two fingers on the ball to dismiss opener Captain JA Davenport with a blinding catch. *The Times* commented that if it had not been taken 'it could hardly have been called a chance'. It was not all play though, there was time to go to the races at Helonan and Gezirah, watch the military tournaments for the English in Cairo and then for the Egyptian Army at Abbassia.

Back in England Teddy, did not make a very auspicious start to his 1909 domestic campaign, making a duck when playing for I Zingari at Charterhouse on 19 May. He then represented MCC against the School in wet weather on a soft pitch and took five for 63 with his lobs. On 8 July, Egypt and Soudan played a one-day game at Lord's, with the wickets pitched parallel to the pavilion. Egypt were 127 all out, but the home side responded with 298 for seven declared. Wynyard put himself down as last man and did not bat. At the close, Egypt were struggling again on 92 for six, with Teddy taking one catch.

Four days later he attended a dinner held at the Savoy Hotel for I Zingari and, at the beginning of August, the two-day Bank Holiday fixture between MCC and Public Schools. Teddy always took great trouble to select strong representative opposition and a suitable Marylebone team to provide as even a game as possible, and the Schools won this game by two wickets. Batting at number five was a sixteen-year-old pupil from St Paul's called Percy Fender, who was a little unlucky when his hard hit return was caught by the bowler, George Ricketts, for 28. Wynyard bowled seventeen overs in the second innings, which was more than anyone else, taking one for 51. In the light of the defeat one might question the captain's tactics in bowling his lobs for such a long spell!

Wynyard then attended Canterbury Week again and was present on Ladies' Day for the game against Hampshire. Although he was amongst the thirteen players named, he was not eventually selected. As he had been closely involved in the formation of Charterhouse Friars CC and had not been picked by his county, he played instead for the new club against Old Wykehamists in a high-scoring draw.

The only first-class match Wynyard played all season was for SH Cochrane's Eleven in the last game of the Australian tour at Woodbridge Cricket Club in Bray, starting on 17 September. Australia won the toss and Monty Noble elected to bat. Opener Warren Bardsley carried his bat for 142 towards the total of 271. Sydney Barnes, a Wisden Cricketer of the Year in 1910, took four for 87 although, surprisingly, Vogler was in the side and did not bowl in the match. Wynyard opened for Cochrane's Eleven and at the close he was 6 not out. The next day, in fine weather, his innings lasted for two and a quarter hours and his defence was just what the situation demanded before he was caught by Noble off Whitty for 36. He had helped to add 93 in an hour and a half with top scorer, Jack Hobbs (56), who had dropped down to number four in the order. In their second innings Cochrane's Eleven ran out of time, finishing six runs short on 99 for six with Wynyard still to bat, in a drawn game.

The winter of 1909/10 saw a further tour to South Africa. The SACA had requested an all-amateur side on economic grounds, presumably because Bailey anticipated considerable future expense with an Australian tour and, hopefully, a triangular tournament to come. MCC always had difficulty in securing the availability of their top amateurs for overseas tours and to find fourteen of them, strong enough to compete with the South Africans on their own territory, was never going to happen. Instead the party of fourteen finally invited comprised six amateurs and eight professionals.

The selectors were Lord Hawke and CB Fry, assisted by Henry Leveson Gower after he had been asked to captain the side back on 17 March. His appointment was an interesting one. Undoubtedly he was a senior and respected figure at MCC and, of course, the captain had to be an amateur, but it is difficult to see any cricketing grounds upon which it was based. Admittedly he had toured South Africa four years earlier but had never played Test cricket and was now thirty-six years of age (only Wynyard was older). His game had hardly improved during the interim and, although he was captain of Surrey, he had barely played, leaving Crawford to skipper the side. Crawford had been invited to tour South Africa again and undoubtedly his batting and bowling would have greatly strengthened the team, but the invitation was withdrawn because during the summer of 1909, he had a public falling out with Surrey over the side Leveson Gower had selected for him to lead against the Australians. Neville Tufnell was the late call up in September and would be the reserve wicketkeeper to Strudwick.

There had to be real doubt, therefore, whether the captain could justify his place in the side for all five Tests, which is doubtless why Fane was given the role of vice-captain. In many ways the Essex amateur was the more logical cricketing choice, but he had been a reluctant captain when taking over in 1907/8 as a result of the illness to AO Jones – the tour that Wynyard had originally been asked to lead. So why was Teddy, as the most senior man, now forty-eight, not skipper?

If it is difficult to see the cricketing grounds for Leveson Gower's appointment then the reason for choosing Teddy is a matter only the selectors can answer. Warsop comments, 'quite what grounds were used in selecting Wynyard for this tour of South Africa are not clear in view of his lack of cricket in 1909. It seems obvious that he was mainly selected as a reserve.' If there was one lesson that should had been learned from four years previously it was that this would be a tough and tiring tour in which allowance had to be made for both illness and injury. There really should have been no room for anyone who could not justify their place in the team.

On 6 November, *The Times*, when reviewing the forthcoming tour, observed that, 'Capt Wynyard though he played very little first cricket in England this season showed by his innings against the Australians for Mr Cochrane's Eleven that he had lost little of his skill and his experience and nerve [and he] should serve the side in good stead.' It is important to put these observations into context. Wynyard scored 30 against the Australians in what was his only first-class game of the season and it had taken place after the touring party had been announced on 31 August. Furthermore, whilst he was undoubtedly both skilled and experienced, he had not displayed on his last tour of South Africa (nor since) any mastery over the leg spin and googly deliveries he was predominantly going to have to face back on matting wickets.

The reason for his selection would seem to have much more to do with his role as the agent in England for the SACA. The triangular tournament had not been held during the summer as Bailey had wished, but the Imperial Cricket Conference was now up and running. The importance of keeping friendly with Bailey and ensuring the tour went ahead smoothly required Wynyard to be out in South Africa in an ambassadorial role. Why else give him the title 'deputy-captain' when Fane was already vice-captain for cricketing matters on the field?

Again, there was a need to be sensitive about the changing political structure. Whilst political union was about to happen between the four colonies, mistrust remained between them, and also between the Boer/Afrikaners and the British. Furthermore the formation of the Union would be on terms that virtually ignored the black population whose rights to vote and own land were taken away. Thus were the seeds of division and discrimination sown that went on to blight the South African harvest for the next eighty years.

This was the political backdrop that Wynyard and Leveson Gower had to face, although their team also had a very strong South African side to compete against. The portents did not look good. Only five of those who played in the Ashes series that summer were chosen or available to tour South Africa: Rhodes, Hobbs, Blythe, Thompson and Woolley. As for the remaining nine tourists, only Wynyard, Fane and Denton had played Test cricket before. The other six players – captain Leveson Gower, Simpson-Hayward, Buckenham, Tufnell, Bird and Bert Strudwick, made their Test debuts during the tour, and the first four of those initiates did not play Test cricket again after this visit to South Africa.

It did appear that some lessons, but not all, had been learned about the itinerary, with only eighteen matches being played, of which thirteen or fourteen (depending upon how the match against The Reef is classified) were first-class. Furthermore, a Test match had been arranged for the first time at Durban, but once again three of the Tests had been concertinaed in at the very end of the South African leg of the tour. There was a hope that the team would then be able to move on to Rhodesia.

There are two very helpful accounts of the tour; John Blythe Smart's *The Real Colin Blythe* and Leo McKinstry's *Jack Hobbs: England's Greatest Cricketer*.

The date of departure had been brought forward by one week to allow greater time for acclimatisation and practice. On 6 November 1909, the MCC tourists left Waterloo by the 11.35 boat express train to join the Union-Castle Line SS *Saxon*. It was a sign of progress that, for this trip, both the gentlemen and the players were travelling first-class on the typical Edwardian mail steamer. Early on in the journey, there was such a rough sea that the passengers were advised to stay on board, even when they reached Madeira.

The weather then improved for the next fourteen days, allowing time for organised practice. Wynyard supervised this and also acted as Master of Ceremonies for the other passengers who wanted to watch the cricketers in action. In spite of restricted space, the promenade deck was transformed into a cricket pitch, with Leveson Gower having arranged for regulation nets to be brought along from Lord's. Matting was put down and drawn taut with stumps fixed into a heavy wooden base. Ayres Limited had patented a slip catching cradle and this was used to sharpen reflexes. There was also time for other recreations. Wynyard refereed the potato, egg and spoon and whistling races as well as the tug of war. He kept fit by skipping whilst others walked briskly around the decks. In the evening Blythe, who was a member in his spare time of the Tonbridge Orchestral Union, participated in the ship's concerts and entertained with an emotional violin solo of 'Ave Maria'.

A photograph was taken of the team on board ship and used to advertise Officers Mess cigarettes. Nine years earlier Wynyard had been captured in the picture of I Zingari against Northern Nomads with a cigarette between his index and middle finger, but there is no way of telling whether he was promoting the same brand!

On 23 November, the team arrived at Cape Town and, once again, was formally welcomed by the mayor at a luncheon held at City Hall. Whilst the captain, Leveson Gower, responded by publicly recognising a great effort would be needed to beat the home side, it was further proof of Wynyard's off the field responsibilities that he also spoke, paying tribute to the reputation enjoyed by South African sportsmen in Great Britain.

Wynyard played in the opening two-day fixture at Newlands against a Western Province Colts Sixteen. Hobbs laid down an early marker with a superb 110 and at the close the score was 320 for seven with Teddy 19 not out. Leveson Gower declared on this overnight score and the match ended in a draw.

When the team moved up to Kimberley, Wynyard encountered extreme temperatures when he opened the batting with Rhodes against a Griqualand West Fifteen. It was a fast pitch and, on 16, the Yorkshireman was caught and bowled by Kenny. Denton was then out for 1, also off Kenny, and he was joined back in the pavilion shortly afterwards by Fane (11) and Woolley (0). Thompson was run out from a smart return leaving Bird with Wynyard to steady the ship. At lunch the score was 75 for five with Teddy having progressed slowly to 18. When play resumed, two wickets fell for one run, and then Simpson-Hayward was bowled for 8 with the score on 90. Buckenham joined Wynyard and a good stand followed. The total had reached 166 when McCarthy bowled Wynyard for a very steady 58, of which 26 had been singles. He had batted in searing heat for three hours, which was a remarkable achievement for a forty-eight year old. Buckenham hit well for 54, and MCC ended up on 190. Wynyard then scored 21 in the second innings and took two wickets with his lobs, as MCC ran out victors by 200 runs.

Even though he had performed well at Kimberley, Teddy did not play in any of the next three games, which were followed by the first Test beginning on New Year's Day at Johannesburg. Wynyard, Tufnell and, surprisingly, Blythe were the three omitted from the England team.

As in 1906, another close opening Test went South Africa's way, but England must have been particularly disappointed after the magnificent opening partnership between Hobbs (89) and Rhodes (66) in the first innings.

Rhodes was a man of humble origins, born on a farm in Kirkheaton, and like Hobbs took great pride in being a professional cricketer. They were both painstaking about their appearance. Schofield Haigh said that 'Wilfred never bought himself a packet of cigarettes in his life' and was described as a 'damned uncooperative old bugger'. He was though a man of the highest integrity who McKinstry said inspired deep respect throughout the cricket world. Hobbs said of him, 'you could always trust Wilfred.'

In short, he was not a man with whom to mess. Early on in this South African tour, Wynyard posted in the professionals' dressing room a list of the players he required to bowl at him in the nets on a particular afternoon. He donned his pads and gloves and strolled out confidently expecting the bowlers to arrive, but no one turned up. 'Blood Orange' was fuming. He was not used to having his orders disobeyed and marched into the dressing room in high dudgeon. He found his note screwed up in the waste paper basket. McKinstry says Wynyard 'had incurred a mix of unpopularity and derision with his high-handed manners'. Rhodes viewed him as being in South Africa 'more or less on a joy ride'. One can but wonder at the reaction of the Yorkshireman had he been on the 1906 tour when Wynyard absented himself to visit the Victoria Falls! If Teddy's selection had, in fact, been to foster good relations with Abe Bailey and the South African cricketing authorities, unfortunately it appears he had not been successful in also fostering good relations with the professionals in his own touring party.

Before the second Test there were two first-class matches. Wynyard did not play in the first against Natal in Durban, but was brought back into the side at Pietermaritzburg, where Leveson Gower drafted Richard Ponsonby, private secretary to the Governor of Natal, into the side as Hobbs, Thompson, Buckenham and Tufnell were all rested. Rain restricted play to two and a half hours on the first day and at one point Natal were 5 for five, but had struggled through to 41 for seven when stumps were drawn. The following morning they were dismissed for 50, with Blythe proving almost unplayable with figures of seven for 20 and Wynyard taking two catches. Teddy, batting down at number eight, made just 1 run before being caught by Saville off Samuelson towards a total of 229. Second time round Natal performed better, reaching 203, but MCC needed only 25 to win. Wynyard opened with Woolley and although the Kent man was out for 4, it was a comfortable win by nine wickets with Teddy making 10 not out.

The team travelled twenty miles north to visit the Howick Falls, named by the Zulu people as KwaNogqaza meaning Place of the Tall One. The tourists then moved back to Durban where they stayed at the Royal Hotel, built of nettle daub and thatch in 1845, near the harbour. On their visits to the city the cricketers visited the skating rink and doubtless this gave Teddy an opportunity to display his skills. On 20 January the tourists lunched with the mayor and the following day the second Test began at Lord's, the first time a Test had ever been played in Durban.

Both sides were unchanged, which was slightly surprising given Blythe's excellent performances with the ball in the two games against Natal. Presumably, the focus was on keeping the batting as strong as possible.

On the fourth night of the match, a banquet was held at the Marine Hotel with a programme of songs, toasts and excellent cuisine: aperitifs, hors d'oeuvres, consommé, sole Florentine, poulet, cotelettes en aspic, roast turkey, salad, gateau-praline, iced pudding. It was the ideal preparation, from a South African point of view, for opponents who had been set 348 to win on the last day. Hobbs and Rhodes progressed to 48, but soon the tourists were struggling on 111 for five. Hobbs fought hard and top scored with 70, but in the end they fell 95 runs short to leave South Africa 2-0 up in the series.

Once more the itinerary dictated that the remaining Tests would all be at the end of the tour. In the intervening month five matches, four of which were first-class, had to be played around the country. Wynyard did not play in either of the two victories against Border and North-East Districts Fifteen (not first-class) at East London and Queenstown respectively. He did, however, play in each of the other three fixtures.

On 11 February he was at St George's Park, Port Elizabeth where Eastern Province were the opposition. They won the toss, elected to bat and found Blythe (five for 21) and Thompson (three for 20) in rampant form and were dismissed for just 45 in only 19.4 overs during the morning session. Hobbs and Rhodes opened, and when Rhodes was out for 31, after another century (102) partnership, Wynyard came to the wicket. The score was taken to 121 when Hobbs was stumped for a splendid 79. Teddy was then out for 5 and MCC went on to 263. Eastern Province only made 79 (Simpson-Hayward five for 14) to lose by an innings and 139 runs.

The next two matches were both against Transvaal at Johannesburg and Pretoria. At the Old Wanderers ground, the home side had six of the Test team playing for them. The weather was hot and the wicket good, as MCC won the toss. Wynyard batted at number five and was caught by Lindsay, falling victim again to the bowling of Vogler, for just 2. MCC made 291 and led on first innings by 21.

When play started on the third day, Wynyard was at the crease in his second innings with Denton, facing the attack of Vogler and Schwarz. The score was 234 and 25 runs were added before Denton was out lbw to Vogler for a superb 138. Wickets then fell quickly with Wynyard being stumped by Ward off White for 7. The innings came to an end shortly after midday for 271. Transvaal needed 293 to win but they fell short by 50 runs.

The match finished on 21 February and the side moved up to Berea Park and, on a hot day, Tip Snooke won the toss for Transvaal and elected to bat. South Africa's Test openers, Zulch and Stricker, had a stand of 215 before Wynyard caught Stricker off the bowling of Rhodes for a magnificent 101. Zulch went on to make 176 not out and at the close Transvaal had reached an impressive total of 371 for three. Leveson Gower used no less than seven bowlers to try and make a breakthrough, including Wynyard who bowled twenty-three overs, taking the wicket of Aubrey Faulkner, for 93 runs. Unfortunately there was then heavy rain and no further play was possible over the next two days.

The final three fixtures of the South African leg of the tour were also the last three Test matches. England's selection was made easy when Blythe dislocated his shoulder and the side was unchanged at the Old Wanderers ground, which meant Wynyard was again not selected. England struck back and the series was very much alive at 2-1. This was thanks to a majestic 93 not out in the second innings by Hobbs, who had suffered sunstroke earlier in the match.

As was the case four years earlier, the team then had to travel all the way back down to Cape Town for the last two Tests, but this time did not have to play any games along the way. For the match at Newlands, Leveson Gower made a brave and honourable decision. Blythe had recovered from injury and was picked for the first time in the series, with the captain dropping himself. Fane took over skippering the side and this did look the strongest combination that could be put into the field, but South Africa won by four wickets and secured another series win.

There was only one day's rest before the fifth Test began. England were forced to make one change as Buckenham was injured; his place went to Tufnell. This meant the only member of the touring party not to play in any of the Tests was Teddy Wynyard. Fane was again the captain and he was particularly complimented for his field placings as his side secured victory by nine wickets.

In the first innings for South Africa, the last man out, Sivert Samuelson, was bowled by George Simpson-Hayward for 15. Probably neither of them realised at the time that this was an historic delivery, the last wicket ever taken in Test cricket by a lob bowler. Indeed, one of the features of this series was the success Simpson-Hayward achieved with his lobs, doubtless helped by the extra spin off the matting wickets. He played in all five Tests and took twenty-three wickets for 420 runs at an average of 18.26. In their second innings, the last man in was again Sivert Samuelson and Blythe bowled him for 7. Again, what no one knew at the time was that it was the last ball ever bowled and the last wicket taken by Blythe in Test match cricket. He captured exactly 100 wickets in his nineteen Tests at an average of 18.63. His best figures were eight for 59 and he took ten wickets or more in a Test on four occasions. He was described as 'a triumph of genius allied to skill'.

England may have lost the Test series 3-2 but the only other match lost had been against Transvaal. They had won ten of the eighteen games played and drawn four. Wynyard had played in six matches, four of which were first-class. He scored a total of 102 runs in seven innings (25 in first-class matches) took nine catches (eight first-class). He bowled thirty-two overs, two maidens for three wickets and 132 runs (one for 102 first-class). Sadly his contribution on the field in his last Test tour was not a significant one. *Wisden* said, 'the feature of this trip was the superb batting of Hobbs who easily adapted to the matting wickets and scored from the famous googly bowlers with amazing skill and facility.'

Unfortunately the tour did not end on a happy note, for two reasons. On the Saturday night of the last Cape Town Test, a banquet was held for the two teams at the Mount Nelson Hotel. Abe Bailey hosted the dinner and said of Morice Bird, 'this is the type of man we want out here as coach, not the professional cricketer.' Hobbs took offence, viewing it as a nasty remark, especially as he had been offered a job as a coaching professional in Natal. Given Bailey's close association with Wynyard, it is unlikely to have improved Teddy's relations with the professionals in the party.

Matters then worsened when MCC announced that the idea previously floated about the tour being extended to Rhodesia had now materialised. The trip would be prolonged by another three weeks and the professionals, who had already been away for over four months, would not receive any extra pay for their exertions. There was also a suspicion that the tour was being organised to allow the amateurs to see the Victoria Falls and go big game hunting. Wilfred Rhodes viewed Wynyard as the 'villain of the piece'. This may not have been entirely fair since Teddy did not actually go on to Rhodesia on this occasion. He had already travelled there four years earlier and it is entirely feasible Rhodes had overheard him extolling the virtues of such a visit to his fellow amateurs and others. In any event, the professionals refused to travel and demanded the terms of their original contract be respected. Their arguments were accepted and they were allowed to return home on the scheduled day of departure, accompanied by Wynyard and Tufnell. The *Winning Post* took a dim view, telling the professionals 'it is not a pretty tale though probably you all thought you were right'. From this distance that seems a very harsh observation.

This only left Leveson Gower, Fane, Simpson-Hayward and Bird to travel north but they co-opted a number of prominent South Africans including Sherwell, Schwarz and Zulch to join them and three further matches were played.

On 16 March 1910, Wynyard and nine other members of the English team boarded SS *Armadale Castle* in Cape Town. During the journey Bert Strudwick fell seriously ill with malaria, although he had started to make progress by the time the ship docked at Southampton on Saturday 2 April. His recovery was aided by the return voyage being calm and it may well have afforded Wynyard the opportunity to improve his relations with the professionals, certainly Hobbs, who on this occasion avoided his usual bouts of seasickness.

Wynyard was a keen collector of memorabilia recording his own career and, when his family put his collection up for auction, the Christies catalogue included '3 appreciative letters from Jack Hobbs'. Furthermore, Teddy's granddaughter still has a scorecard of the Middlesex v Surrey game in August 1926 to which is affixed a signature of Hobbs, recording his highest first-class score of 316 not out. Clearly a mutual respect developed and existed between them.

Perhaps there was another reason why Wynyard was in good humour on the journey back. The name below his on the passenger list was Miss L Worts.

Calm before the storm: Teddy teaches catching to a young
public school pupil at Lord's in 1914

17

GOODERHAM AND WORTS AND WYNYARD 1910-14

1910 saw the end of the Edwardian era. King Edward VII died on 6 May, to be succeeded by George V. Just over three weeks after the King's death, Wynyard played his first game of the domestic season at Lord's. He was now forty-nine years of age and only played two more first-class matches in his career, although he continued to represent MCC in a number of their other fixtures.

In early June, he made 85 not out against the Royal Artillery at Lord's, as well as taking three for 54 with his lobs. The only first-class fixture Wynyard played during this summer was against Oxford University at Lord's, beginning on 20 June. Oxford were captained by their wicketkeeper, Guy Pawson, who won the toss and batted. His side made 254 with Teddy taking two for 29. *The Times* observed:

> It was very interesting to see the very indifferent way several of them shaped to the not very high class lobs of Captain Wynyard. In old days it was a common sight to see batsmen of great skill playing nervously and badly against lobs and in this match the batsmen seemed unable to hit them at all.

Not very high class – I wonder how Teddy reacted to that harsh but probably accurate assessment?

In reply to a total of 254, MCC made only 108, with Teddy opening the batting and making the top score of 35. He was bowled by another leg spin/googly bowler, Philip le Couteur, a Rhodes Scholar, who ended with figures of six for 22 from eight overs. *The Times* commented, 'Capt Wynyard, who knows as much about the googly as anyone was fairly beaten.' They should have added that he may have known about the googly, but it appeared he still had not completely mastered how to play it! The ball that took his wicket then flew from the stumps into the wicketkeeper's face and struck him below the eye. Pawson had to retire, but fortunately the injury was not serious.

'Not more learned, but steeped in a higher learning' is the motto of the Quaker founded Haverford College in Pennsylvania. On 7 July their cricket team visited Lord's for a one-day game against MCC that ended in a draw, with Wynyard dropping himself down to number eleven and being run out without scoring. Just over a week later he scored 61 against a team representing Egypt and Soudan who lost by 227 runs.

August saw the traditional bank holiday fixture between MCC and the Public Schools whose captain that year, Robert St Leger Fowler from Eton, took a hat-trick in MCC's second innings, but it was not enough to prevent a victory by two wickets.

Wynyard then travelled to Ireland to play for Woodbrook against Warwickshire at Bray. The county side declared on 412 for nine, with both Willie Quaife and Dick Lilley making centuries (124 and 118 respectively). Teddy bowled nine overs, taking one for 36. When he batted it was at number six and he made 16 towards 91. Following on he was caught and bowled by Frank Foster for 36, but his side lost by an innings and 53 runs.

The following year saw the 1911 Census. Teddy was living at 11, Elm Park Gardens in Chelsea, with his two older sisters Eleanor and Lily along with four servants. Teddy was described as 'late Captain 8th Regiment, Pensioned and Private Means' and shown as a 'Visitor' whereas Eleanor was 'Sister of the Head' but 'the Head' was 'staying away'. This must have been a reference to their younger half brother, Henry Buckley Wynyard. In 1912 he was married to Nellie Fotheringham in Adelaide, Australia but on 19 December 1913 their first child, Anthony, was born at the Elm Park Gardens address.

Teddy did not play any first-class cricket in the summer of 1911, but on 17 June he was back at Charterhouse to play for Free Foresters, who had an easy win over the School. He opened with JWHT Douglas and made 32 in a total of 249.

The Public Schools were back at St John's Wood for the August bank holiday fixture and their captain was Maxwell Woosnam from Winchester College. Mick Collins has written a biography about him, *All Round Genius: The Unknown Story of Britain's Greatest Sportsman*. After playing at Lord's he went up to Cambridge in 1911 and earned Blues at cricket, football, golf (off scratch), lawn and real tennis. The justification for the claim in the title is that, in addition to Max's university achievements, he became a household name after the war in football and lawn tennis, playing for Manchester City and winning Olympic gold at Antwerp in the men's doubles and silver, partnering Kitty McKane (whose married name was Godfree), in the mixed doubles, losing 6-4, 6-2 to the strong French pairing of Suzanne Lenglen and Max Decugis. In 1921, at the Wimbledon Championships, he won the men's doubles and was runner-up in the mixed doubles, this time partnered by Phyllis Howkins (later Covell). He went on to be appointed Britain's Davis Cup captain.

His opposing captain at Lord's in 1911 was another highly accomplished and versatile sportsman in Teddy Wynyard and a closely fought draw ensued with Woosnam scoring a magnificent 144 in the first innings.

The American Cricket Club from Germantown, Philadelphia toured the British Isles that summer, playing thirteen games between 28 July and 25 August. Teddy played in two of the fixtures in Ireland, and turned out first for Woodbrook at Bray. Aubrey Faulkner was also in the side. Germantown, who lost the match, could not cope with Faulkner's leg breaks and googlies and he took eight for 77 in the second innings. Wynyard and Faulkner stayed in Ireland to play for Phoenix at Phoenix Park, Dublin on 23 and 24 August in another comfortable victory over their American visitors.

During the winter of 1911/12, Pelham Warner took an MCC side to Australia but was taken ill. Johnny Douglas captained the team in all five Tests when the Ashes were regained. On 1 May 1912, there was a dinner for the victorious team held at The Trocadero in London. Lord Desborough, President of MCC, was in the chair, and a menu of the evening signed by ninety-seven cricketers and guests was put up for auction in 2016 with an estimate of between £3,000 and £5,000. The cover was signed by the tourists (bar Strudwick and Vine) as well as by guests including Wynyard, Ranjitsinhji and Arthur Conan Doyle, amongst an extensive list of other luminaries.

The summer of 1912 finally saw the coming to fruition of Bailey and Wynyard's plans for a triangular tournament between England, Australia and South Africa. Australia had insisted, however, that the South Africans must first visit Australia. That tour had taken place in the winter of 1910/11 when Australia comprehensively won the five Test series, 4-1. The following winter they, in turn, had lost by the same margin to England. The Australian camp was not a happy one.

At a selectors' meeting on 3 February 1912, captain Clem Hill had not only traded insults but also blows with a fellow selector, Peter McAlister, leading to his resignation. Hill asked for Frank Laver to manage the team for the Triangular Tournament, but the ACB insisted upon appointing George Crouch, whereupon six senior players, Hill, Warwick Armstrong, Victor Trumper, Tibby Cotter, Vernon Ransford and Hanson Carter, all declared themselves unavailable to tour.

The consequence was that the touring Australian team, captained by Syd Gregory, was a considerably weakened one. By the same token the South Africans, captained by Frank Mitchell and Louis Tancred, were without Vogler and probably past their peak. CB Fry captained the England team, who were the favourites on their home patch. There were nine three-day fixtures in all with each nation playing the other three times at five different venues (Old Trafford, Lord's, Headingley, Trent Bridge and The Oval).

The new King showed his support for the tournament when he attended at Lord's on 28 July during the second Test between Australia and South Africa. His Majesty arrived at the ground at 4.15 pm and was received by the Duke of Devonshire (President of MCC), Francis Lacey (MCC secretary), Teddy Wynyard and Sir Spencer Ponsonby-Fane. The King was taken to the Committee Room and the game was suspended for a few minutes until he had taken his seat. Ten minutes later, at the fall of the second wicket in South Africa's second innings, tea was taken and during the interval both sides were presented to him. The King then watched for a couple of hours from the President's box. He left shortly before the drawing of stumps with South Africa doomed to defeat.

In the final reckoning, England prevailed over Australia and retained the Ashes, with South Africa coming a poor third, losing five times and drawing once. The perceived view remains to this day that the tournament was a failure. *The Daily Telegraph* wrote, 'Nine Tests provided a surfeit of cricket and contests between Australia and South Africa are not a great attraction to the British public.' A somewhat parochial view but, sadly, it was probably accurate. There were mitigating factors. The most significant one was the weather. The summer of 1912 was one of the wettest since records began, with the three months of June, July and August receiving twice the amount of the annual average rainfall. Indeed the coldest, dullest and wettest August for the whole of the twentieth century happened to be in 1912.

The big imponderable is how the tournament would have fared had it been played when Bailey and Wynyard wanted, three years earlier in 1909. They had hoped the competition between the only three Test playing nations at that time would be repeated every four years. Unfortunately any enthusiasm remaining for that to happen after the disappointments of 1912 disappeared forever with the outbreak of war two years later.

On 27 June 1912 Wynyard played his last ever first-class game. If it was not going to be for Hampshire, it was entirely appropriate that it should be at Lord's for MCC and not without significance, as he helped pick the team, that the captain should be Ranjitsinhji. Their opponents were Oxford University who ran up an impressive 406.

Wynyard came in at number eight for his last first-class knock (he did not bat second time around) and *The Times* observed, 'Captain Wynyard is still a beautiful player and his innings was most enjoyable to those who like to study method in batting.' He went on to make 27 not out towards the total of 302.

Oxford then stumbled to 26 for three when Bardsley and Harry Surtees Altham came together. They soon settled down and began to make runs against bowling that was not very difficult. Altham played attractive cricket with a lot of his runs coming off the back foot through the leg side. Bardsley was out for 46 whereupon, in the next forty-five minutes, Crutchley helped Altham put on 75 runs. The partnership was broken when as *The Times* reported, 'one of Captain Wynyard's lobs got rid of Mr Altham.' It was Teddy's last first-class wicket and his figures read two overs, one maiden, one for 5. The following day Oxford declared on 232 for seven and MCC were 23 for three when stumps were drawn, not only on the game but on Wynyard's first-class career that had begun thirty-four years earlier in 1878.

As he was the last victim of Wynyard's lobs, it is only fitting Altham should have the final word. In his *Hampshire County Cricket*, he assessed Wynyard as:

> A man of arresting presence and strong personality. Though never a good starter, he was a pugnacious batsman of high quality, combining with a strong and watchful defence a wide variety of attacking strokes of which the most individual was the pull-drive when he would drop on his right knee to pick up the over pitched, or even at times good length ball on or outside the off stump and hit it like a good iron shot wide of mid on; alternatively he might drive 'skimmers' over mid-off or extra cover. He was a fine slip field, could keep wicket very adequately and liked bowling lobs.

1913 saw even closer ties between Teddy and Charterhouse. On 5 July the General Meeting of the Old Carthusian Cricket and Football Club was held at Verites, Charterhouse, and Wynyard was voted its President. It was a position he held until the end of the First

World War. Unfortunately, Richard Webster, Lord Alverstone, was unable to attend through illness, but it was agreed a grant should be made to Charterhouse Friars, the cricket club of which Teddy was also President. In the School match against Old Carthusians, the pupils won the toss and batted making 183 on a perfect wicket. Wynyard then opened and scored 65 towards his team's total of 303.

The Charterhouse Friars began a cricket tour on 23 July and the following Friday and Saturday, according to *The Carthusian*, Wynyard 'found time to play among his many duties a large part in knocking off the 205 runs' needed for victory against the Aldershot Command. One of those duties was, of course, to organise MCC's matches, and on 17 July he had been at Lord's for the one-day fixture against the Royal Academy of Arts. Teddy's lobs again proved treacherous outside the first-class arena and he took five for 66 off 11.3 overs as the visitors were dismissed for 207. He opened the batting and made exactly 100 out of his side's 169. The Royal Academy won on first innings by 38.

There were no Test matches in England that summer and so there was greater focus on the games at Lord's, including the traditional August fixture against the Public Schools, who were captained that year by a tall fast bowler, John Heathcoat-Amory from Eton. In later life, he married Joyce Wethered, arguably England's greatest ever lady golfer. The Public Schools made only 180 on a beautiful wicket, with Wynyard taking one for 12. In their response MCC totalled 327, with Harry Altham top scoring with 83; next best was Teddy, batting at number seven, with 54. *The Times* commented, 'Capt Wynyard's innings was quite in his best manner and was a valuable object lesson of good batting.' On this occasion MCC were far too strong, dismissing the Schools for 143 to win by an innings and 4 runs. Teddy bowled just three overs and took two for 11.

Wynyard's close association with the growth of public schools cricket saw him make a significant contribution to the first *Public School Cricket Year Book* in 1914, recording the performances of the previous summer. He gave his thoughts on the six best school sides of the year and wrote a seven-page article for the editor, Albert Lane-Joynt, who had played for Radley that season before going up to

Oxford. The annual was priced at one shilling and a copy was sent to the King. In the preface, Lane-Joynt tendered his heartiest thanks to Wynyard, not only for his article, 'but for the interest he has taken in the book since the idea was first broached'. He continued:

> It is not, perhaps, always sufficiently realized what an immense debt of gratitude is owed to Capt EG Wynyard and FE Lacey for the trouble which they annually take not only over the Easter classes at Lord's – which is very considerable – but in the care with which they choose the representative sides in August, a most invidious task and the general interest they take in School cricket throughout the season.

The editor explained that he approached Wynyard to help him select the six best sides because 'he has done more than anybody else to bring about the increased opportunities now given to Schoolboy players'.

The comments about Wynyard and his own article provide an interesting insight into Teddy's character. During the Easter holidays, arrangements were in place whereby the sons of members could be coached at Lord's, but preferably not those who had already earned their school colours. Over 100 boys a year benefited from this tuition, with responsibility for the arrangements resting with Wynyard and Lacey. ACM Croome wrote about the Easter classes for the *Year Book* and observed:

> Capt Wynyard is out on the practice ground all day and his personality pervades the place. There is abundant tolerance for honest incapacity, but woe betide anybody who is late for his practice or shows the least sign of slackness. And the director of the proceedings has eyes in the back of his head. While he is conducting a fielding practice in the centre of the ground he manages to see exactly what is happening in a dozen nets surrounding it on all sides. Nor does he ever forget his impressions of any youngster who has ever come under his notice. The result is that he can tell at a glance whether the proper amount of progress is being made in this or that net. If he is dissatisfied he strolls across to the place, and in a minute or two the coach gets the needed hint, or the pupil hears the winged words which suit his case.

Wynyard's own article, which had previously appeared in *the London Evening News,* had the catchy title 'The Advantages of Coaching at Cricket and Some Suggestions to Coaches'. Teddy wrote that coaching 'should never be of a kind to check the individuality of pupils ... but where correction is necessary, no sort of doubt as to the reasons for the correction must be allowed to remain in the pupil's mind.' When commenting on other manuals dating back to Old John Nyren's *The Young Cricketer's Tutor,* he thought, 'possibly the necessary keynote of simplicity has not always been struck in these works ... plain simple explanations are best.'

In other words, as a coach he was a disciplinarian but one who could show understanding towards a boy trying his best and not wanting to suppress his freedom of spirit whilst keeping everything as simple as possible.

Reverting from theory to practice, at the end of August, Teddy played alongside Harry Altham, Bernard Bosanquet and Henry Leveson Gower in a twelve-a side match for Harlequins against a side organized by Lionel Robinson at Old Buckenham Hall in Attleborough. Robinson had gathered together a strong side for this fixture including Johnny Douglas, Archie MacLaren, Leonard Moon, Aubrey Faulkner, and Reggie Schwarz. Teddy took four wickets as the opposition were dismissed for 266, then scored 31 and 9, although it was in a losing cause.

Wynyard was now fifty-two but it was no barrier to him donning his football boots again, albeit to play in goal for AH Tod's Eleven against Charterhouse on Saturday 27 September. He was also now competing at real tennis, which was hardly surprising, given the close association between the sport and MCC with the courts at Lord's. On Saturday 15 November 1913, however, Teddy was a member of the team from the Prince's Club that played against Oxford University in the Merton Street Court, part of Merton College. *The Times* observed 'Capt Wynyard has never played much tennis, but his footwork, his strength and his eye show that that this is another of the many ball games at which he would have excelled.'

Just under a fortnight later, on Thursday 27 November, he was playing again, but this time for MCC against Cambridge University at the Clare and Trinity College court. It was a significant fixture. Although there had been a real tennis court at Lord's since 1838, this was the first inter-club match that MCC had ever played. It was a six-a-side fixture with each competitor playing two singles matches. The Cambridge team included Max Woosnam, who won both of his matches. In his two games Teddy won one and lost the other as Cambridge went on to win by seven matches to five.

As 1913 neared its end, his mind turned from affairs of a sporting nature to those of the heart. The photograph opposite page thirteen in the *Public School Year Book* depicts a dapper, immaculately suited man of military bearing, sporting a straw boater with perfectly polished shoes and nonchalantly standing with his left hand in his jacket pocket. There lingers a suspicion this may not have been a current portrait, but anyone looking closely may well have wondered if there was a lady whom Captain EG Wynyard DSO was trying to impress!

The modern traveller to Canada who is visiting Toronto may well take the tourist bus in order to see all the local attractions. If so, one of the stops along the route is Gooderham and Worts in the heart of the Distillery Historic District. The Distillery ceased trading in 1990 and, for a while, the site became the number one film location in Canada and was the second-largest outside of Hollywood. In December 2001 the land was purchased and transformed into a pedestrian-only village entirely dedicated to arts, culture and entertainment: a conversion comparable to that of Covent Garden Market in London.

Its origins date back to the arrival from England in 1831 of Suffolk mill owner James Worts. He set up a business that processed grain from Ontario and then shipped it on via the port. He built a prominent stone windmill on the Toronto waterfront near to the mouth of the Don River. His business partner was William Gooderham, who had also emigrated from East Anglia. Worts married Gooderham's sister, Elisabeth, who died in 1834. In the same year their eldest son William died aged just seventeen and, overcome by grief, Worts committed suicide by drowning himself in the well of the windmill. Gooderham continued with the business and assumed responsibility for the rearing of Worts' children. In 1845, Worts' eldest surviving son, James Gooderham Worts (known as James junior) who had been born in 1818, was made a partner and the firm renamed Gooderham and Worts.

In 1859 a new distillery was constructed on Mill Street at a cost of nearly $200,000. By 1871, the annual whisky and spirits production of Gooderham and Worts totalled 2.1 million gallons, accounting for nearly one half of the total spirits produced in Ontario, and it was at one time, the largest distillery in the world.

James junior died in 1862 from malaria leaving over $1,500,000. He had married Sarah Bright on 1 October 1840 and their seventh child, born in 1853, was James Gooderham Worts II. He also entered the family distillery business and was married twice. His first wife, Julia Dwight, died at the age of just twenty and on 21 January 1879, he married his second wife, Mary Louise Elliott. They had four offspring together, although one boy died at or shortly after birth. Their eldest child was Sarah Louise Worts, born in Toronto on 26 November 1879.

The family were living at that time in the St Lawrence Ward of the city, but Sarah's father died of uremia (renal failure) aged just thirty-one when Sarah was barely five years old. Her maternal grandparents, Charles and Elisabeth Elliott, were of Irish descent, and Mary took Sarah and her two other children to live with them in Cobourg, ninety-five kilometres east of Toronto. Sarah was eleven years old at the time of the 1891 Census, which revealed a household of nine, as three of her mother's siblings were all still at home.

By the time of the 1901 census, whilst there was no record of Sarah Louise Worts, there was a Louise Worts, born in Ontario on 27 November 1879, living in Esquimalt, Victoria at the southern tip of Vancouver Island. Louise was shown as the head of the house with forty-year-old May Marmion as her guest (probably her governess-cum-chaperone), along with an eighteen-year-old Chinese domestic servant by the name of Teng.

Given Worts was not a particularly common name and her position as head of the household was consistent with someone who was part of a wealthy distillery family, there is little doubt that Louise and Sarah Louise were one and the same person. There is clear evidence that she was known as Louise throughout her life, signing her name in that fashion, and it was also the name shown on her own son's birth certificate.

In 1903, Louise Worts travelled on board SS *Cymric* from New York to Liverpool arriving on 7 September. She returned home, but just over two years later was on RMS *Majestic* when she left New York again bound for Liverpool, arriving on 29 November 1905. She was fast becoming a regular transatlantic traveller and, in 1909 was on the White Star liner *Megantic* that travelled from Montreal via Quebec to Liverpool, accompanied by 26-year-old Norah Figgis. The ship docked in England on 14 August and her excursions continued to South Africa.

At Cape Town, on 16 March 1910, she was on the SS *Armadale Castle* and found ten of the returning MCC touring party as her fellow first-class passengers. Louise was an independent, intelligent and well-travelled woman, and in Teddy Wynyard she met a dashing, exceptionally well-travelled, self assured, retired Army Officer who had won the DSO. The sea was tranquil, the ambience serene and there were seventeen days to socialise. Louise was thirty years of age, while Wynyard had his forty-ninth birthday on the penultimate day of the voyage.

Upon their return home, when the 1911 Census was taken, it showed Louise as a British resident living at 53 Abingdon Court, Abingdon Villas in Kensington. She had a cook and house parlourmaid looking after her. Teddy was only 1.3 miles away in Chelsea. As the adage reminds us, 'something worth having is something worth waiting for,' and it was not until Monday 2 February 1914 that the following marriage announcement appeared in *The Times*:

WYNYARD : WORTS. On Friday 30th January at St James's Westminster by the Lord Bishop of Willesden CAPTAIN EG WYNYARD DSO eldest son of the late William Wynyard to SARAH LOUISE daughter of JAMES G WORTS of Toronto, Canada.

The marriage certificate revealed Teddy was residing at 8 St James's Square and Louise at Baileys Hotel in South Kensington. The witnesses were Henry Buckley Wynyard (the groom's half brother) and

Nellie Marmion (a teacher and younger sister of May who had been living with Louise in British Columbia at the turn of the century).

On a sadder note, in May 1914, Wynyard was MCC's representative at the funeral of RE Foster, who had died from diabetes at the age of just thirty-six. 'Tip' was cremated at Golders Green on Friday 15 May. On the following day there was a service at the Priory Church in Malvern followed by the internment of his ashes at Malvern cemetery. In addition to Teddy, the mourners included Foster's parents and five of his brothers. Worcestershire CCC sent a floral tribute consisting of three stumps, the centre one being half down with bails at its base.

In June, the centenary of the present Lord's ground was celebrated by a special match between the victorious England team from the winter tour to South Africa, captained by JWHT Douglas, and the Rest of England, captained by CB Fry. On the second day (23 June), King George V attended and both captains were introduced to him. In the evening a banquet was held at the Hotel Cecil in the Strand where Lord Hawke presided with an Old Carthusian, Prince Albert of Schleswig-Holstein, sitting to his right. It was said, 'never, perhaps, have so many famous cricketers, young and old, been gathered together.' 100 years later, on 8 October 2014, MCC celebrated the bicentenary in a marquee on the Lord's outfield with Prince Philip, Duke of Edinburgh, in attendance. The menu contained a photograph of the 1914 banquet showing the packed hall in the Hotel Cecil with members and guests enjoying what was described as 'a spectacular' meal with different wines accompanying each course before eight separate toasts were proposed. Try as hard as I might, I cannot identify Teddy Wynyard.

Back in 1914, Teddy had four days in which to recover before attending Old Carthusians' Day on Saturday 27 June at Charterhouse, when over 200 old boys travelled to the school for the event including Prince Albert of Schleswig-Holstein. For the first time Charterhouse had on display the portrait in oils of Lord Alverstone donated by the Old Carthusians. The focus of the day was the twelve-a-side cricket match in which Wynyard captained Old Carthusians against the School.

On 13 July, a two-day game began at Winchester and Teddy top-scored for I Zingari with 73 out of 278 against the Greenjackets. At the close of the first day their opponents were 229 for five. It was difficult, though, for anyone to concentrate properly on cricket during this time.

On 28 June 1914, the chauffeur for Archduke Franz Ferdinand had taken a wrong turn in the streets of Sarajevo, unwittingly affording Gavrilo Princip, a Bosnian Serb, an attempt at assassination. He was successful, and the next thirty-seven days saw ultimatums, bluff, misunderstandings, delay and failed diplomacy, culminating in German troops crossing the border with Belgium to attack Liège. On 4 August 1914, the British Prime Minister, Herbert Asquith, having guaranteed military support to protect Belgian neutrality, felt he had no option other than to declare war on Germany.

Thus the curtain came down on the theatre of cricket, bringing the final act of the golden age to its close. Simultaneously the curtain rose on a theatre of bloodshed, where suffering was revealed on such a scale that we are still trying to comprehend its magnitude to this day.

The dashing captain:
Teddy pictured in the 1914 Public School Cricket Year Book

18

MAJOR WYNYARD'S WAR AND PEACE 1914-23

After barely seven months of married life together, Teddy and Louise Wynyard had to contend with life at war.

Following the 4 August declaration by the Prime Minister, the War Office immediately requisitioned The Oval and Hobbs' benefit against Kent had to be transferred to Lord's. On 6 August, MCC, after deliberations by its committee and officers (including Wynyard as Assistant Secretary), issued a statement to the effect that 'no good purpose' could be served by cancelling matches. On 27 August, WG Grace wrote to *The Sportsman* strongly advocating the closure of the season, and Lord Roberts was openly critical of those continuing to play. On Monday 31 August, *The Times* reported a new statement emanating from MCC to the effect that, as the continuance of first-class cricket was hurtful to the feelings of a section of the public, they had decided to withdraw from the matches in the Scarborough Festival for which they had undertaken to send teams. Surrey cancelled their last two fixtures and effectively brought the Championship to an end, although MCC still declared them as County Champions at a committee meeting in November. 1914 had seen Hampshire achieve their highest placing yet when they finished fifth. Indeed, they won five of their last six matches; their last three games against Lancashire, Essex and Kent had been at Dean Park for the Bournemouth Festival beginning on 24 August. Teddy was amongst those spotted basking in the sunshine down at the coast for the Essex game.

One might be tempted to think, at the age of fifty-three and recently married, Wynyard would view this as a war for the younger man. After all, men who had previously served in the Army were accepted only up to the age of forty-five and the initial call for 100,000 volunteers was comfortably exceeded. But anyone believing that Teddy might ever view this as somebody else's fight simply did not know their man. At the beginning of September 1914, Wynyard used his contacts in London to lobby as intensely and vigorously as he could for a return to the Army and active service. He was only partially successful. In spite of his age, he was recalled and given the temporary rank of Major with his old King's Liverpool Regiment, but he was denied the opportunity of fighting at the front.

He may still have thought this was a possibility or it could simply just have been good common sense now that he was married, but on 12 October 1914 Teddy visited his solicitor, Richard Wood at 9 Lincoln's Inn, to make a fresh will. He appointed Louise as his sole executrix and bequeathed everything to her.

In May 1915, Wynyard was attached to the Army Ordnance Corps at Aldershot, where the skills he had displayed as an adjutant in India twenty-five years earlier were now put to excellent use as the war escalated and the organisational requirements and structure of the Ordnance Corps became increasingly more complex.

In November 1916, Wynyard was appointed to the Middlesex Regiment and, from then until the end of the war, he was the Commandant of the Thornhill Labour Camp in Aldershot. There is limited information in the public domain about these camps, especially the one at Thornhill. There is not a reference of any kind to it in the records and database of the Hampshire Cultural Trust, who run the Aldershot Military Museum.

Warsop says that Thornhill Labour Camp was located in Southampton, and Thornhill is indeed a suburb of that city. However,

Teddy's entry in *Who's Who* for 1918 indicates that he was living at Glebe House, Church Lane, Aldershot – a town established in the 1850s as the Army's permanent training camp. Thornhill Barracks were located there for use by the Royal Army Service Corps. In *The Final Over: The Cricketers of Summer 1914*, Christopher Sandford says Wynyard was 'the commandant of a military prison in Aldershot' but the prison was known as the Glasshouse, so named because of its glass roof and the reason why military prisons became known as glasshouses.

There are public documents referring to Wynyard as part of the Labour Corps. This Corps was first raised in 1915 and manned by officers and other ranks who had been medically rated below the A1 condition needed for front-line service. Given his age, Teddy fitted into that category. The use of the words 'Commandant' and 'Labour Camp' in such an authoritative source as *Who Was Who 1929-1940* suggests that Thornhill was an internment camp in the Aldershot area. During the early stages of the war, military and civilian prisoners were housed in the same camps, although usually separated from each other within them. As the conflict progressed, different camps evolved, and by January 1918 there were 566 different places of internment over a wide range of locations throughout the country. The accommodation and layout of a camp was dependent upon the institution being used (schools, disused factories, stables, farms, castles) but the standard installation usually consisted of huts resembling army barracks surrounded with thick barbed wire and patrolled by armed soldiers.

The role of the commandant was vital in terms of setting the tone for the camp. The person needed to be a strict disciplinarian, and Wynyard fitted that bill. It would be nice to think he also brought to the task touches of humanity and individuality, but he had to be careful because there was close public scrutiny of the lifestyle afforded to the internees. Barely a family had been untouched by the loss of a loved one and there was great unease about the enemy being seen to enjoy their life in captivity.

This was very clearly illustrated by the libel action brought by Margot Asquith against the owners of *The Globe*, who inferred she had sent presents from Fortnum and Mason to German officers at Donington Hall and may even have visited and played lawn tennis with them. Her Leading Counsel made clear that such conduct would be unpatriotic by anyone, let alone the Prime Minister's wife. The case was not defended and she was awarded £1,000 damages plus an indemnity in respect of her legal costs. Press comment was to the effect that these officers were enjoying what most people considered to be lavish hospitality at Donington Hall, although Panikos Panayi's *Prisoners of Britain* asserts 'that the reality remained different'.

Whilst it was frowned upon for internees to enjoy themselves, there remained plenty of opportunities for Commandant Wynyard to participate in armed forces cricket matches, although in 1917 his army responsibilities forced him to resign as Assistant Secretary of MCC. He was replaced by Eton-educated William Findlay, who had taken over at Surrey following the death of Charles Alcock and went on to succeed Lacey as MCC Secretary in 1926, holding that post for ten years. He became President with Plum Warner's support in 1951.

In *The Charm of Cricket Past and Present*, Major CHB Pridham, who had been a cadet at Sandhurst when Wynyard was an instructor there, told a curious tale about one cricket match in wartime. It took place at Aldershot in September 1918 between Aldershot Command, captained by Teddy, and the Household Brigade. It was a three-day game, which was unusual during the war. Pridham was umpiring and JWHT Douglas was bowling, with SGA Maartensz (of Incogniti and Hampshire) standing as wicketkeeper. Pridham described the incident in the following way:

> The wicketkeeper made an appeal for stumping one of the Brigade batsmen, a fraction of a second after the wicket had been broken by a gust of wind. This occurred directly *after* the ball had left the bowler's hand but *before* it had reached the striker.

Pridham did not reveal his decision but said:

The incident caused considerable discussion during the tea interval that day, but no one seemed able to come to what they considered to be the correct decision. Wynyard stated he had never heard of or seen a like incident during his exceptionally wide experience of the game in many parts of the world, though he was the greatest and most widely travelled of all Army cricketers.

The author referred to his having spent many months 'in muddy trenches and hospital beds'. Surely neither he, nor Wynyard given his Zingaro pedigree, would have wanted to dispatch such a batsman, on a welcome break from war's horrors, back to the pavilion in such circumstances.

Whilst Wynyard could not continue with his role in St John's Wood he was, nevertheless, able to pursue his love of golf. When he took up his duties in wartime Aldershot he became a member at nearby Camberley Heath Golf Club and formed a golf society of his own, open to all ranks, which he named the Jokers. Sandford said of Wynyard that 'nature seemed to have cast him in a lifelong role as a prankster'. I am not persuaded by that portrayal, although he clearly possessed a lighter and more jovial side to his character.

Aldershot at this time had a rough, tough and uncouth reputation, with drunkenness and prostitution rife. This was perhaps not too surprising because, after all, this was where many soldiers were being trained and it would be their last taste of 'Dear Old Blighty' before being sent to the front and an uncertain future. One might not consider it the ideal location, in which to bring up a family? Yet circumstances dictate, especially in wartime, and on 23 May 1918, Louise gave birth to their only child, a son, who they named Edward James Buckley Wynyard.

Edward's arrival must have been an occasion of great rejoicing for both Teddy and Louise as there is the hint they may have feared not being able to have children. On 25 March 1916, when they had been married for over two years, Teddy returned to his solicitor in Lincoln's Inn and made a Codicil to his Will. It provided that, in the event of there being no issue of his marriage living at his death, his half brother Henry was to receive the portrait of Colonel William Wynyard by Sir Joshua Reynolds which was then at Langford

Parsonage in Essex, and also the gold hunter repeating watch which had been left to Teddy by his uncle. If Henry predeceased him then the bequests should go to Henry's first son, provided he survived Teddy and reached twenty-one.

Henry and his wife Nellie already had a son, Anthony, and on 4 January 1917, they became proud parents of a daughter, Margaret, born in their home at 55 Drayton Gardens, Kensington. Henry's occupation was shown as a law student when he had been engaged in the Royal Naval Volunteer Reserve in October 1914. He served on the training ship HMS *President* moored at Blackfriars but was ultimately discharged on grounds of ill health.

This period in history, however, was much more readily associated with unhappy memories. The other Wynyard brother, William, whose home was at Langford Parsonage, had died on 22 August 1915 at Strathpeffer Ross, New Brunswick, Canada when only fifty-one years old. The war was only to add to the losses suffered by Wynyard in his circle of extended family, friends and playing colleagues.

The Battye family were cousins and had their own proud military tradition. Lieutenant Cyril Wynyard Battye died on 21 March 1916 aged just twenty-one when his Vickers fighter biplane suffered engine failure in Wiltshire. Just over eighteen months later, 43-year-old Lieutenant Colonel Clinton Wynyard Battye was cut down by machine-gun fire. The saddest story was the death of Teddy's nephew, Damer Wynyard, who was wounded at Mons in August 1914. Whilst back in England, he was promoted to captain and married Olive, daughter of His Honour Judge Wakely. He returned to the front and barely four months later was killed in action defending Hill 60 near Ypres. His name is commemorated on the Menin Gate Memorial there.

Teddy was particularly close to the Leatham family. On 26 September 1915, Brevet Major Bertram Leatham, described as 'the best officer that the Green Howards had turned out in the last forty years', was killed at Hulloch by a German sniper's bullet.

Whilst war does not discriminate between social classes with casualties coming from all walks of life, Wynyard had devoted an enormous amount of his time to coaching as well as promoting public school cricket. Tragically, many of that generation of boys who had passed through his tutelage never had the chance to put what he had taught them into practice. Instead, their pitifully short lives were ended, as Rupert Brooke noted, in 'some corner of a foreign field that is forever England'. Public schools lost on average five years worth of students, with one in five perishing. From Charterhouse alone, 686 old boys died.

Albert Lane-Joynt, when editing the first issue of *The Public School Cricket Year Book 1914*, placed a notice seeking advertisers for the next year and expressed hope he may be able to include sections on preparatory schools and old-boy cricket. He was at Oxford when war was declared and renounced university life to join the Dorset Regiment. He was attached to the Machine Gun Corps when, on 26 February 1916, he too was killed by a bullet from a German sniper. Lane-Joynt never did have the opportunity to edit a second edition of the year book.

Andrew Renshaw's *Wisden on the Great War: The Lives of Cricket's Fallen 1914-18* contains the definitive roll call and among those listed are many who played alongside Wynyard whether for county, club, country or on tour, as well as those who opposed him. Evelyn Bradford of Hampshire, Wilfred Curwen and Attwood Torrens of the MCC party to New Zealand in 1906/7; Leonard Moon and Colin Blythe who had toured South Africa in 1905/6 with Gordon White amongst the opposition; Kent's Kenneth Hutchins who had served with Wynyard's old regiments; Australian fast bowler Albert 'Tibby' Cotter (who Jack Hobbs described as the fastest bowler he faced in international cricket) – these were just a handful of those who fell.

Finally, at the eleventh hour on the eleventh day of the eleventh month of 1918, the Armistice was signed. Just as peace was breaking out, so there was an outbreak of a particularly aggressive virus that caused 250,000 fatalities in Britain alone. On 18 November 1918, only seven days into peace time and after surviving the carnage of the last four years, a 43-year-old major, mentioned three times in despatches, wounded twice and awarded the Military Cross, succumbed to influenza in the military hospital at Etaples just south of

Boulogne. His name was Reginald Oscar Schwarz. Fate could hardly have dealt him a crueller hand.

The *London Gazette* recorded that, 'as from 8 April 1919, Temporary Major EG Wynyard DSO (Capt Retired pay) of the Infantry Labour Corps relinquished his temporary commission on grounds of ill health but retained the rank of Major.' Under a week later there was a further notice announcing that Wynyard had been awarded the OBE for 'valuable services in connection with the War Military Division'.

Teddy's health problems which could be traced back to his days in Burma had recurred, but he was only invalided out when the war was over and his contribution had been recognised by the high honour awarded to him. It was time to leave Aldershot and he, Louise and baby Edward moved to Buckinghamshire. They set up home at Kingswear House in Burkes Crescent, Beaconsfield. It remains to this day a magnificent Edwardian mansion, with five bedrooms and gardens stretching to nearly one acre.

Just before Wynyard relinquished his commission, he played his part in the creation of the Army Cricket Association, whose stated aim was 'to foster and encourage cricket in all ranks' and it was intended to arrange Command Leagues for that summer.

County cricket recommenced, albeit with a reduced programme of matches played over just two days. Worcestershire, who were in financial difficulties, did not enter a team for this season.

Teddy played for I Zingari against Charterhouse and then, on Saturday 14 June 1919, Royal Military College were I Zingari's opponents at Sandhurst. He commented, 'lovely hot day, AC Gore, bowled very well. We had very little bowling.' Teddy continued to arrange I Zingari matches and in Arrowsmith's history of the club, the author observed:

> I Zingari became a by-word for producing sides of elderly non benders ... there were also among them too many who regarded it as their duty to bring up the young the hard way and teach them to mind their P's and Q's and the young at that time were not newly left schoolboys but men who had fought in the war.

He did not name names, but there must be a strong suspicion that Wynyard was in his sights given the comments by Gerald French and the story told later by Masterman about their tour of Canada together. Teddy then played for Free Foresters against Royal Fusiliers in a match starting at Lord's on 16 June. The Fusiliers were dismissed for 122. The Free Foresters side included Lionel Palairet, the Reverend Frank Gillingham and Lionel Tennyson, and they took a commanding lead when they responded with 274. Palairet made 40 and Teddy wrote 'Coo played a beautiful first knock'. He did not do so badly himself; going in at number eleven, he scored an impressive 33 for a last-wicket partnership of 69 in a match that the Foresters won by eight wickets.

5 July was Old Carthusians' Day and 400 former pupils attended with one amongst them (who was not named by the school magazine) arriving by aeroplane! The traditional cricket match began at 11.30 am. Wynyard opened but was bowled for 13 by Raymond 'Crusoe' Robertson-Glasgow, who went onto play for Somerset and became a famous cricket writer and journalist. At 1 o'clock, in his capacity as the last President, Teddy took the chair at the first AGM since 1914 of the Old Carthusian Cricket and Football Club. He stood down from the committee and AH Tod took over as the newly elected President. Lunch was then taken in a marquee erected on Founder's Court before play resumed. Unfortunately there was bad weather in the afternoon and the cricket had to be abandoned.

18 August saw Hobbs' benefit match at The Oval against Kent (his first having produced a meagre return because of the outbreak of war) with Jack Crawford back for Surrey. Meanwhile, north of the river at Lord's, Teddy Wynyard was opening for MCC in a two-day game against Buckinghamshire. It was a military-looking side that turned out alongside him. Batting at number three was Oliver Leese, who rose to be Lieutenant General and commanded the Eighth Army in the Italian Campaign throughout most of 1944. Unfortunately Wynyard was out for 1, but he did take four for 10 off 9.3 overs, including one caught and bowled, with his lobs.

Wynyard was now fifty-eight years of age and whilst still involved in cricket and hockey (at which he had been representing Hertfordshire County), it is clear his attention was increasingly being consumed by the less physically demanding sport of golf. He had played the game for a number of years and at the turn of the century, when he was an instructor at Sandhurst, had been a member at nearby Royal Ascot Golf Club. In 1910 he changed to Royal North Devon, the oldest club in England playing on its original land. Even though the club was very prestigious, it was not an obvious one for Wynyard to join given that, before the war, his summers were spent as Assistant Secretary at Lord's. In any event, after the war and once he had moved house, he became a member at the Beaconsfield Club. He was also enthusiastically organising fixtures for the Jokers in his capacity as Chief Joker. He issued each member with a card simply bearing the words 'Cricket, Golf, Curling.' It is unknown how much curling was actually played but he referred to the cricket and golf matches as 'frolics', although as Masterman pointed out 'the rigour of the game was always insisted upon'.

On 15 August, the Jokers played cricket at Victoria Barracks, Windsor against a twelve-man Coldstream Guards side. The Guards made 227 with Wynyard taking four wickets, all bowled, but his Jokers were dismissed for 165 with Teddy, going in last, making 5 runs. This fixture was a regular occurrence and the first time Masterman played in it; he recalled Wynyard giving him:

> The terse order: 'Go in first, and make a hundred.' Military bowling was not very formidable – but military umpiring was. I had made two or three (or was it even nought?) when a ball, well outside my leg stump, struck my pads and I returned unhappily to the pavilion. Teddy made no comment, but a year later on the same ground he won the toss. 'You were unlucky last time,' he said. 'Go in first and make that hundred you should have made last year.' I did not venture to disobey him twice.

On 19 September, Teddy was one of a number of well-known Corinthian football players who played at the Stoke Poges Golf Club. There was an eighteen-hole contest in the morning, under handicap, which resulted in a three-way tie between Tip's brother,

Geoffrey Foster (85 scratch), former Sussex cricketer George Brann (82+3=85) and Teddy Wynyard (99-14=85). It must be stated that the performances of Foster and Brann off scratch and plus three were particularly creditable. The fact that Teddy played off fourteen makes him a little more mortal in sporting terms, but the spirit of competition clearly burned deep. Old Carthusians Charles Wreford-Brown and AM Walters were amongst others who played, and the Stoke Poges Club gave a magnificent challenge bowl for the singles that was to have the names of the three winners inscribed as the joint-holders for 1919. It was agreed the trophy would be played for annually over the course. In the afternoon foursomes, Charles Wreford-Brown offered silver-mounted Malacca canes as the prizes, but Wynyard, partnered by AM Walters, was not a recipient – their match was lost 6 down.

In the evening, Wreford-Brown presided at the General Meeting of the Corinthians Football Club, and it was affirmed the club would compete for cups and prizes only on special occasions as may be determined by the committee – a last bastion of resistance to the encroachment of professionalism and the perceived (and actual) declining standards of sportsmanship.

At the MCC AGM on 5 May 1920, Wynyard was nominated to sit on the MCC committee. It was also proposed that a gateway be erected in St John's Wood Road with iron gates and a bust to commemorate WG Grace – a landmark for cricket lovers ever since. Whilst Teddy was no longer Assistant Secretary, he was now back at the heart of MCC affairs.

He was still playing cricket, turning out in particular for I Zingari and MCC. When the Metropolitan Police were MCC's opponents on 14 August, they simply could not handle Wynyard's lobs and Aubrey Faulkner's leg breaks. They were the only two bowlers needed, and ended with figures of five for 56 and five for 35 respectively with, quite remarkably, every batsman being bowled. Wynyard graciously did not use either Faulkner or himself when the Police followed on. They had reached 79 for two by the close and, although the match was drawn, MCC were treated as victors on the first innings.

Wynyard had already embarked upon a series of turn-of-the-century tours around the world to play cricket. He was now a married man with a young son, but the opportunity arose for him to take his family with him on the 1920 Incogniti tour to North America and Canada. It also afforded Louise the opportunity to let her family in Toronto see Edward junior for the very first time.

Incogniti are the third oldest wandering club after I Zingari and Free Foresters. Their ethos is 'the desire to play a fair and honourable game to a sporting conclusion' and they insist upon the 'proper way of playing, the joy derived from playing for a finish and playing with the opposition rather than against them'. Members have included Reggie Schwarz, Bosanquet, Sir Arthur Conan Doyle and Harold Gilligan.

The thirteen tourists were captained by a fellow Joker, Evelyn Metcalfe, who had toured Egypt with Wynyard in 1909. In addition to Teddy, the most notable players in the group were a young nineteen-year-old Oxford student, Douglas Jardine; the first New Zealand Test captain, Tom Lowry; and film actor, Desmond Roberts. The tourists had a decidedly Eton and military air and included Captain Robert St Leger Fowler, who captained Eton in the 1910 match against Harrow known as 'Fowler's match'. He scored 21 and 64, but Harrow needed only 55 to win. He then proceeded to take eight for 23 to dismiss the opposition for 45. *Wisden* recorded, 'in the whole history of cricket, there has been nothing more sensational.' In the same year he also captained Public Schools against Wynyard's MCC. In 1924, much to Wynyard's delight, Fowler made his debut for Hampshire, but only played three matches because he died of leukaemia only a year later, aged just thirty-four.

The tourists were to play nine matches on the tour but Wynyard actually only played in one game, although doubtless his organisational abilities were utilised in the management of the tour, especially since he was already known in North America from his previous tour before the war.

On 21 August 1920, Teddy, Louise, their two-year-old son and his nurse, Clara Freeman, were on board the SS *Mauretania* when she set sail from Southampton, and the team arrived in Philadelphia on 30 August. Next day they played a two-day game against Frankford, which they won by an innings and 21 runs. Teddy played in the next game against twelve players from Philadelphia Cricket Club at St Martin's ground beginning on 3 September. The home side made 255 and 120. Wynyard bowled in the first innings with figures of nought for 7 but did not bat when Incogniti made 406 for seven declared. That was his only playing contribution to the tour.

After playing their last match in Toronto the party began their journey home, but Teddy and his family were not with them. They stayed on to see Louise's family and friends. They remained for another month, leaving on board the Canadian Pacific RMS *Empress of France* that arrived back at Liverpool on 10 November 1920. They travelled south to their new home as they had moved locally within the Beaconsfield area, to the Red House at Knotty Green, where they lived for the rest of Wynyard's life.

At the MCC AGM on 4 May 1921, FS Jackson was appointed the new President and Wynyard, along with Lord Harris, proposed Russell Bencraft to rejoin the Committee. The annual dinner, in morning dress afterwards, was at a cost of twenty-one shillings to members. Teddy continued to play for the Marylebone Club and, after securing victory by four wickets against London University, was at Lord's on Wednesday 4 July to watch the first day of the Varsity match. Gilbert Ashton captained Cambridge and he had the remarkable distinction of having his two brothers, Hubert and Claude, in the side with him alongside Percy Chapman and Alexander Doggart (father of future England cricketer Hubert Doggart). Oxford had Jardine, Greville Stevens and Robertson-Glasgow in their ranks but lost by an innings and 24 runs. Apart from watching the cricket, Teddy was at St John's Wood that day to honour the ninetieth birthday of Hampshire stalwart, Canon Charles Theobald.

Theobald had narrowly missed out on playing in the Varsity match seventy years earlier and in his day played against the likes of Alfred Mynn, John Wisden, Julius Caesar and John Lilywhite, as well as knowing Fuller Pilch. Wynyard was joined by Lord Harris and Francis Lacey when he went to the box to offer 'many happy returns' to the Canon, and conveyed apologies from FS Jackson who had been unavoidably detained in the House of Commons.

Following the previous autumn's Incogniti tour, the Philadelphia Pilgrims returned the compliment by visiting England and playing twelve matches over a period of a month beginning on 29 July. The highlight was the two-day game against MCC, captained by Lord Harris, at Lord's on 11 and 12 August. The presence of Harris in the side prompted *The Times* to wax lyrically about the man who had captained England before WG Grace. The Marylebone Club batted first achieving 348 with Wynyard going in at number six, making 17, and Harris, following him at seven, knocking up 25. The Pilgrims made 230 (Wynyard two for 68, Fowler five for 78) and 87 to lose by an innings and 31 runs. Wynyard could thank Francis Brooke for one of his wickets. Charles Morris, who had scored 73, hit Wynyard off the full face of the bat down the leg side and could hardly believe his eyes when the wicketkeeper pulled off an absolutely blinding catch. Harris fielded at mid off on a fast wicket and outfield, which *The Times* considered 'a wonderful performance'. Their correspondent continued:

> It was delightful to see Major EG Wynyard turn out again. He is a 'mere boy' at 60. He is, however, as keen on his bowl as he was at 35 or even 45 years of age... he went in too late to give us another classic innings. He did not care at the moment – the moment of caring has passed.

On 16 August, the Pilgrims were the guests of Sir Rowland Blades MP at the House of Commons. Teddy was amongst those meeting the American cricketers along with Austen Chamberlain, who had been Chancellor of the Exchequer until April and was now Leader of the House, and such cricketing dignitaries as Lord Harris, FS Jackson, AC MacLaren, Pelham Warner and Reggie Spooner. In his speech, Chamberlain said, 'the highest praise an Englishman could pay to cricket was when he described an action which no gentleman would do as "not cricket". The phrase was colloquial because "our national game has profoundly affected our national character".'

Given the way our modern day politicians talk about the special relationship between the UK and America, it was particularly interesting to read the comments that Chamberlain then addressed to the Pilgrims: 'wherever they went in the country they would find the same sense of kinship with the US, the same determination and earnest desire to act with them wherever possible for the peace of the world and the advancement of civilisation.'

On 6 October, Teddy returned to his solicitor, Richard Wood in Lincoln's Inn, to make further family arrangements. In the second Codicil to his Will he appointed Colonel HC Moorhouse and William Herbert Cawthra to be Edward's guardians in the event of Louise's death. Harry Moorhouse was a good friend of Wynyard and a fellow Joker. They had toured Egypt together and played in three non first-class games against the Public Schools. He became Lieutenant-Governor of Nigeria and held that position until 1925. Although William Cawthra, a barrister by profession, was visiting England at the time the Codicil was made, his home was in Forest Hill, Toronto. One of his forebears had joined forces with Louise's grandfather, James Gooderham Worts junior, to establish Canada's first infectious disease centre at Toronto General Hospital. The Cawthra family were famous for their business, social and cultural contributions to the City, and their successors continue to play significant roles in Toronto to this day.

While the quality of both people to be guardians was not in doubt, they may well have had to perform their duties at a distance. Perhaps Teddy realised this because on 30 March 1927 he made a third codicil directing that Frank Hubert Hollins of 70 Brook Street be guardian if the others named failed to act. Hollins toured Canada with Wynyard and his family during 1923.

Wynyard, having put his affairs in order, then quietly settled down to life in the Red House with Louise and Edward. There is no public record of Teddy playing any cricket during 1922 but that is not to say he did not do so, and on 27 July he was on hand to greet the visiting Canadian team when their boat docked down at Southampton. They were to play eleven matches under the captaincy of Norman Seagram. Dr Russell Bencraft accompanied Wynyard and they handed over a personal letter of welcome from the MCC President – now Frederick Thesiger, First Viscount Chelmsford. The

Canadian cricketers must have looked upon Wynyard as one of their own because, after they had returned home, they sent him a telegram in November asking him to put together a team to visit the following autumn.

As he started to put his plans together, Teddy had another duty to perform in the library at Charterhouse on 9 December 1922. He stepped in to replace his old captain, Toronto-born Edward Parry, and presented a replica of the 1881 FA Cup winner's medal to the School. It was a gift from the surviving members of the team as a memorial to the dead. AH Tod, who had been in the cup-winning side and only retired as a master in 1920, was present on the evening, as was the eminent amateur footballer, AM Walters.

The Carthusian reported that Wynyard spoke very well about 'the honour their victory had given to Charterhouse and the honour Charterhouse conferred upon them by receiving their gift'. He continued by saying no praise could be high enough for Parry, who as captain might have had equals but never a superior, and Charterhouse had, in its football, a priceless heritage. When Teddy left Charterhouse, he had gone to a rugby-playing school and, although *The Carthusian* makes no specific reference to the point, he may well have seized the opportunity (it would have been in character to do so) and suggested his old school broaden its sporting horizons. The magazine does record the Headmaster's response when he assured 'Major Wynyard that Charterhouse would begin to think of playing rugby only when Rugby School took to soccer'!

1923 saw a more active Teddy on the golf course and on the cricket field. On 2 May he attended the AGM of MCC, where he remained a committee member. A month later, at sixty-two years of age, he played at Lord's for MCC against London University. It was a single-innings match in which the Marylebone Club were the victors by 187 runs, with Teddy scoring 27, taking one catch, and two wickets for 7 runs off just 3.4 overs. He then played alongside Jardine at Chislehurst for I Zingari against West Kent in a twelve-a-side fixture.

Wynyard's time, however, was largely taken up with putting together the Free Foresters side he had been invited to take to Canada for a late season tour. Although Yorkshire had already won the County Championship, the season still had a fortnight to run and this hindered Wynyard in terms of the strength of the side he could select to go with him.

It was this tour that enabled John Masterman to become properly acquainted with Teddy, whom he acknowledged to be one of his boyhood heroes. Masterman had been born in 1891 and educated at Worcester College, Oxford. He was an exchange lecturer at the University of Freiburg when the First World War began and was interned as an enemy alien for four years in a detention camp in Ruhleben. When the conflict was over he returned to England and became a tutor in Modern History at Christ Church, Oxford.

Masterman is best known for his role with the intelligence services during the Second World War. Ian Fleming worked in his department and there is a belief that he adapted Masterman's name to Jill Masterson, a character in *Goldfinger*. Indeed, Masterman occasionally used the pseudonym of Masterson himself during the wartime years.

The journalist, author and historian, Ben Macintyre describes Masterman as:

A cold fish, apparently without romantic feelings for either sex, but cricket was different ... something about the game attracts the sort of mind also drawn to the secret worlds of intelligence and counter-intelligence – a complex test of brain and brawn, a game of honour interwoven with trickery, played with ruthless good manners and dependent on minute gradations of physics and psychology and tea breaks ... [Masterman] was highly intellectual, intensely conventional and faintly priggish, with a granite sense of moral duty. He was the embodiment of the British Establishment ... He neither smoked nor drank and lived in a world of High Tables and elevated scholarships, exclusively inhabited by wealthy, privileged, intelligent English men ... [he] represented English traits that were once considered virtues *noblesse oblige*, hard work, and unquestioning obedience to the norms of society. By his own account he was almost obsessively anxious to conform to accepted standards.

Certain similarities in character and beliefs with Wynyard, but enough of a difference not to make them automatically the friends they became in spite of their thirty-year age gap.

There were fourteen in the touring party and many, in addition to Masterman, were Teddy's fellow Jokers and friends including Lieutenant Colonel JC Hartley (who had been on Warner's tour to South Africa in 1905/6), Captain Robert St Leger Fowler and Frank Hollins (Eton and Lancashire). *The Times* was very complimentary, saying, 'the team of Free Foresters that went out for a short cricket tour to Canada ... [were] under the able and kindly management of Major EG Wynyard.' A photograph was taken of the tour party showing the captain looking thinner and greyer, with a gaunt face indicating that, at sixty-two years old, age was starting to catch up with him.

On 24 August 1923, Teddy, Louise and their young son, Edward junior, boarded SS *Montlaurier* along with the other cricketers, bound for New York and Toronto. When the ship docked in Canada, on 1 September, the side was met by Mr George Ferrabee, who accompanied them back to Montreal where they were taken to the Hotel Windsor, which for decades billed itself as 'the best hotel in all the Dominion'.

Fowler led the side when Wynyard did not play in either of the games in Montreal and the first match when the team moved on to Toronto, where the tourists were entertained for dinner at the Military Institute as well as being taken to the Toronto Exhibition to see a procession of pedigree cattle from all over the world. Teddy captained the side in the next match against Eighteen Boys of the United Colleges. The Boys batted first and made 146 but simply could not cope with the wily old lobster as Teddy took five for 10 in just eight overs. At the end of the first day, the Free Foresters were struggling on 111 for eight, but progressed next day to 136 with Masterman making 18 and Wynyard 14. The main destroyer was Lyon who took six for 57. He was the son of a famous Canadian golfer, George Lyon, who had won the gold medal at the 1904 Olympics in St Louis. It was the last time golf was an Olympic event before Justin Rose won in 2016, so Lyon had the unique claim of being the reigning Olympic Champion for 112 years.

In their second innings, the Colleges were dismissed for 109 (Masterman two for 20, Wynyard one for 5) and Free Foresters made 63 for four (Masterman 13, Wynyard did not bat) in a drawn match. Teddy did not play in the next fixture, but on Monday 17 September the team were driven through delightful scenery to Hamilton for their two-day game against Fifteen of Hamilton and District. The Free Foresters fielded a side of twelve players led by Wynyard. Hamilton made only 124 (Masterman one for 18, Wynyard two for 6) but the tourists responded with 265 (Masterman 17, Wynyard 20 not out when batting last). Hamilton more or less equalled their first innings knock with 123 to lose by an innings and 18. Fowler was again the star turn with seven for 20, but Wynyard weighed in with three for 21 (two bowled and one lbw).

In his *Blackwood's Magazine* article published in 1974, Masterman's recollection of events over half a century later was a shade awry. First he talks of the tour being in 1922 and then of Wynyard playing in 'only three or four of the matches'. In fact, the tour was a year later and Wynyard played in only two games, with the match against Hamilton being his last. However Masterman commented that whilst he had not seen Teddy play in his great days, 'there were traces of greatness still to be seen', and cited a shot he played 'which few could have equalled'. He explained:

> The bowler was medium or slow-medium and he delivered a half volley just outside the leg stump. Ranji would have glanced the ball past fine leg with almost majestic contempt: Teddy treated it differently. He jumped off both feet and made a half-turn to his left in the air, and then, coming to ground exactly at the right moment, drove – yes, *drove* – the ball for six between fine and long leg. Surely a miracle of timing. Incredible, you might say, but I saw him do it – and he was sixty-one [actually sixty-two].

This appears to be a repeat of the 'back stroke' Wynyard had played in his 411-run partnership with Bertie Poore, twenty-four years earlier. Masterman also had another story to tell about Wynyard on this Canadian tour:

Off the field, as well as on, he demanded the best behaviour of all members of his side. Once in Canada, I was instructed to go out to dinner with him to play bridge with two of his friends. (He was not a good player, but it was *lèse-majesté* to hint any criticism of his bids or play.) We had an agreeable and remunerative evening and returned about midnight to our hotel. I was, therefore, very surprised when he fell upon me at breakfast next morning. 'You behaved very badly last night when we came home; in this country it is thought most discourteous to keep your hat on in the lift.' I felt a little ill-used, since the only occupant of the lift besides ourselves had been an elderly man, sitting on the floor, his clothing dishevelled, his head resting on his knees and it seemed, sunk in a drunken slumber.

It is worth remembering, when considering this rebuke, that far from being a recalcitrant young cricketer just out of school, Masterman was now thirty-two years of age and a respected Oxford tutor renowned as a stickler for 'obedience to the norms of society'. So much for Wynyard mellowing with age and marriage! Nevertheless, it is important to realise that upholding standards had been drilled into him from an early age. At Charterhouse, it was always considered an offence against public taste to wear a bowler hat within the school precincts. This may explain Wynyard's sensitivity on the issue and expectation that others would comply with a Canadian social convention (even if it was not sufficiently well established for Masterman to be aware of it and the victim was a comatose drunk, at midnight, who was hardly going to take umbrage!)

Originally an invitation to travel south and play in Philadelphia had been declined on grounds there would be insufficient time, but the tour was extended, and on Saturday 29 September there was the first of two two-day games against All Philadelphia. It seems likely Wynyard did not make this leg of the journey because he, Louise, Edward and their nurse Clara Freeman made their departure from Montreal on board SS *Montclare* and did not arrive back at Liverpool until 21 October. After all his travels, Teddy's final cricketing tour abroad was over.

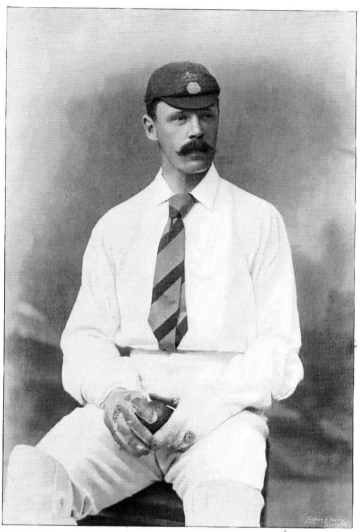

One of the best-known photographs of Teddy, from
Famous Cricketers and Cricket Grounds (published 1895), shows a
relaxed man wearing both wicketkeeping gloves and a tie

19

STUMPS ARE FINALLY DRAWN

1924-36

Whilst Teddy and his family were on their way back from Canada, his two elder sisters, Eleanor and Lily, were on board *Anchises* and also Liverpool-bound. They had been in Adelaide for six months visiting their half brother, Henry. He had emigrated with his wife, Nellie, to set up home in the country where they had married before the war.

Once home, Teddy took himself off to play golf with the Jokers, and 6 March 1924 proved to be a memorable golfing day at the New Zealand Club in Surrey. The opponents were Royal Wimbledon and the match was halved. Wynyard won his singles 3 and 2 but in the afternoon, partnering Harry Moorhouse who was presumably on leave from his posting in Nigeria, lost 2 and 1. Let *The Times* act as the record for the morning's events:

Major EG Wynyard, the Chief Joker, emphasised his exalted position by holing the short sixteenth in one and therefore laid himself open to the usual penalty. It is understood, however, that by an unwritten law of the Companionship he has to present, in addition, a new driver to each of his subordinates, a liability which was sufficient to affect his golf in the afternoon.

The reporting of Jokers' matches in *The Times* may have had something to do with their golfing correspondent, Bernard Darwin, being a Joker himself.

Darwin was brought up by his grandfather, the British naturalist Charles Darwin, when his mother died just four days after his birth. He was educated at Eton and Trinity College, Cambridge, where he won his golfing blue. He entered journalism and covered golf for *The Times* from 1907 to 1953. He was a member at Royal Wimbledon and became Captain of the R&A in 1934. Over forty years after his death, he was elected to the World Golf Hall of Fame in 2005.

In addition to his golfing works, Darwin was an authority on Charles Dickens, and his biography of WG Grace, first published in 1934, is a succinct and easy to read account of the Doctor's life in just 120 pages. It is reverential and by its very nature superficial, but what makes Darwin's literary style so enjoyable is his understated and self-deprecating sense of humour, which is nowhere better demonstrated than in his reports of Jokers matches.

In the spring of 1925, it was time again for the Jokers to play against Royal Wimbledon, but this time at Wynyard's home course at Beaconsfield. The match report stated that, 'the men of Wimbledon came to Beaconsfield to play a return match against the myrmidons of Major Wynyard, and the Jokers, belying their name, made a serious and successful effort to win a match.' Darwin waxed poetical:

On every side Field Marshalls gleamed, With Admirals the Ocean teemed, And there are some golfers as well. Major Wynyard, like the Duke of Plaza Toro, led his regiment from behind and set a good example by beating Colonel Malcolm. Mr Bond, who has always been a thorn in the Jokers' side was actually beaten by an adversary who played much better than he expected and generally the Jokers had a good day of it.

That player continued to be in great form with both club and pen and, two years later, observed:

The teams that play against Major Wynyard's Jokers are always carefully graded to suit the varying and usually senile capabilities of their adversaries. Apparently the charitable process can be carried too far for the Jokers have now beaten Royal Wimbledon first of all at Wimbledon and yesterday [6 April] at New Zealand in two successive matches, which is altogether too good a joke. Major MacRae, who is probably one of the half dozen longest drivers alive when he really gets under the tail of the ball, found that the fir trees rather cramped his style, and was comfortably beaten by one who seldom hits far enough to reach them.

Modesty indeed, as Darwin reached the semi-finals of the British Amateur Championship in both 1909 and 1921.

Meanwhile at the MCC AGM in May 1924, Teddy and Henry Leveson Gower had to retire from the committee by rotation, having served for four years. Wynyard was still playing and in July turned out alongside his old partner, Bertie Poore (now a retired Brigadier General), for I Zingari against the Royal Naval College at Dartmouth. Poore took three wickets and Wynyard scored 46 to revive old memories. Poore was still playing for his local club side at Hinton St Mary, thirty miles from Bournemouth.

On 25 August 1924, Wynyard played for MCC against Hampstead Cricket Club in a one-day game at Lord's. Hampstead had been founded in 1865, but a cloud hung over them because the lease of their ground was to terminate at the close of the following season and the land was so valuable as a building site (*plus ça change, plus c'est la même chose*) that a large sum of money had to be raised if it was to be preserved for cricket. It is pleasing to report they play at Lymington Road to this day.

Wynyard made 26 out of 224, but 20 runs were still needed by Hampstead when the official finishing time was reached. *The Times* reported that Teddy (and this speaks volumes for his approach to the game) allowed extra time so that his opponents could 'convert a moral victory into an actual one'. Play eventually finished at 6.45 pm with Hampstead on 225 for three.

There is no record in Cricket Archive or *The Times* of Teddy playing cricket during the 1925 season, but on 30 July 1926 he turned out for I Zingari at Highclere against Woolton House. He had two victims including the dismissal of Denis Hill-Wood, who went on to become Chairman of Arsenal FC. The match ended in a draw.

On Saturday 18 June 1927, Teddy returned to Charterhouse for the consecration by Theodore, Bishop of Winchester, in the presence of the Archbishop of Canterbury, of the school's War Memorial Chapel designed by Sir Giles Gilbert Scott. Scott was part of the procession into the church that included Wynyard, Lieutenant General Sir Robert Baden-Powell, AH Tod, AM Walters, Charles Wreford-Brown and Field Marshall Lord Plumer, who had been the Commander of the Second Army British Expeditionary Force, amongst other dignitaries. The tablet at the entrance poignantly read: '1914-18. You who enter this Chapel think upon the Carthusians in memory of whom it was built who died for their country and remembering them quit you like men be strong.'

The procession then passed the statue of Haig Brown into the Chapel where the Headmaster and Lord Plumer paid tribute to 'the silent and invisible congregation'.

On 28 July 1928, over fifty years after he first played at Lord's, Wynyard turned out for MCC in a one-day single innings match against Lords and Commons. Overnight rain persuaded the visitors to insert their opposition, and Teddy opened the batting. Unfortunately, in the words of *The Times* correspondent, he did not celebrate the occasion of his anniversary 'with one of his long innings but he took a wicket later in the day with his lobs and that was an event in itself.' The match was drawn thanks to a game-saving innings by Waldron Smithers, the MP for Chislehurst, of whom *The Times* commented 'some of his strokes have never even appeared in some men's dreams'.

Back at the Red House, it appeared Louise was having trouble with her domestic staff. In January she had placed an advertisement in the personal columns of *The Times* seeking a 'good, plain cook' from the middle of February. In March a further advertisement appeared, this time for a parlour maid to live in. By October the household requirements had increased because it was stated there were already four maids kept but another parlour maid or experienced house-parlour maid was now needed for early November, again with an offer of accommodation. These employment issues seem to have been resolved satisfactorily because no further advertisements appeared, at least in *The Times*, during the following year.

On 26 March 1929, Wynyard was present at the Mansion House for a dinner in honour of I Zingari, with around 250 members in attendance. It was a formal affair with white tie and I Zingari sash being required dress for the evening. The host was the Lord Mayor of London, Sir Kynaston Studd, the eldest of three brothers who had played together in the same Cambridge side. The guests included Prime Minister Stanley Baldwin; the Governor (previously known as the Grand Master) of I Zingari, the sixth Earl of Dartmouth; and a large number of the cricketing dignitaries of the day.

After the toast of 'the King', the noted baritone Kennerley Rumford, who had withdrawn from Wynyard's Free Foresters team to tour Canada, sang the I Zingari song. The Earl of Dartmouth then proposed the toast 'I Zingari', to which Lord Harris was one of the three speakers who replied. The famous Romanian violinist, Georges Boulanger, played a solo and then there were toasts by the Lord Mayor and Stanley Baldwin. In all there was a combination of nine toasts and/or speakers with two musical interludes – one trusts it was a bibulous evening!

While Wynyard's cricket was now mainly for I Zingari, his golf thrived as he partnered Roger Wethered in a win for the Jokers against Oxford University Golf Club. In 1931 Teddy was made an Honorary Life Member of the Oxford Graduates' Golfing Society.

The next couple of years saw Wynyard having to cope with the loss of two of his closest family. On 26 December 1929, at Crafers in Adelaide, Teddy's half brother Henry died at forty-nine years of age. Just over two years later, on 3 January 1932, Teddy's youngest sister, Amy died at Beaconsfield, aged sixty-six.

In 1931, Teddy had attended the annual dinner of The King's Liverpool Regiment at the Café Royal in June. The following month, on 25 July, he was back on the cricket field, captaining MCC against Lords and Commons. Nearly thirty years before, Teddy – an instructor at Sandhurst – captained Gerald French. The experience was repeated after Wynyard had passed his seventieth birthday in his last recorded game. French confirmed this in *The Cornerstone of English*

Cricket and recalled that when Wynyard led the MCC team on to the field, there were ominous clouds in the sky. The portents for play were not good. Wynyard proceeded to:

> ...address the umpires in these words, which I have never forgotten, 'we have come out here to play cricket, we don't go in for rain.' Almost, at once the storm broke, and for some time we stood out in pelting rain, until finally, when it had become difficult to see one wicket from the other, even our zealous captain was obliged to give in. But I feel sure there was not one of us who would have jibbed at staying out indefinitely with Teddy Wynyard's inspiriting example before us.

It appears that age had not greatly mellowed Teddy. Douglas Jardine, another autocratic leader who had played under Wynyard on the Incogniti tour of North America, was about to lead England on the now-infamous Bodyline tour to Australia. Furthermore, Wynyard was very well acquainted with the two managers for that tour, Plum Warner and Richard Palairet (brother of Lionel).

Jardine, like Wynyard, had been born in India and there were certain similarities in their characters. Jardine's daughter, Fianach, said her father 'could be harsh in his judgments when others did not live up to the high standards he set for himself'. *The Times* obituary recorded that 'he stuck to his guns with a tenacity which nothing could disturb'. Jardine was still an Oxford undergraduate at an impressionable age, when he toured with Wynyard, but whilst there may well have been empathy between them, Douglas' character traits seem to have already been well formed. One of his Winchester masters, Rockley Wilson, when learning that his former pupil was going to captain the team in Australia, observed that 'he might well win us the Ashes but he might lose us a dominion'. Prophetic words.

Jardine's own account of the tour, *In Quest of the Ashes*, was revised and updated in 2005 with a foreword by Mike Brearley. He agreed with Bob Wyatt that the use of 'persistent short-pitched leg theory was against the spirit of the game'.

Whilst that may be the opinion of one of England's great captains, what did Wynyard think when news of the controversy reached him? The first important point to note is that Teddy had been a member of the MCC committee during the previous decade and still knew all the key figures well. It is unlikely that he would have been in disagreement with the views expressed by the MCC Secretary, and fellow Joker, William Findlay. As a member of the leading amateur clubs of the day, it would be unthinkable, viewed from the other side of the world, that an English amateur player could perform an unsportsmanlike act. I Zingari's whole ethos centred upon the way in which the game was played, and Jardine was a Zingaro. He had even worn his I Zingari tie when he boarded *Orontes* bound for Australia.

As the true facts started to emerge, one can imagine a reluctant recalibration of opinion on Wynyard's part. In the biography of his old record-breaking batting partner, Bertie Poore, Jeremy Lonsdale wrote 'Poore is said to have expressed some distaste for the Bodyline tactics and a possibly apocryphal quote "By gad, if they did that to me I'd fix bayonet and charge the blighters!"' Perhaps a similar reaction disturbed Louise's peace and quiet at the Red House!

Wynyard continued to run sides and remained a member of the I Zingari committee until his death. Arrowsmith said, 'it was not to be expected that such a forceful character would be a docile member of a committee and Sir Francis Lacey sent to the Governor of I Zingari, who had been unavoidably absent, an account of a meeting in April 1934 that concluded "they are good boys, your I Zingari officers. Even Teddy submitted to order".'

Lacey had organised the Easter classes at Lord's since 1902 and had been assisted for a large part of that time by Wynyard. In 1932 it was the turn of Teddy's son, Edward, to benefit from this tuition. The lessons paid off, because on 13 August 1934 he captained the side in the annual match for schoolboys under sixteen chosen from the Easter classes and an eleven selected by Mr Carleton Tufnell (father of Neville, who had toured South Africa with Teddy in 1909/10). Edward, who was at Eton College, won the toss and elected to bat. His side reached 151 for two at lunchtime, thanks largely to a brilliant century by JM Pollen of Downside who scored 106 out of 126 in 105 minutes. When the third wicket fell early in the afternoon, Edward walked to the crease and saw the ball well from the start. He made two good off drives for 4 and 2 in the first over he faced.

He should have had an extra run but the umpire called 'one short', which happened, unusually, no fewer than six times in the team's innings. *The Times* reported, 'Wynyard played bright cricket until playing over a ball from Richardson and was mainly responsible for the 30 runs added for the fourth wicket.' He actually made 18. At tea the score was 268 for seven, but Edward opted not to declare and the last three wickets added just another 11 runs. Also in the side from Eton were H Tennyson (eldest son of the former England captain and great-grandson of the poet) and John Jacob Astor VII (youngest child of Nancy Astor, the first female MP to take her seat in the House of Commons), who scored 1 and 11 respectively.

Tufnell's side were dismissed for 244, just 35 runs behind. When the Lord's Eleven batted again there were six consecutive maidens bowled to Pollen and Tennyson (were they batting to captain's orders?), but Edward (who did not bat in the second innings) declared on 140 for three leaving ninety minutes for Tufnell's side to make 176, but it was finally agreed to draw stumps with their score on 104 for two.

Life was now more sedate for Teddy resting back home, but the winter of 1935/6 afforded an opportunity for him to see James Wynyard, from the New Zealand branch of his family, play for the All Blacks on their UK tour.

The summer of 1935 saw the visit of a South African touring team and on 13 May a dinner was held at Carpenters Hall for them, hosted by Surrey, and their President, Henry Leveson Gower. Jack Hobbs was in attendance and he had previously suggested that South Africa should only be allotted three Tests because they had never won a Test in England. Sir Abe Bailey was in typically belligerent form. He said there was too much interference in cricket and that it was becoming too professionalised, was lacking in amateur spirit with no leadership or policy. He continued, 'the person who showed most sport should always be the real leader. Was MCC or the Board of Control the dictator? That question was often asked.' It appears Bailey still remembered the difficulties of over a quarter of a century before in trying to set up a triangular tournament and, more recently, the tactics adopted in the Bodyline series. He then turned his sights from Jardine to Hobbs. 'Should the Boat Race cease because Oxford had not won for many years or horse racing be curtailed because the Aga Khan was unbeatable on the English racecourse?' Bailey ended by saying there was a spirit of adventure in cricket. The South African team stood for a straight life and a straight bat, representing South Africa, a society of equals, on a mission of friendship and unity, and they would, he knew, rise to the occasion.

He was to be proved correct because the team captained by Herbert Wade beat Bob Wyatt's England 1-0 to win both a Test and the series for the first time in this country.

Teddy Wynyard had been Abe Bailey's representative before the war and had very close associations with South African cricket, but *The Times* did not list him amongst those present. If he was not there, it was the clearest possible sign that, approaching his mid-seventies, he was now slowing down and withdrawing more and more into life at home with Louise at the Red House.

1936 witnessed the Berlin Olympics and Gubby Allen's England beating the touring Indian side 2-0 in a three Test series. Derbyshire won their only County Championship up to the present time, but Teddy never did witness Hampshire achieve the distinction.

Summer gave way to autumn and, as Gubby Allen prepared to take an MCC side to Australia for another Ashes series, sadness descended upon the Red House. On 30 October 1936, surrounded by his family, the innings of Major Edward George Wynyard finally came to its close. The cause of death was shown on the certificate as 'bronchitis, auricular fibrillation and arterio sclerosis'. Irregular heartbeat, thickening of the walls of the arteries and a chest infection will have meant fatigue and breathlessness during the final, frustrating days for this man of action.

The obituaries naturally listed his many accomplishments both on and off the sporting field. *The Times*, on the following day, described 'Ted Wynyard' as 'one of the greatest all-round athletes of his generation'. Plum Warner, in similar vein, when writing for *The Cricketer*, called him:

A magnificent all round athlete ... unquestionably the best cricketer produced by the Army ... Major Wynyard was a natural and adaptable batsman, with a marked individuality of his own. He possessed every stroke, and was particularly fond of the pull, which he used to make by going down on his right knee and hitting at the pitch of the ball. A superb fieldsman in almost any position, especially the slips and at short leg, he was also a very fair wicketkeeper and a useful under-hand bowler.

Major CHB Pridham, the cadet at Sandhurst under Teddy who had umpired one of his wartime matches, wrote an appreciation of his former tutor. He thought:

Perhaps Wynyard's chief characteristic was his adaptability for he was uniformly successful wherever he played, in all classes of cricket, in many climes, and on all kinds of wickets ... for several seasons, in Hampshire's second-class days, he kept wicket for the county in first-rate style, in addition to being far and away their best batsman.

The 1937 *Wisden* was also fulsome in the obituary it published:

Wynyard was over 6 feet in height and finely built ... a brilliant player of most games and excelled on the cricket field, where his commanding figure could not escape attention ... He used to say that he made 150 centuries in all kinds of cricket of which he kept a record. [He was] a fine, free hitter [who] used a great variety of strokes, especially those in front of the wicket. He had a grand drive, a powerful 'hook', a good cut, back strokes of a forcing description and a rare pull in making which he dropped to his right knee and drove the ball on the half volley over mid-on. He developed also a special method of hitting left handed bowling over cover point in most effective fashion. While he could field admirably anywhere, he excelled at slip and mid-on.

How many accounts make mention of that trademark shot off one knee!

The Times carried a notice that the funeral of the 'beloved husband of Louise Wynyard' would take place at the 800-year-old Penn Parish Church on Monday 2 November 1936 at 12 noon. The Rector of Beaconsfield, the Reverend RBP Wells, and the local the Reverend EA Smith both assisted Prebendary LJ Percival, one of Wynyard's golfing Jokers, to officiate at the funeral service.

The weather could have been kinder to them all. It was unsettled, mild in temperature but cloudy with local rain and drizzle, as the mourners in sombre mood congregated at the church. These included a large cross-section of relatives, friends, teammates and colleagues from the fields of cricket, football, golf, the military and Old Carthusians; reflecting the wide breadth of Teddy's interests. Amongst those present were Ronnie Aird, Sir Stanley Cochrane, William Findlay, Colonel Hartley, JT Hearne, Henry Leveson Gower, AM Walters and Pelham Warner.

It was pleasing to see that the great Middlesex and England professional Jack Hearne was in attendance. He had been the destroyer of Australia, taking ten wickets in the match, when Wynyard had made his Test match debut. Hearne died in April 1944 at his home in nearby Chalfont St Giles, where he had been the rector's warden at his local parish church.

Teddy was buried in the Penn church cemetery. Louise, Edward, Eleanor and Lily Wynyard, having bid farewell to a husband, father and brother for the final time, solemnly made their way home to the Red House.

The day of the funeral saw the official launch of the BBC Television Service from Alexandra Palace in London. For a man who had been born in India shortly after the Indian Mutiny, where the means of communication had been extremely basic, the seventy-five years of his life had seen enormous change: telephone, automobile and now television, not to mention four different monarchs and a catastrophic war that was meant to end all wars. Teddy was now at rest. The war that was under three years away really was one the next generation would have to fight.

Wynyard's affairs were easy to administer as he left everything to Louise. Probate was granted on 21 January 1937 with effects of £1,651 and 10 shillings gross (£1,332 7s 1d net, or £81,640 in today's money).

Teddy's two elder sisters died within two years of one another. Eleanor passed away on 2 October 1940 at 7 Vale Road, Tunbridge Wells, aged eighty-two; Lily died in 1942.

Louise continued to live at The Red House until after the Second World War, when she moved to 41 Melbury Court at 240-280 Kensington High Street. In June 1950, Louise attended the marriage of her son to 21-year-old Ann Cowan. They also lived in a property called the Red House, but on Welford Road, Chapel Brampton. They had three daughters, Georgina (born in 1951), Ann (1954) and Edwina (1960). Edward died aged seventy-three in Northampton in September 1991 and his widow, Ann, died in November 2006.

Louise lived to enjoy seeing her grandchildren grow up, and was still living at Melbury Court when she passed away on 24 November 1972. She was just two days short of her ninety-third birthday. She had made a will in 1966 leaving everything to her son apart from legacies for her long-standing housekeepers, Florence McGraith and Mabel Bricknell. When probate was granted on 6 March 1973 she had effects totalling £20,613 (£245,300 in today's money).

Louise left a specific instruction in her will that she wanted to be buried in the grave of her husband. Clearly their relationship had been a very close and loving one.

Teddy Wynyard had not been cricket's only major loss in 1936. The great lob bowler George Simpson-Hayward, who had often toured with Teddy, died on 2 October aged sixty-one; ten days later Bernard Bosanquet passed away at his home in Ewhurst, Surrey, on the day before his fifty-ninth birthday. At the end of the year, on 10 December, the game lost one of the great professionals of the Golden Age, whose career had intertwined at critical points with that of Wynyard: Robert Abel.

Whereas Wynyard had been born into a military family, educated at public school and enjoyed private means that enabled him to travel the world playing cricket when he retired from the Army, Abel came from completely the opposite end of the social spectrum. He was four years older than Teddy, born at 18 Commercial Road, Rotherhithe in 1857, and was the son of a lamplighter. He stood only five feet, four inches tall, was of slim build and had been spotted playing club cricket in Southwark Park. He made his professional debut for Surrey in 1881 and for England seven years later. He was Wisden Cricketer of the Year for 1890 and scored 2,000 runs in each season from 1895 to 1902. In 1899 he carried his bat for 357 towards Surrey's 811 against Somerset at The Oval. He had an unconventional technique for his day with a predilection for cross-batted shots but, CB Fry said, 'he gathers runs like blackberries everywhere he goes.'

Abel had suffered from eye problems ever since he contracted a rheumatic infection following diphtheria in 1893. The following year, in preparation for the day when he might no longer be able to play, he opened Abel and Lane, a sporting outfitter and cricket bat manufacturer at 310 Kennington Road near The Oval. By 1902, however, the business was in trouble. Abel dissolved his partnership with Lane and set up on his own. He retired from first-class cricket in 1904 but his poor eyesight limited his coaching opportunities at The Oval and Dulwich College. After the First World War, life was not kind to him. His wife died in 1923 and his business again fell into debt. In 1927 he sold out to Charles Riggs and a fund was set up for him by the *Daily Mail*, as well as financial assistance being provided by Surrey. Sadly by the end of his life he was blind and died six weeks after Teddy, at 43 Handforth Road, just around the corner from The Oval.

Bobby Abel was one of five professionals who requested more money to play in the deciding Test against Australia in 1896, the game in which Wynyard made his international debut. It is difficult to think of two men more different in terms of physique, background and lifestyle than Abel and Wynyard, but their shared love of the game has eternally linked them together on celluloid, walking side by side from the Assistant Secretary's garden to the Lord's Pavilion, on the occasion of WG's fiftieth birthday match 120 years ago.

It is a treasured reminder of the Golden Age of Cricket that will forever be with us.

The 1896 England team with whom Teddy
made his international debut.
Back: W Hearn (umpire), TW Hayward, AFA Lilley,
T Richardson, JT Hearne.
Middle: AC MacLaren, KS Ranjitsinhji, WG Grace (captain),
FS Jackson, EG Wynyard.
Front: R Abel, R Peel.

20

REFLECTIONS FROM THE PAVILION

Wynyard died long before I was born, so there was never an opportunity to meet him and make my own character assessment. But would we have been compatible in any event?

There are so many questions I would have wanted to ask him. What did he think of the way football had developed since his own FA Cup winning days? What were the conditions like in the Burmese jungle and, by contrast, how would he describe life with the English society during those halcyon winter days in Davos? What could he recall of the men whose paths crossed with his, ranging from Aubrey Smith and Baden-Powell at Charterhouse, to the cadet Churchill at Sandhurst, Conan Doyle in Switzerland and the MCC dressing room, not to mention just about every famous name in the Golden Age of Cricket from Grace through Trumper to Hobbs? How did he feel about the demand for more money by the professionals in 1896, and what was really behind his dispute with Ranjitsinhji? Why did he decline the captaincy of England in Australia in 1906? How friendly was he with Jardine on their tour to America together, and what was his opinion of Bodyline?

How would he have reacted to my questions? Would he have recognized a love of shared sporting interests and been the jovial Joker
or, instead, could he have resented the interrogation bringing the
autocratic side of his character to the fore? Might I have witnessed
what Jessop described as 'a violent tirade' from Blood Orange, leaving me 'shaken and exhausted' as appears to have happened to Ranjitsinhji when he ate those hothouse grapes? This contrast between
dark moods and jovial prankster would be a fruitful area of research
for the modern-day psychologist, but I fancy Wynyard would have
been a reluctant patient even if such advanced analysis had been
available in his day.

It is tempting to apply a little basic amateur psychology and say
that Teddy's character must have been shaped by his family circumstances, the early loss of his mother and spending his adolescent
years in all-male Victorian boarding schools. He then lived for nearly eight years on the Indian subcontinent with the Army and, on his
return, trained military cadets at Sandhurst. Even after retirement he
went hunting in the wilds of Newfoundland with his friend Hesketh
Vernon Hesketh-Prichard and travelled around the world on various
cricketing tours. Whilst there is evidence that he was close to his
four sisters, none of whom married, there is nothing else to suggest
close female companionship until he met and married Louise, by
which time he was fifty-two years of age. It is clear they had a close
and loving relationship and Masterman did say in his later years that
Wynyard mellowed, although he could also testify that it was only
to a certain extent!

Teddy's character is not one though that fits neatly into a text-
book case study. The stern, occasionally hot-headed disciplinarian
was not hide bound by convention and had a sense of fun. He was
prepared to pass students off as cadets on an important military parade and skilful enough to imitate WG Grace to dupe his colleagues
as well as his superiors. He had experienced the horrors of jungle
warfare where he witnessed the decapitation of a fellow officer, but
still had the courage, allied to presence of mind, to assume command and save the day as well as the lives of the men under him –
recognised by the award of the DSO. His disposition required him

to find the answer within himself and deal with whatever problems and traumas life threw before him. The observations of French and Masterman indicate that he expected others around him similarly to accept responsibility for their own lives and conduct.

When mulling over a title for this biography, I had considered 'A Man of His Time' because so many aspects of Wynyard's background and character (Public School, Army, Empire and Amateur Sport) were typical of his generation and social class. Someone who was a stickler for discipline, a domineering personality, expecting to have his orders obeyed, would not be tolerated in the same way today as over 100 years ago. I do not know Teddy's politics or views on race and class, but again some of his friends and associates (Major Spens and Abe Bailey for example) held opinions decidedly to the right – not uncommon within the military and aristocracy until the Second World War. On reflection though, I felt a title restricting him to a particular period in history did not give sufficient credit to his wider attributes and, above all else, to everything he achieved in his life. If there was one point that was unassailably true, it was he had lived his allotted seventy-five years to the absolute full. What is more, his style of attacking play was very twenty-first century, and whilst he may have revelled in the one-day and T20 game, I would not have liked to be in the dressing room when he was presented with the coloured clothing to wear and saw the cheerleaders gyrating to loud music every time a boundary was scored. I also wonder what he would have thought about his *Vanity Fair* depiction being used by Post Office Telecommunications in 1979 to advertise their Cricket Score Service?

I then considered plagiarising Robert Bolt and use 'A Man for All Seasons'. After all, Wynyard had played and been successful across a range of sports at all times of the year. He was the International Tobogganing Champion at his very first attempt in the winter of 1895, had won the FA Cup in the spring of 1881, played cricket in a number of summers around the world, leaving the autumn (and other times) for golf and the multitude of games he chose to play, ranging from hockey to racquets and real tennis. Teddy was not alone in the Victorian and Edwardian eras by excelling at a wide variety of different activities. David Frith called his biography of Stoddart *England's Finest Sportsman*, Iain Wilton described CB Fry as the *King of Sport* and Mick Collins thought Max Woosnam was an *All-Round Genius* who was *Britain's Greatest Sportsman*.

Should I make a similar claim on my subject's behalf? After all, *The Times* had called Wynyard 'one of the greatest all-round athletes of his generation'. Undoubtedly he reached a high standard very quickly in just about every sport (and as we have seen there were many of them) at which he tried his hand. How 'great' though was he at any one of them? What would he have achieved had his Army duties not prevented him from playing during the prime years of his life?

Certainly that is a question worth asking about his rugby and football careers, although it is difficult to see how he could have continued to play both at the highest level and a choice would need to have been made. It seems likely it would have been football, given that he started playing for Old Carthusians and, when he was just twenty years of age, had scored a goal to help win the FA Cup. Football at that time was rough and physical, which suited his style of play, but by the time of his return from six years away in India and Burma, it had developed tactically. With the creation of the Football League football had become more professional, making it very different from the game he had played.

To an extent, similar considerations apply to the development of his cricketing career. He made his first-class debut for Hampshire when he was little more than seventeen years of age, and although he played cricket extensively and very successfully in India, by his own admission the standard was not very high. By the time of his permanent return he was nearly twenty-nine, and disregarding what he eventually went on to achieve, it is hard not to think that his twenties ought to have been his most prolific run-scoring years. Although his posting to Sandhurst increased his opportunities to play, the Army still had priority. With the introduction of the County Championship in 1890, Hampshire matches were not treated as first-class. Wynyard tended to play primarily for them towards the end of each season and it was his three consecutive centuries in 1894 that acted as the catalyst for their promotion to the elite ranks.

The next five seasons between 1895 and 1899 saw Wynyard in his pomp, and it is worth remembering he was already thirty-four at the start of that period. His highest ever score of 268 was achieved in 1896 against Yorkshire, and in that year he finished second in the national batting averages behind Ranjitsinhji. He also made his Test match debut, and ultimately it is the performances at this highest level by which greatness is truly measured.

Teddy played in only three Tests and the last two were nearly ten years after the first. He batted six times, scoring 10, 3, 29, 0, 0 and 30. A total of 72 at an average of 12 which, it must be conceded, is far from great. The innings do merit closer scrutiny though. In the first match against Australia, the wicket was badly affected by rain and Grace gave instructions to the incumbent England batsmen (Wynyard and Hayward) that he wanted Australia to be batting by 12.30 pm on the last day. In the two Tests in Johannesburg in 1906, when Wynyard was nearing forty-five years of age, he had to face four of the greatest leg spin/googly bowlers of any generation plying their trade on matting wickets that were particularly responsive to their skills. It is also worth noting that the England scores when Teddy walked out to the crease in all of his Tests were 114 for five, 56 for five, 6 for two, 55 for two, 62 for four and 25 for four. In other words, every occasion was a crisis, except possibly for the second innings of the first South African Test. He never really had the luxury of a large score on the board and the freedom to bat with little pressure upon his shoulders.

The jury must remain out on his prowess as a Test match cricketer. The question mark hanging over him would only ever have been removed had he been able to go on either of the 1898 or 1906 tours to Australia. Whilst I remain of the opinion that he is unlikely to have been successful on the second of those tours, given his age and lack of first-class cricket, it is important to remember that the hierarchy at MCC held him in such high regard they invited him to captain the side.

Outside of Test cricket, the next most important games at that time were viewed as those between Gentlemen and Players. Teddy played in the most famous of all those fixtures, when WG celebrated his fiftieth birthday. Again, his scores of 12 and 0 hardly stand out. Nevertheless, he played five Gentlemen v Players matches in all, scoring an aggregate of 357 runs with a top score of 137 at an average of 44.62, which is more than respectable.

Teddy had retired from the Army in 1903, freeing him to play cricket when and where he wanted, but he was forty-two years of age and only played eleven more first-class games for his county. He chose instead to organise and play in matches for MCC (for whom he became Assistant Secretary in 1907) and the amateur nomadic sides, I Zingari, Incogniti and Free Foresters. He also toured extensively overseas, represented South African cricket in the committee room at Lord's and played a key role in the formation of the ICC.

In any summary of Wynyard's cricketing career, mention must be made again of his sixth wicket stand of 411 with Bertie Poore – still standing as a Hampshire record – and to his all-round athleticism as a fielder or wicketkeeper, and his cunning underarm lobs. His sixty-six first class wickets were at an average of 32.27 that was only marginally better than his batting average of 33. Although it is said the umpire should have looked favourably upon his lbw appeal against White at a crucial point in the first Test at Johannesburg, lob bowling was a dying art by the end of his career. Nevertheless, his lobs could still be deadly when deployed in the annual match against the schoolboys of Charterhouse.

His statistical record amassed during the Golden Age of Cricket stands up to objective scrutiny and analysis of his ability. Does it really matter then whether that much over used word 'great' should be applied to him? What is surely relevant is his great love of the game. He continued playing until he was over seventy and from middle age had sought to pass on his knowledge by coaching the next generation. Surely that is a far greater testimony to Teddy Wynyard than a bare restatement of the number of runs, wickets and catches he registered during what was, unquestionably, an illustrious career.

I decided that whilst 'A Man for All Seasons' did reflect Teddy's wide range of activities, I would use it as a chapter heading, as it still did not quite capture the vital essence of the man.

Gerald French wrote, 'Wynyard was the type of man who would excel at anything adventurous.' The circumstances under which the DSO was won, deer hunting in the wilds of Canada and hurtling headfirst, without any crash helmet, on a sled down the icy roads of Switzerland, provide ample support for such an observation. He was undoubtedly 'A Man of Action' but that description had already been applied to his father. I wanted a title that was unique to him. So why not simply 'Teddy', and let his story speak for himself?

For me, there is one event that stands head and shoulders above all others and was his defining moment. To quote Baptista in Act 2, Scene 1 of Shakespeare's *The Taming of the Shrew*, 'Tis deeds must win the prize.' Hampshire's own Jane Austen, wrote in *Sense and Sensibility*, that 'it isn't what we say or think that defines us but what we do'.

At 2.30 pm on 9 December 1893, Teddy Wynyard did not have any prizes in mind. He was a highly proficient figure skater and was enjoying his time on Lake Davos with his friend, GR Wood. About a quarter of mile away, a local Swiss peasant by the name of Munkert was skating along with his collection of edelweiss flowers in his hand, when suddenly the ice broke beneath him. Wynyard acted instinctively. He did not wait to see if others might go to the rescue or seek to direct them in what they should do to help. There was no thought of class or race but simply that another human being was in peril. He did not give a second's thought to his own life or safety but simply skated to the spot, roped himself up and dived straight into the icy waters. He could not find Munkert but refused to give up. He tried, again and again, to save the local man but he too then lost consciousness and it was only thanks to the efforts of his friend, Wood, that he did not lose his own life.

What better epitaph could there be to Teddy? Selfless, humane and courageous: Major EG Wynyard DSO, OBE.

Acknowledgements

I am deeply indebted to so many people for assisting and encouraging me to achieve my lifetime ambition of writing this cricket biography.

My biggest thanks must go to my long-suffering family. My very special wife, Elisabetta, whose love and support over more than forty years can best be illustrated by her conversion to the great game, travelling around the Test match grounds of Australia and in more recent years, driving and accompanying me to Lord's. I could not have achieved anything in life without her. My wonderful children Marco, Francesca and Alessandra, and their other halves, Nicole, Tom and Matt have all had to endure long periods of silence while I pored over this manuscript and the name Wynyard has been a constant topic of conversation at the dinner table. Since November 2016, my twin grandsons, Daniele and Edoardo, have not only brought great joy and fun, but have also been the inspiration for me to finish my task.

I have also sorely tested relationships by asking very good friends to read a first draft that was far too long and then give me their opinions. The fact they all did so without murmur or complaint speaks volumes for their kindness and generosity of spirit. A very big thank you, therefore, to Daniel Servini, David John, Ron Sharp, Peter Stibbard, Nigel Brooke-Smith, Colin Barlow and Dr Ray Choy. When a fresh set of eyes was needed to read the final draft before submission to the publisher, Colin Davey and Francesco Giacon came to my aid and I am most grateful to them for their help. Finally, I must also mention my very good friend Tony Grieco, who had promised to be one of my proofreaders, but sadly succumbed to the same illness as me before I had finished my first draft. He is sorely missed, but I sincerely hope his sports-mad wife, Caroline, enjoys this book.

My research was made easier by the help and assistance of a number of people. Mrs Catherine Smith, the archivist at Charterhouse School, gave me access to their digitised records including back issues of *The Carthusian*. *The Times* archive, *Wisden* and Keith Warsop's *EG Wynyard: His Record Innings-by-Innings* for ACS Publications were regular points of reference. Justine Tracey of Aldershot Military Museum; Dr Anthony Morton (courtesy of a very kind introduction by Peter Donovan), Curator of the Sandhurst Collection; Lawrence of Forces War Records; Bill Gordon, Pavilion Curator of the Kia Oval and Colin Maynard, when Assistant Secretary of MCC, all answered my questions with great efficiency for which I thank them all.

When my first draft was completed Edwina Wynyard (Teddy's granddaughter) showed kindness and enthusiasm for my project. Patrick Ferriday, Mark Rowe and Roger Mann have all given me their invaluable time and help, but it is to Scott Reeves of Chequered Flag that I owe the greatest debt of gratitude for his advice, support and commitment to publishing my work. Thanks also to Keith and Jennifer Booth for proofreading the book before it went to print. All mistakes, though, remain very firmly mine alone.

Last, but most certainly not least, there is a very important group of people I must thank. I started writing at the time of my retirement, but unfortunately this coincided with my need for a closer association with the medical profession. In order of treatment the expertise of Mr Malachy Gleeson, Mr Jeffrey Webster, Mr Stephen Cannon, Mr William Aston, Dr Paul Nathan and Dr Nihal Shah along with all their very helpful and kind staff, including those at Lloyds Pharmacy Homecare, Elstree Cancer Centre and Pinner Ward at Bishops Wood hospital, have enabled me to complete this book. The work of the Cancer Treatment and Research Trust at Mount Vernon Cancer Centre has helped so many people like me. I cannot thank them all enough.

BIBLIOGRAPHY

Books

Allen, Dean. *Empire, War & Cricket in South Africa: Logan of Matjiesfontein.* Zebra Press, 2015

Altham, HS, Arlott, John, Eagar, EDR, Webber, Roy. *Official History of Hampshire County Cricket.* Wyman and Sons, 1957

Alverstone, Lord and Alcock, CW. *Surrey Cricket: Its History and Association.* Longman and Co, 1902

Arrowsmith, RL, and Hill BJW, revised by Wintour, Tony. *I Zingari.* JG Publishing, 2006

Arthur, Max. *Symbol of Courage: A History of the Victoria Cross.* Pan Macmillan, 2004

Bailey, Malcolm. *From Cloisters to Cup Finals.* JJG Publishing, 2009

Baily's Magazine Sports and Pastimes. December 1897

Baldry, AJ *Sir Joshua Reynolds PRA.* George Newnes, 1900

Bingham, Rev CW. *The Family of Wynyard.* Library of Congress, Washington

Booth, Keith. *The Father of Modern Sport: The Life and Times of Charles W Alcock.* Parrs Wood, 2002

Booth, Keith and Booth, Jennifer. *The Haywards: The Biography of a Cricket Dynasty,* Chequered Flag, 2018

Boswell, James. *L123 Catalogue of Papers at Yale University*

Bowen, Rowland. *Cricket: A History of its Growth and Development Throughout the World.* Eyre and Spottiswoode, 1970

Brown, Paul. *Goal: Post Victorian Football.* Superelastic Publishing, 2012

Bruce, George. *The Burma Wars 1824-1886.* Hart-Davis, MacGibbon

Buckton, Oliver S. *Secret Selves: Confession and Same-Sex Desire in Victorian Autobiography.* University of North Carolina, 2009

Burns, Michael. *A Flick of the Fingers.* Pitch Publishing, 2015

Butler, Bryon. *The Illustrated History of the FA Cup.* Headline, 1996

Cairns, WE. *Social Life in the British Army.* London, J Long, 1900

Cannon, Richard. *The Historical Record of the 17th or Leicestershire Regiment of Foot.* London, Parker, Furnivall and Parker, 1848

Canynge Caple, S. *The Springbok at Cricket 1888-1960.* Littlebury and Co, 1960

Chalke, Stephen. *Summer's Crown: The Story of Cricket's County Championship.* Fairfield Books, 2015

Chaplin, Arnold. *A St Helena's Who's Who.* 1914, revised Fonthill Media, 2013

Churchill, Winston. *A Roving Commission: My Early Life.* Collins, 1930

Collins, Mick. *All Round Genius.* Aurum, 2006

Conan Doyle, Arthur. *The Maracot Deep and Other Stories (including The Story of Spedegue's Dropper).* Cambridge Scholars Publishing, 2009

Conan Doyle, Arthur. *Memories and Adventures.* Oxford University Press, 1989

Coren, Michael. *Conan Doyle.* Bloomsbury, 1995

Cornwell, Bernard. *Waterloo.* William Collins, 2014

Crosthwaite, Sir Charles. *The Pacification of Burma.* 1912, republished Frank Cass, 1968

Darwin, Bernard. *WG Grace.* 1934, republished Duckworth, 1978

Douglas, Christopher. *Douglas Jardine: Spartan Cricketer.* George Allen and Unwin, 1984

Ferriday, Patrick. *Before the Lights Went Out.* Von Krumm Publishing, 2011

French, Lt Col the Hon Gerald. *The Cornerstone of English Cricket.* Hutchinson and Co, 1950.

Frith, David. *England versus Australia: A Pictorial History of Test Matches since 1877.* Macdonald Queen Anne Press, 1977

Frith, David. *'Stoddy': England's Finest Sportsman.* Von Krumm Publishing, 2015

Frith, David. *By His Own Hand.* ABC Enterprises, 1990

Frith, David. *My Dear Victorious Stod.* Lutterworth Press, 1977

Frith, David. *The Golden Age of Cricket 1890-1914.* Omega Books, 1983

Gibson, Arthur and Pickford, William. *Association Football and The Men Who Made It.* Caxton, 1905/6

Gibson, Harry. *Tobogganing on Crooked Runs.* 1894, republished Kessinger Publishing, 1910.

Grace WG *Cricketing Reminiscences and Personal Recollections.* 1899, republished Hambledon Press, 1980

Grayson, Edward. *Corinthians and Cricketers.* The Sportsmans Book Club, 1957

Green, Benny (ed). *Wisden Anthology 1860-1900.* Queen Anne, 1979

Green, Benny (ed). *Wisden Anthology 1900-1940.* Queen Anne, 1980

Green, Stephen (ed). *Backward Glances.* MG Richards, 1976

Ingram, John. *The Haunted House and Family Traditions of Great Britain.* London, Gibbings and Co, 1897

James, CLR. *Beyond a Boundary.* Random House Group, 2005

Jardine, DR. *In Quest of the Ashes.* republished Methuen, 2005

Jenkins, Roy. *Churchill.* Macmillan, 2001

Kaye and Malleson. *History of the Indian Mutiny 1857-58.* Allen, 1889

Kynaston, David. *Bobby Abel: Professional Batsman.* Secker and Warburg, 1982

Kynaston, David. *WG's Birthday Party.* Night Watchman Books, 1998

Lambie, James. *The Story of Your Life: A History of The Sporting Life Newspapers 1859-1998.* Matador, 2010

Layne-Joynt, AW. *The Public School Cricket Year Book 1914.* Hammond, 1914

Lazenby, John. *Test of Time: Travels in Search of a Cricketing Legend.* John Murray, 2005

Leatham, AE. *Sport in Five Continents*. William Blackwood, 1912

Lewis, Tony. *Double Century*. Hodder and Stoughton, 1987

Lonsdale, Jeremy. *The Army's Grace: The Life of Brigadier General RM Poore* . Spellmount Ltd, 1992

MacIntyre, Ben. *Double Cross*. Bloomsbury, 2012

Major, John. *More Than a Game*. Harper Perennial, 2008

March, Russell. *The Cricketers of Vanity Fair*. Webb & Bower, 1982

Mason, Tony and Riedi, Eliza. *Sport and the Military: The British Armed Forces 1880-1960*. Cambridge University Press, 2010

Masterman, JC. *On the Chariot Wheel*. Oxford University Press, 1975

McKinstry, Leo *Jack Hobbs: England's Greatest Cricketer*. Random House, 2011

Midwinter, Eric. *The Illustrated History of County Cricket*. Kingswood Press, 1992

Mockler-Ferryman, Major AF. *Annals of Sandhurst: A Chronicle of The Royal Military College*. Heinemann, 1900

Nicholls, Mark. *Investigating Gunpowder Plot*. Manchester University Press, 1991

Nisbet, John. *Burma under British Rule and Before*. Archibald Constable, 1901

O'Meara, Barry. *An Exposition of some of the Transactions that have taken place at St. Helena*. Book on Demand, 1819

Panayi, Panikps. *Prisoners of Britain*. Manchester University Press, 2012

Parker, Eric. *Hesketh Prichard*. T Fisher Unwin, 1924

Pollard, Jack. *Australian Cricket: The Game and The Players*. Hodder and Stoughton, 1982

Pridham, Major CHB. *The Charm of Cricket Past and Present*. Herbert Jenkins, 1949

Rae, Simon. *WG Grace: A Life*. Faber and Faber, 1998

Ranjitsinhji, Prince. *Jubilee Book of Cricket*. William Blackwood, 1897

Rayvern Allen, David. *Sir Aubrey*. JW McKenzie, 2005

Reeves, Scott. *The Champion Band: The First English Cricket Tour.* Chequered Flag, 2014

Renshaw, Andrew. *Wisden on the Great War: The Lives of Cricket's Fallen 1914-18.* John Wisden, 2014

Rice, Jonathan. *The Presidents of MCC.* Methuen, 2006

Rivett Caniac, Col S. *The Presidential Armies of India.* Allen and Co, 1890

Ross, Alan. *The Cricketer's Companion.* Eyre and Spottiswoode, 1960

Sandford, Christopher. *The Final Over: The Cricketers of Summer 1914.* Spellmount, 2014

Sissons, Ric. *The Players: A Social History of the Professional Cricketer.* Kingswood Press, 1888

Smart, John Blythe. *The Real Colin Blythe.* Blythe Smart, 2009

Smyth, Brigadier Sir John. *Sandhurst.* C Tinling, 1961

Thant Misunt-U, *The River of Lost Fortresses.* Farrar, Straus and Giroux, 2006

Thomas, Hugh. *The Story of Sandhurst.* Hutchinson and Co, 1961

Tod, AH. *History of Charterhouse.* GH Bell and Sons, 1919

Tomlinson, Simon. *Amazing Grace.* Little, Brown, 2015

Tyerman, Charles. *A History of Harrow School 1324-1991.* Oxford, 2000

Warner, PF. *The MCC in South Africa.* Chapman and Hall, 1906

Warner, PF. *Gentlemen v Players 1806 to 1949.* George G. Harrap, 1950

Warsop, Keith. *EG Wynyard: His Record Innings-by-Innings.* ACS Publications, 2004

Wilde, Simon. *A Genius Rich and Strange.* Kingswood, 1990

Wilde, Simon. *Wisden Cricketers of the Year.* John Wisden, 2013

Wilson, James. *Court and Bowled.* Wildy, Simmons & Hill, 2014

Wilton, Iain. *CB Fry: King of Sport.* Metro, 2002

Wisden Cricketers' Almanack, various

Wynne-Thomas, Peter. *The History of Hampshire County Cricket Club.* Christopher Helm, 1988

Yapp, Nick, *A History of the Fosters Oval,* Pelham, 1990

Magazines, newspapers and journals

The Ancestor

Bell's Life in London

Bell's Life in Sydney and Sporting Chronicle

Blackwood's Magazine

The Carthusian

Charterhouse archives and register

Cricket

The Cricketer

The Cricket Field

Morning Post

The London Gazette

The New Light of Myanmar

The Sportsman

The Times

Wisden Magazine

Websites

Haigh, Gideon. 'So much done, so little to do: Abe Bailey', ESPN Cricinfo espncricinfo.com

Norten, Rictor. 'The Life of John Addington Symonds', Gay History and Literature rictornorton.co.uk

Cricket Archive cricketarchive.com

STATISTICS

Compiled from
Keith Warsop, *EG Wynyard: His Record Innings-by-Innings*

Batting and fielding
Test matches

Year	M	Inn	NO	HS	Runs	Avg	100s	50s	Ct
1896 (Aus)	1	2	0	13	10	6.5	0	0	0
1906 (SA)	2	4	0	59	30	14.75	0	0	0
TOT	**3**	**6**	**0**	**72**	**30**	**12.00**	**0**	**0**	**0**

Bowling
Test matches

Year	Overs	M	Runs	Wkts
1906 (SA)	4	0	17	0

(six-ball overs)

Batting and fielding
All first-class matches

Year	M	Inn	NO	HS	Runs	Avg	100s	50s	Ct/St
1878	1	2	0	1	1	0.50	0	0	1
1880	3	5	0	24	46	9.20	0	0	3
1881	1	2	0	42	43	21.50	0	0	1
1883	4	7	1	61	172	28.66	0	1	2
1887	2	3	0	7	14	4.66	0	0	2
1888	1	2	0	27	27	13.50	0	0	0
1890	2	3	1	91*	129	64.50	0	1	9
1893	1	2	0	10	12	6.00	0	0	1
1895	13	26	0	69	581	22.34	0	4	19
1896	13	23	2	268	1038	49.42	4	3	20/1
1897	12	22	0	80	713	32.40	0	5	15/2
1898	8	13	2	140	391	35.54	1	0	14/2
1899	18	32	1	225	1281	41.32	2	8	23
1900	4	6	0	107	310	51.66	1	2	1
1901	3	5	0	59	180	36.00	0	2	3
1903	8	14	2	72	379	31.58	0	3	6
1904	11	20	0	147	642	32.10	1	3	8
1904/5 WI	8	14	0	157	562	40.14	2	2	9/1
1905	10	18	1	115	583	34.29	1	3	7
1905/6 SA	6	10	2	54*	156	19.50	0	1	1
1906	9	18	2	137	614	38.37	1	2	3
1906/7 NZ	2	3	3	48*	86	-	0	0	1
1907	2	3	0	38	82	27.33	0	0	0
1907 USA	2	4	0	13	22	5.50	0	0	1
1908	3	6	1	59	130	26.00	0	1	5
1909	1	1	0	36	36	36.00	0	0	0
1909/10 SA	4	5	1	10*	25	6.25	0	0	7
1910	1	2	0	35	36	18.00	0	0	0
1912	1	1	1	27*	27	-	0	0	0
TOT	**154**	**272**	**20**	**268**	**8318**	**33.00**	**13**	**41**	**162/6**

Highest score: 268 for Hampshire against Yorkshire at Southampton on 16/17 July 1896

Bowling
All first-class matches

Year	Overs	M	Runs	Wkts	Avg	Best
1883	46	7	119	2	59.50	1-28
1895	22	6	77	2	38.50	2-22
1896	39	7	140	2	70.00	1-0
1897	65	15	184	9	20.44	4-47
1898	35.1	8	95	6	15.83	3-13
1899	285.4	56	749	27	27.74	6-63
1900	5	0	23	0	-	-
1901	58	16	140	5	28.00	2-36
1903	29.3	2	96	3	32.00	3-47
1904	18	1	58	0	-	-
1904/5	5	0	28	0	-	-
1905	51	6	199	5	39.80	3-45
1905/6	4	0	17	0	-	-
1906	12	0	49	1	49.00	1-39
1909/10	25	1	102	1	102.00	1-93
1910	19	4	49	2	24.50	2-29
1912	2	1	5	1	5.00	1-51
TOT	**721.3**	**130**	**2130**	**66**	**32.27**	**6-43**

1884 = four-ball overs, 1895-1899 five-ball overs, 1900 onwards six-ball overs

Batting and fielding
Hampshire non-first-class matches

Year	M	Inn	NO	HS	Runs	Avg	100s	50s	Ct/St
1887	8	15	0	75	327	21.80	0	2	5/2
1888	5	8	0	22	76	9.50	0	0	8/1
1890	8	16	4	114*	455	37.91	1	2	9/12
1891	1	2	0	28	34	17.00	0	0	0
1892	2	3	0	32	41	13.66	0	0	5/0
1893	5	9	0	154	450	50.00	1	2	6/0
1894	5	8	1	117	465	66.42	3	1	1/0
TOT	34	61	5	154	1848	33.00	5	7	34/15

Highest score: 154 against Warwickshire at Southampton on 10,11,12 August 1893

Bowling
Hampshire non-first-class matches

Year	Overs	M	Runs	Wkts	Avg	Best
1888	4.1	1	11	2	5.50	2-11
1890	5	1	10	2	5.00	2-10
1892	17	5	39	0	-	-
1893	4	0	28	0	-	-
1894	21	6	56	1	56.00	1-13
TOT	51.1	13	144	5	28.80	2-10

1884 = four-ball overs, 1890-1894 five-ball overs

Batting and fielding
All Hampshire matches

Year	M	Inn	NO	HS	Runs	Avg	100s	50s	Ct/St
First-class	71	129	4	268	4312	35.80	7	22	88/3
Non-f-c	34	61	5	154	1848	33.00	5	7	34/15
TOT	**105**	**190**	**9**	**268**	**6160**	**34.03**	**12**	**29**	**122/18**

Bowling
All Hampshire matches

Year	Overs	M	Runs	Wkts	Avg	Best
First-class 4-ball	46	7	1549	49	31.61	6-63
First-class 5-ball	377.3	77				
First-class 6-ball	131.3	22				
N-f-c 4-ball	4.1	1	144	5	28.80	2-10
N-f-c 5-ball	47	12				
All 4-ball	**50.1**	**8**	**169.3**	**54**	**31.35**	**6-63**
All 5-ball	**424.3**	**89**				
All 6-ball	**131.3**	**22**				

First-class centuries

Score	For	Against	Venue	Year
268	Hampshire	Yorkshire	Southampton	1896
225	Hampshire	Somerset	Taunton	1899
157	Lord Brackley's XI	Jamaica	Kingston	1904/05
147	I Zingari	Gentlemen of England	Lord's	1904
140	Hampshire	Leicestershire	Southampton	1898
137	Gentlemen	Players	Scarborough	1906
121	CI Thornton's XI	Cambridge University	Fenner's	1896
115	MCC	Cambridge University	Lord's	1905
112	Hampshire	Sussex	Hove	1896
111	Hampshire	Warwickshire	Southampton	1896
108	Hampshire	Worcestershire	Southampton	1899
107	Hampshire	Somerset	Bath	1900
101	Lord Brackley's XI	West Indies	Bridgetown	1904/05

Wynyard's 225 was also his highest first-class partnership of 411 with RM Poore (304)

INDEX

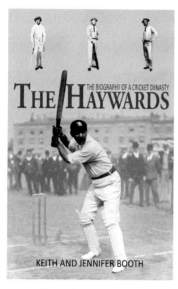

THE HAYWARDS

THE BIOGRAPHY OF A CRICKET DYNASTY

by Keith and Jennifer Booth

Four players, three generations, two counties, one famous family.

The mourners who attended the funeral of Daniel Hayward in 1852 lamented the loss of a fine cricketer, but little did they realise that his family would continue to star in English cricket for another 60 years. One son was a stalwart of Cambridgeshire cricket; the other would help pioneer and popularise cricket as a famous member of the All-England Eleven. A grandson would eclipse them all, becoming one of the greatest batsmen of all time and the second to score a century of centuries.

Together the Haywards featured in nearly 900 first-class or equivalent matches, scored nearly 50,000 runs and took over 750 wickets. They witnessed the growth of cricket from its early days as a pastime for gentlemen to an international sport with huge crowds. They took part in the first overseas cricket tour, spurred the rise of county cricket and battled for the Ashes.

Using extensive archival research, Keith and Jennifer Booth shine the spotlight on four fascinating characters, elevating the Hayward name to rank alongside Grace and Lillywhite as one of cricket's foremost families.

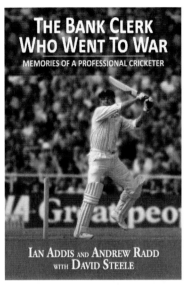

THE BANK CLERK WHO WENT TO WAR

MEMORIES OF A PROFESSIONAL CRICKETER

by Ian Addis and Andrew Radd with David Steele

'Who's this grey-haired bleeder?'

Few people expected the slim, bespectacled 33-year-old who made his Test debut at Lord's in 1975 to be the one to rescue England after a first Test thrashing in the Ashes – especially after he took a wrong turn in the pavilion on his way to the middle. Yet David Steele faced down the fearsome pace duo of Lillee and Thomson, saving the honour of English cricket by drawing the remaining three matches and finishing top of the England batting averages. It propelled him into a national hero and led to him becoming the BBC Sports Personality of the Year.

A dogged and determined batsman cast from the same mould as his contemporary, Geoffrey Boycott, Steele also stood up to the destructive bowling of the West Indies, twice helped take Northamptonshire to the brink of the County Championship, was named a Wisden Cricketer of the Year and won the NatWest Trophy with Derbyshire.

In this authorised biography produced with the help of hours of interviews with David Steele, Ian Addis and Andrew Radd dig into the memories of a cricket icon whose Churchillian efforts with the bat made him the unexpected saviour of English cricket.

HOWZAT FOR A GREAT CRICKET BOOK?

Chequered Flag
PUBLISHING

www.chequeredflagpublishing.co.uk